OUT OF HIDING: HOLOCAUST LITERATURE OF BRITISH COLUMBIA

OTHER BOOKS
BY ALAN TWIGG

Gidal: Letters and Photos, the Unusual Friendship of Yosef Wosk and Tim Gidal (Douglas & McIntyre, 2021)

Tolstoy's Words to Live By, ed. (Ronsdale, 2020)

Moon Madness: Dr Aall, Sixty Years of Healing in Africa (Ronsdale, 2019)

Undaunted: The Best of BC BookWorld, ed. (Ronsdale, 2013)

The Essentials: 150 Great BC Books & Authors (Ronsdale, 2010)

Tibetans in Exile: The Dalai Lama & the Woodcocks (Ronsdale, 2009)

Full-Time: A Soccer Story (McClelland & Stewart, 2008)

Thompson's Highway: British Columbia's Fur Trade, 1800–1850 (Ronsdale, 2006)

Understanding Belize: A Historical Guide (Harbour, 2006)

Aboriginality: The Literary Origins of British Columbia (Ronsdale, 2005)

First Invaders: The Literary Origins of British Columbia (Ronsdale, 2004)

101 Top Historical Sites of Cuba (Beach Holme / Dundurn, 2004)

Intensive Care: A Memoir (Anvil Press, 2002)

Cuba: A Concise History for Travellers (Penguin Books, 2002; Harbour, 2004)

Twigg's Directory of 1001 BC Writers (Crown Publications, 1992)

Strong Voices: Conversations with 50 Canadian Writers (Harbour, 1998)

Vander Zalm: From Immigrant to Premier: A Political Biography (Harbour, 1986)

Hubert Evans: The First Ninety-Three Years (Harbour, 1985)

For Openers: Conversations with 24 Canadian Writers (Harbour, 1981)

OUT OF HIDING
Holocaust Literature of British Columbia

AN HISTORICAL SURVEY

IN APPRECIATION OF ROBERT KRELL

ALAN TWIGG

RONSDALE PRESS

OUT OF HIDING: HOLOCAUST LITERATURE OF BRITISH COLUMBIA

RONSDALE PRESS
3350 West 21st Avenue, Vancouver, B.C., Canada V6S 1G7
www.ronsdalepress.com

Type: Minion Pro 11.5 pt on 15
Front cover photo: Jennie Lifschitz, courtesy of Rachel Mines
Paper: Ancient Forest Friendly Enviro 100 edition, 60 lb. Husky (FSC), 100% post-consumer waste, totally chlorine-free and acid-free.

Ronsdale Press wishes to thank the following for their support of its publishing program: the Canada Council for the Arts, the Government of Canada, the British Columbia Arts Council, and the Province of British Columbia through the British Columbia Book Publishing Tax Credit program.

Library and Archives Canada Cataloguing in Publication

Title: Out Of Hiding: Holocaust Literature of British Columbia / Alan Twigg.
Names: Twigg, Alan, 1952- author.

Description: Includes bibliographical references.

Identifiers: Canadiana (print) 20220143277 | Canadiana (ebook) 20220145814 | ISBN 9781553806622 (softcover) | ISBN 9781553806639 (HTML) | ISBN 9781553806646 (pdf)

Subjects: LCSH: Canadian literature—British Columbia— | LCSH: Holocaust survivors' writings.. | LCSH: Holocaust survivors' writings—History and criticism | Holocaust, Jewish, German (1939-1945), in literature. | LCSH: Holocaust survivors—British Columbia. | LCSH: Jews—British Columbia. | LCSH: Jews, Canadian—British Columbia.

Classification: LCC PS8131.B7 T85 2022 | DDC C810.9/35840531809711—dc23

At Ronsdale Press we are committed to protecting the environment. To this end we are working with Canopy and printers to phase out our use of paper produced from ancient forests. This book is one step towards that goal.

Printed in Canada by Island Blue, Victoria, B.C.

More than anyone in Canada, Robert Krell
has continuously carried the torches of healing,
investigation and discourse about the Shoah since
the 1970s to counteract ever-encroaching racism,
denial and willful ignorance. This digest honours
the steadfast leadership he has provided.

This book is also dedicated to Ronald Hatch,
who was always extraordinary as a publisher,
editor, environmentalist, mountaineer,
professor, husband, father and friend.

ABOUT THE COVER

Vancouverite Jennie (Lifschitz) Mines—photographed as a schoolgirl in Liepaja, Latvia—was probably the only Canadian-born citizen to survive the concentration camps as a Jew and the first Holocaust camp survivor to return to Canada. She was born in Montreal in 1924 and she endured captivity in the Liepaja ghetto in Latvia and two concentration camps—at Kaiserwald (in Riga, Latvia) and Stutthof (near Gdansk, Poland). The latter was the first German concentration camp established beyond Germany's 1937 borders (in September of 1939) and the last camp liberated by the Allies (in May of 1945). Under her maiden name Jennie Lifschitz, she returned to Montreal as a Canadian citizen in 1946 and spent most her life on the West Coast. [Emigration of Jews from Europe was not officially sanctioned in Canada until Order-In-Council #1647 on April 29, 1947.]

Consult entry for MINES, Rachel (her daughter) for more info.

ACKNOWLEDGEMENTS

I am grateful to Holocaust educators Gene Homel and Robert Krell, book designer David Lester, publisher Ronald Hatch—whose series of Holocaust-related books is exemplary and under-appreciated—and especially Yosef Wosk for his enduring faith in the Sherwood Forest of our friendship. *Out of Hiding*, in the words of Sir Martin Gilbert, reveals "the backward march of mankind." It is therefore essential for some disturbing images to appear. It is hoped that parents and other educators, at their discretion, will not choose to censor reality.

All proceeds will go to the B.C. Civil Liberties Association.

— A.T.

"I think the world will forget about Auschwitz. Apparently, the portion of people who remember anything about how many Jews were killed in the Holocaust, what Auschwitz was, what the Holocaust was, and so on, is not all that much above 50%.

"... in terms of remembering it as something in your gut, something that arouses an emotion, something that has a personal connection to you, I don't think it's going to last all that much longer."

— DR. PETER SUEDFELD

(panelist, Hillel House, UBC, International Holocaust Remembrance Day, January 27, 2020, 75 years after the end of WW II)

"As human,
we are both perpetrator and victim,
guilty and innocent at the same time,
but never all at once."

— YOSEF WOSK

(explorer, scholar, essayist, rabbi)

CONTENTS

[Countries in parentheses signify where the Holocaust was chiefly experienced or the country for which information is most relevant—not necessarily birthplaces of individuals.]

Foreword

I AM NOT A JEW. I AM NOT A GERMAN. I simply believe it is the responsibility of everyone on the planet to know more than just a little about the Holocaust. It is our collective responsibility to teach our children—with details—about why the Shoah is unique among the many genocides.

No other political regime has ever systematically murdered at least 1.5 million babies and children. As Dorothy Macardle wrote in her pioneering work titled *Children of Europe* in 1949, "the systematic slaughter of innocents stands out in history as the most coldly vicious proceeding that has ever emanated from human brains."

Never before or after has a modern, industrial state mobilized all of its resources to systematically commit murder at least six million times in about eight years (from Kristallnacht in 1938 to 1945) and no other government has established a separate killing ground to murder approximately 50,000 women (at Ravensbruck, north of Berlin).

No other regime has so thoroughly and consistently degraded its victims. Estimates vary but the United States Holocaust Memorial Museum claims Germans created 980 concentration camps, 30,000 slave labour camps, 1,150 Jewish ghettos, 1,000 prisoner-of-war camps and 500 brothels where women were sex slaves.

AT AGE 17, WHEN I was on Crete, living alone in a cave at Matala, in early 1970, I went for a walk, got lost and came to a rocky field overlooking the sea. It was unusually cold, in January.

Coming towards me, with a walking stick, was a much older man, grizzled, unshaven. To me, he appeared ancient and fearsome; I was barely shaving. A farmer perhaps? There were no sheep so he was not likely a shepherd.

He didn't know any English; I knew not a word of Greek. Our meeting was like some Cretan equivalent of *Waiting for Godot*, but not comic. Nobody on earth knew where I was. The hairy eyeball he gave me was universal.

"Allemagne?" he asked, in French.

In worse French, I replied, "Canadien."

As soon as he was satisfied that I was not German, my inquisitor shuffled off, free to ignore me. My nationality was all that mattered to him. I could have been a shrub or a rock. I was as intimidating to him as a butterfly.

Fifty years have elapsed. I know now that when this man was much closer to my age, Cretan renegades lived in those hills and caves during World War II, chain-smoking their hand-rolled cigarettes and fighting back. Cretans, descendants of Minoans, would not be beaten. You could burn down their churches full of people, you could torture and humiliate them, but the Greek patriots on this dry island maintained their rock-hard resistance.

The man I met on the bluff overlooking the sea must have been one of those resistors. Since that meeting in the hills above Matala, I've gathered enough knowledge of World War II to know that approximately 83 percent of Greek Jews were murdered and Greek Jews were involved in the only recorded uprising at Auschwitz [see the Stella Harvey entry]. Two hundred Greek Jews chose to be gassed rather than facilitate the murders of other innocents within the *Sonderkommando* units at Auschwitz.

I believe such stories of the Holocaust must be passed along, from generation to generation, regardless of your ancestry. Such education must be undertaken with an abiding awareness that the conveyor belt massacres—for profit—were perpetrated by so-called ordinary people. Most certainly it can happen again.

I believe each society ought to gather their particular Holocaust stories and claim them as their own, regardless of your skin colour or faith, or your lack of faith. Such stories must be taught in schools, as mandatory as math.

Out of Hiding is therefore a secular book about the Holocaust, from a regionalized framework, in which all perspectives matter, to help prevent the ongoing obliteration of necessary knowledge. I was not taught anything about the Holocaust in school or at home. The school system where I live never provided in-depth, mandatory education about the Holocaust. (In 2003, a Kelowna high school teacher named Graeme Stacey appealed to the Board of Education to grant him permission to start a course entitled "The Holocaust: A Blueprint for Modern Societal Tragedy" but the focus of a new and optional Genocide Studies 12 course was not restricted to the Holocaust.)

I believe human beings are capable of (very) good and (very) bad behaviour whether one is white, black or any of the myriad of gradations in-between; whether one is female, male or any of the myriad of gradations in-between; and whether one is indigenous or newly arrived from Timbuktu. If we fail to know what human beings are capable of, we fail our inner selves.

Currently, there is what I call a "Nice-ification" of the Holocaust. It walks hand-in-hand with avoidance to the ovens of oblivion. Even Jews who write their memoirs in their old age lean towards self-censorship. Elie Wiesel once said, "Although I mention the camps during my lectures, I cannot describe what happened there. For many years I could not utter the word 'Auschwitz.'" Persecuted Jews naturally wish to spare their grandchildren the details of how truly horrific the Shoah was. Therefore, as we retreat further from 1945, the hideous details of Nazi cruelty are being eroded, reduced and essentially censored.

Who knows what really happened at the Xin'an massacre of 207 B.C.? Or at the sacking of Carthage in 146 B.C.? Or Masada in 73 A.D.? Charlemagne's massacre at Verden in 782? The "Massacre of the Latins" at Constantinople in 1182 (estimated 70,000 killed)? From 1885 to 1908, Belgium's King Leopold II was complicit as a mass murderer with approximately ten million victims, in the same league as Stalin and Hitler, but probably less than 1 percent of the current world population can speak intelligently for more than thirty seconds about the 23 years of genocide in the Belgian Congo under his rule.

We have a Remembrance Day in Canada for soldiers but there is no Remembrance Day for those who were killed in pogroms and genocides. The darker truths about the Holocaust are thus jettisoned from history.

I have no political or religious agenda. My goal as a journalist (rather than as an historian) is to be as informative, accurate, engaging and dignified as possible—in that order—for as many people as possible, lest we forget. With this in mind, accents on "foreign" names have been jettisoned to facilitate easy comprehension, particularly for younger readers. Ditto for intimidating footnotes.

I have no direct or ongoing affiliation with any organization. Due to Covid-19 and the fact that I don't Zoom, I have had precious little liaison with the Vancouver Holocaust Education Centre (VHEC) beyond the acquisition and transfer of Buchenwald photos taken by Dr. Tom Perry Sr. Any errors are therefore entirely my own. I hasten to add I am an admirer of the Vancouver Holocaust Education Centre as an institution and I urge my fellow British Columbians to support it. Robert Krell served as VHEC's founding President of the Board of Directors from 1983 to 1998. Robbie Waisman took over from Krell as President in 1999, followed by Jody Dales. Rita Akselrod, Ed Lewin and Phillip Levinson. The current president is Corinne Zimmerman, daughter of Holocaust survivors Henry and Sally Zimmerman. Roberta Kremer succeeded Ronnie Tesler as Executive Director in 1996, followed by Frieda Miller and now Nina Krieger.

Out of Hiding has been conceived and executed by one independent journalist, on his own volition. Its aim is to serve as many people as possible. The best learning comes from curiosity and compassion. Even the digitally-dull, super-hero movies of today verify that confrontation with evil is a universal subject. Nowhere in living memory is this confrontation more undeniable than the Holocaust. Soon it will not be in living memory.

Hence this undertaking.

—A.T.

> "All we know and learn from the Holocaust strengthens us, as we may confront other genocides elsewhere or in the making."
>
> —TOM SZEKELY
>
> *Vancouver Holocaust survivor*

I ESCAPED FROM AUSCHWITZ

INCLUDING THE TEXT OF THE AUSCHWITZ PROTOCOLS

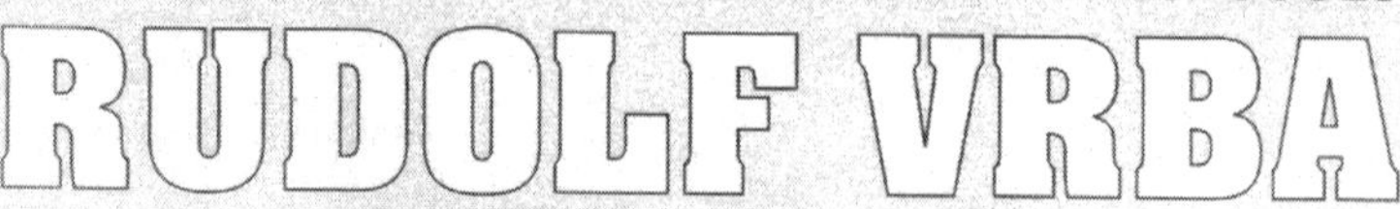

Preface by Sir Martin Gilbert

PART ONE

Leaders

VRBA, Rudolf

THE MOST IMPORTANT author of British Columbia is not Pauline Johnson, Douglas Coupland, William Gibson, David Suzuki or Alice Munro. It's Prisoner #44070, aka Rudolf Vrba, one of the most significant chroniclers of the Holocaust.

Historian Ruth Linn estimates there were about 500-700 attempts to escape from Auschwitz-Birkenau, and most failed. Some seventy-five of these attempts were made by Jews; only five Jews made it successfully to freedom. The most significant of these five was Rudolf "Rudi" Vrba, the main author of the most authoritative report on the true nature of the concentration camps, co-authored with co-escapee Alfred Wetzler.

Before Vrba, less convincing reports had been rendered by Polish escapees such as Kazmierz Halon (February, 1943) and Witold Pilecki, Jan Redzei and Edward Ciesielski (April, 1943). Rudi Vrba was the co-author of the first authoritative report with reportage of mass murder that was accepted as credible by the Allies. He called Vancouver home for the last thirty-one years of his life.

In conversation in 2001, Vrba described to the author of this book how he and Alfred Wetzler escaped. On Passover Eve, April 7, 1944, they hid inside a woodpile, in a previously prepared chamber, for three days and nights, using kerosene-soaked tobacco spread around the woodpile to keep guard dogs from sniffing them out and alerting search parties. The pair fled overland towards Slovakia after the SS cordon around the camp was withdrawn on April 11. There is a precise summary of how Vrba and Wetzler escaped in Vrba's book, *I Cannot Forgive.*

After a perilous, eleven-day journey, both men reached their homeland of Slovakia where they were taken into separate rooms at the headquarters of the Jewish community. They dictated separate reports that resulted in the Report on Auschwitz death camps, dated April 25, 1944, in Zilina, Slovakia. Their 33-page report became known in the historiography of the Holocaust as the "Vrba-Wetzler Report" and formed the most important reportage in the "Auschwitz Protocols." It describes the geography of the Auschwitz camp, the methodology of the gas chambers and a history of events in Auschwitz since April 1942.

Siegfried Lederer had previously fled from Auschwitz on April 5, 1944, in the company of a Nazi corporal named Viktor Pestek who had fallen in love with a Jewish woman in the camp. Pestek was able to obtain a Nazi uniform for Lederer who subsequently alerted Jews in the Theresienstadt Ghetto in Czechoslovakia about the mass murdering of Jews. Vrba and Wetzler escaped only six days after Lederer, so, essentially, they were alerting Jewish authorities around the same time, but Vrba and Wetzler had developed a system for corroborating their reports and so their descriptions and numbers were harder to dismiss.

The following month, two more Jews, Czeslaw Mordowicz (Prisoner #84216) and Arnost Rosin (Prisoner #29858), escaped from Auschwitz on May 27, 1944. Their seven-page "Rosin-Mordowicz Report" was added to the Vrba-Wetzler Report and a less-influential report made by escapee Jerzy Tabeau, known as "The Polish Major's Report," to comprise the Auschwitz Protocols (essentially three reports originally entitled "The Extermination Camps of Auschwitz and Birkenau" (visit the Vrba entry on ABCBookWorld for a transcript).

COURTESY DNA PRODUCTIONS, SLOVAKIA

In 2020, Slovakia's Oscar submission for best international film was director Peter Bebjak's *The Auschwitz Report*, about Rudolf Vrba's remarkable escape with Alfred Wetzler.

Mordowicz was recaptured by the Nazis and returned to Auschwitz but he succeeded in chewing off his tattoo so the SS failed to identify him as an escapee. Both he and Rosin survived the Holocaust.

Due to his ability to speak German, Vrba first worked sorting the belongings of gassed victims. He was therefore able to count the incoming trains and maintain a tally as to the number of victims. Then, as block registrars with relative freedom of movement, both Vrba (born Walter Rosenberg) and Wetzler were able to observe preparations underway at the new Birkenau compound for the eradication of Europe's last remaining Jewish community, the 800,000 Jews of Hungary. It was their summary (the Vrba-Wetzler Report) that finally revealed to the Allies the true nature and extent of the Holocaust.

Vrba also chiefly wrote a report that was given to the Papal Nuncio in Slovakia, then forwarded to the Vatican. The Regent of Hungary was informed of the report's contents. The Vrba-Wetzler Report II not only attempted to rationally estimate the scale of mass murder at Auschwitz, it also described methodology. As such, it's one of the most important documents of the 20th century. Copies are kept in the Franklin D. Roosevelt Library in New York, in the Vatican archives and at the Yad Vashem archives and memorial in Jerusalem.

The methodology of mass so-called "extermination" was described as follows:

> At present, there are four crematoria in operation at BIRKENAU, two large ones, I and II, and two smaller ones, III and IV. Those of type I and II consist of 3 parts, i.e.: (A) the furnace room; (B) the large halls; and (C) the gas chamber. A huge chimney rises from the furnace room around which are grouped nine furnaces, each having four openings. Each opening can take three normal corpses at once and after an hour and a half the bodies are completely burned. This corresponds to a daily capacity of about 2,000 bodies. Next to this is a large "reception hall" which is arranged so as to give the impression of the antechamber of a bathing establishment. It holds 2,000 people and apparently there is a similar waiting room on the floor below. From there a door and a few steps lead down into the very long and narrow gas chamber. The walls of this chamber are also camouflaged with simulated entries to shower rooms in order to mislead the victims. This roof is fitted with three traps which can be hermetically closed from the outside. A track leads from the gas chamber to the furnace room. The gassing takes place as follows: The unfortunate victims are brought into hall (B), where they are told to undress. To complete the fiction that they are going to bathe, each person receives a towel and a small piece of soap issued by two men clad in white coats. They are then crowded into the gas chamber (C) in such numbers there is, of course, only standing room. To compress this crowd into the narrow space, shots are often fired to induce those already at the far end to huddle still closer together. When everybody is inside, the heavy doors are closed. Then there is a short pause, presumably to allow the room temperature to rise to a certain level, after which SS men with gas masks climb on the roof, open the traps, and shake down a preparation in powder from out of tin cans labeled "CYKLON For

> use against vermin," which is manufactured by a Hamburg concern. It is presumed that this is a CYANIDE mixture of some sort which turns into gas at a certain temperature. After three minutes everyone in the chamber is dead. No one is known to have survived this ordeal, although it was not uncommon to discover signs of life after the primitive measures employed in the Birch Wood. The chamber is then opened, aired, and the "special squad" carts the bodies on flat trucks to the furnace rooms, where the burning takes place. Crematoria III and IV work on nearly the same principle, but their capacity is only half as large. Thus, the total capacity of the four cremating and gassing plants at BIRKENAU amounts to about 6,000 daily.

By the end of June 1944, the Vrba-Wetzler Report had reached the governments of the Allies, but it was hardly soon enough. Estimates vary as to exactly how many prisoners were killed in the combined work camp/death camp of Auschwitz-Birkenau, likely over a million, but it is clear there were more murders than in any other death camp. For the rest of his life, Vrba would claim that some Jewish leaders, most notably Hungarian-born Rudolf Kastner—known for negotiating directly with Adolf Eichmann and saving 1,684 Jews on the so-called Kastner train to Switzerland—had failed to promptly and adequately alert the Jews of eastern Europe as to the dangers of mass murder, thereby resulting in the deaths of thousands who might have been spared or at least been forewarned to fight or flee.

The whistleblowing of Vrba and Wetzler nonetheless prompted diplomats in Budapest (the Swede Raoul Gustaf Wallenberg was one of about ten) to save thousands of Jews by issuing false exit visas. Eventually, the contents of the yet-to-be-named pair's combined reportage in the Auschwitz Protocols was provided to the public by the *New York Times* on November 26, 1944.

Vrba's expert witness testimonials from 1944 to 2006, when he died in Vancouver, made him perhaps the most important witness of the Holocaust. As a result, he was featured in numerous documentary films, most notably the pathbreaking *Shoah* directed by Claude Lanzmann (Paris, 1985), as well as *Genocide* (in the "World at War" series) directed by Jeremy Isaacs (BBC, London, 1973), *Auschwitz and the Allies* directed by Rex Bloomstein, in collaboration with Martin Gilbert (BBC, London, 1982) and *Witness to Auschwitz* directed by Robert Taylor (CBC, Toronto, 1990).

Vrba also appeared as a witness for various investigations and trials, such as the Frankfurt Auschwitz trial of 1964. In Canada, he was called upon to provide testimony at the seven-week trial of Ontario's Ernst Zundel in 1985, when Zundel was found guilty of misleading the public as a Holocaust denier. In 2001, the Czech Republic's annual One World International Human Rights Film Festival established a film award in Vrba's name.

According to his curriculum vitae, Rudolf Vrba was born Walter Rosenberg in Topolcany, Czechoslovakia, in 1924 as the son of Elias Rosenberg (owner of a steam saw-mill in Jaklovce near Margecany in Slovakia), and Helena (nee Grunfeldova) of Zbehy, Slovakia. At the age of fifteen he was excluded from the High School (Gymnasium) of Bratislava under the so-called "Slovak State's" version of the Nuremberg anti-Jewish laws. He worked as a labourer in Trnava until 1942. In March 1942 he was arrested for being Jewish, and on June 14, 1942, he was deported first to the Majdanek concentration camp. He was transferred to Auschwitz on June 30, 1942.

As Prisoner #44070, Vrba worked in Birkenau's "Canada" warehouse sorting confiscated belongings, giving rise to his belief that massive and unprecedented theft was also a fundamental motive for the Holocaust. After escaping, Walter Rosenberg joined the Czechoslovak Partisan Units in September of 1944 and adopted Rudolf Vrba as his *nom de guerre*. He fought until the end of the war in a unit commanded by Milan Uher ("Hero of the Slovak National Uprising in Memoriam") and was decorated with the Czechoslovak Medal for Bravery, the Order of Slovak National Insurrection and Order of Meritorious Fighter. He subsequently legalized his undercover name, Rudolf Vrba, and became a citizen of Great Britain.

Rudi Vrba after World War II in Prague. Pre-eminent WW II historian Sir Martin Gilbert has stated Vrba's actions saved the lives of at least 100,000 Jews.

Vrba graduated in chemistry and biochemistry from the Prague Technical University in 1951 and obtained a post-graduate degree from the Czechoslovak Academy of Science in 1956. After research at Charles University Medical School in Prague until 1958, he worked for two years as a biochemist at the Ministry of Agriculture in Israel. He then became a member of the Research Staff of the British Medical Research Council in London (1960–1967). When Vrba immigrated to Canada in 1967 and became Associate of the Medical Research Council of Canada, he began to use Rudi as his common first name. He worked for two years (1973–1975) in the United States as a Lecturer and Research Fellow at Harvard Medical School before joining the medical faculty at the University of British Columbia in 1976 as associate professor of pharmacology. Specializing in the chemistry of the brain, Vrba published more than fifty original scientific papers and also undertook research pertaining to cancer and diabetes.

The author of this book invited Rudolf Vrba to make a rare public appearance in Vancouver as a guest speaker at the sixteenth annual BC Book Prizes awards banquet in 2001; otherwise, he was rarely, if ever, cited as a B.C. author. In 1997, he provided a keynote address for the annual Kristallnacht Commemorative Program at the Vancouver Jewish Community Centre on November 9, speaking on "Money and the Holocaust: The Role of the Holocaust in German Economic and Military Strategy, 1941–1945." Vrba expressed his belief that the theft of Jewish property was a prime motivation for the murders of six million Jews between 1941 and 1945. His speech was based on his extensive research and his unique perspective as a slave labourer in the Kanada section of Auschwitz–Birkenau where confiscated Jewish clothing and goods were processed.

The last time I saw Rudi Vrba, we met for coffee on West Broadway. He seemed fine, jovial, fatherly. We discussed our mutual friend, Stephen Vizinczey, and he left me with some parting advice: "Whenever something bad happens, something upsetting or irritating, like locking your keys inside your car, or somebody steals your bicycle, stop and ask yourself, am I going to remember this a year from now?

The anxiety will subside." Quite simply, Rudi Vrba knew things about life that other people didn't know.

Rudi Vrba died of cancer in Vancouver on March 27, 2006, at age eighty-one, predeceased by his elder daughter, Dr. Helena Vrbova, and survived by his first wife, Gerta Vrbova, his second wife, Robin Vrba, and his daughter, Zuza Vrbova Jackson. Vrba's papers were gifted by Robin Vrba to the Franklin D. Roosevelt President Library and Museum in New York. Efforts were made to have Rudi Vrba buried in the oldest Jewish cemetery on the B.C. mainland, part of Mountain View Cemetery in Vancouver, but it was ultimately decided that his final resting place would be a seldom-visited cemetery, known to few people, where there is only a simple headstone.

As an author, Vrba most significantly published a memoir, *I Cannot Forgive* (1963), with an Irish-born journalist in London, Alan Bestic, that has been translated worldwide. The first Hebrew edition of Vrba's memoir was not published until 1988. His follow-up version, *I Escaped from Auschwitz* (2002), covers the intricacies of life inside Auschwitz–Birkenau, including an attempted revolt and a love affair, with excellent Appendix material. It is lucid, frank and riveting.

If there is an overriding message for *Out of Hiding*, Vrba's concluding words in his life story will do nicely: "It is of evil to assent to evil actively or passively, as an instrument, as an observer, or as a victim. Under certain circumstances even ignorance is evil."

WAISMAN, Robert

ROMEK WAJSMAN was born in 1931 in Skarzysko, Poland, as the last child in a family of eight, six years younger than his nearest sibling. This detail matters. During a happy childhood within an Orthodox Jewish household he was catered to and treasured—and in this way he was inadvertently trained to be wise beyond his years. A childhood beating received at the hands of some Gentile friends, only a few blocks from his home, first made him question the security of his existence. Then the Nazis were advancing. "My father used to say that there was nothing to worry about," he has recalled. "You can't just go and kill people on a wholescale level without some people in other nations sitting up and taking notice and saying 'Now wait a minute. What are you doing here?' That was my father's theory."

Soon Skarzysko became a rail depot for advancing German troops. The Wehrmacht used chemical bombs. Black smoke was billowing. "We were all running. And what I recollect is my mother giving me a soaked towel, and (saying) 'Keep it on your face . . . ' so this was the first brush with war and bombs and what was to come." The Wehrmacht arrived and literally asked for a cup of tea. His mother showed them hospitality. Discussion ensued when they left. "You see, they're not monsters. They don't have horns." It was still possible to rationalize a hopeful future. Some Poles told themselves that at least the cultured Germans could make sure that Communism wouldn't come.

Many Poles tried to adapt to defeat but tolerance was one-sided. Romek witnessed a Pole being shot to death in the street. The Nazis soon needed labourers. While a few able-bodied men disappeared into the woods, others who tried to run away were shot. Poles became afraid to go out. Particularly Jews. All of his four brothers acquired work permits. Everyone tried to retain optimism. "It was expected locally that either Russia or America or England would come to the rescue and defeat the Germans and restore Poland and every other country," he has recalled.

The entire family was forced to pack their belongings and move into a ghetto, rife with typhoid, in 1941. There were rumours that other ghettos were much, much worse. Deprivations and cruelties were rationalized until one evening a man who had escaped from Treblinka came into their ghetto residence, bringing them first-hand news about the mass murders being committed in the camps. Romek was told by his mother to go out and play but he disobeyed and hid behind curtains. He could hear the man from Treblinka shout, in frustration, "If you don't want to believe me, don't believe me!"

Panic ensued. It was true. All those people who were being forced

JENNIFER HOUGHTON PHOTO COURTESY OF ROBBIE WAISMAN

All Holocaust memoirs are not created equal. As one of the youngest survivors of Buchenwald, Romek Wajsman (at left), known in Canadian society as Robert or Robbie Waisman, was nursed back to health and rehabilitated alongside Nobel Prize winner Elie Wiesel (at right) in France. His unprecedented story of perseverance and survivalist acumen appears wondrous in retrospect.

to leave on trains, never to be heard from again, were not being resettled. "As a child," Romek later recalled, "I remember thinking to myself, being Jewish was really not the most wonderful thing in the world and being Chosen, as sometimes we read in the Bible."

The Wajsman family secured work permits, except for Romek and his mother. In the early days, it was still assumed that women and children would not be harmed.

Romek's father hatched a plan to protect Robbie. He was the youngest, the precious one. They packed him a little suitcase. A couple with a horse and buggy arrived. Both his parents rode with him to the couple's farm. They reassured him that he would only have to remain at the farmhouse until it was safe. It was only for a short time. He was obliged not to make a fuss. But after three weeks he was extremely homesick. He was accustomed to his mother's arms and her kiss good night. He was special at home. Abandoned, he was nothing.

"I put my suitcase together and ran home," he later said. "It took me about a day. I came home exhausted . . . . The only spanking I ever received was that time. And while he was doing it, my father was screaming, 'You know it cost me all kinds of trinkets of jewelry' [given to the farmer]."

This was the first time Romek risked his life to be reunited with his family.

The ghetto was not safe for children. Next-to-useless as labourers, they were being exported by the Nazis for execution. Consequently, Romek's eldest brother woke him at three o'clock in the morning and put him on a truck. Covered with potato sacks, without any permit, he was smuggled out of the ghetto and hidden in a hayloft. At age eight, Romek Wajsman was instructed to stay in hiding for two days and two nights. At night he would descend the ladder and forage for food in the garden.

When his brother returned, as promised, Romek asked if they were going home. He was told there was no home. The ghetto had been liquidated. Of the approximately 1,500 children in Skarzysko, Romek and his sister would be among the handful who survived. Romek asked his brother about his mother. Where was she? His brother said she had been resettled. Lacking a work permit, she had been sent to Treblinka. Later, he would learn she was gassed to death.

Romek's response to this tragedy was to go blank, to vow to live. The way to survive was to work. Some fifty years later, while watching the movie *Shoah*, depicting a rail journey to Treblinka, he would be jolted into a flood of grief. Until liberation, he knew he must win in the deadly chess game of survival. It was 1942. His father, sisters and brothers were working in a forced labor camp at Skarczysko. It was a munitions factory. He succeeded in persuading his brother, Abraham, who drove a transport truck, to smuggle him into the prison camp. This was the second time he would risk his life to be reunited with his family.

A German metalworking company, HASAG, was producing ammunition and equipment, including anti-aircraft shells. Romek excelled at painting 3,200 of these per day. His prodigious work rate earned his survival. "I was revered and looked up to for being a wunderkind. That allowed me to live. That's the way you had to look at it. Anytime there was some higher-up from the Gestapo people, they would come to take a look." Romek was painting the S onto anti-aircraft shells much faster than adults. Nonetheless, children were routinely sent to the gas chambers. There was absolutely no certainty that he might not be selected for death while walking to and from the barracks. "I didn't consider myself a child. You grow up very fast when you have to. I very quickly learned to walk tall and look twice the size that I was."

The obligatory assembly line-ups in the camp were harrowing. On a whim, he could be selected as a child bound for Treblinka. Sometimes he had to improvise. Once he was placed in the doomed line-up for older people and children. He did not panic. During the frenzy that ensued, he made an extraordinary gamble. He went up to the Nazi in charge and pleaded to be put in the line-up for old people and children, the line he was already in. Sure enough, the Nazi supervisor refused to grant his request. The supervisor roughly pushed him into the line-up with his father and the other workers. This was the third time he risked his life to be reunited with his family.

At all costs, they had to avoid the next selection process. His father devised a plan for Romek to escape and join the Polish partisans. "Don't worry," his father said. "I'll find you after this mess is over." A guard was bribed. A portion of the electrified fence was made safe. Romek was small. He could crawl underneath. He used a stick to lift up the wire. He made contact with the Partisans. He ran errands for them. One of them was going to teach him to handle a gun. But the Partisans were mean-spirited survivalists. "I was totally despised in that group because, again, I was a Jew." It was easy to distinguish a Jewish boy. He could be a liability. He stood out. "I realized very quickly that my chances of survival weren't very good and I looked for the same hole to get back into the camp. My chances for survival were better in the camp than they were outside." For the fourth time he risked his life to be reunited with his family.

It's conceivable that Romek Wajsman is the only person in human history to sneak his way back into a concentration camp a second time. There, when an older co-worker noticed the holes in Romek's shoes, he gave Romek a scrap of leather from a refuse pile. A Nazi guard noticed this act of kindness and promptly accused the gift-giver of stealing from the Third Reich. The good Samaritan was promptly shot. Blood splattered onto Romek. The horror-stricken look on the face of the gift-giver would plague his dreams for the rest of his days. Romek blamed himself for the death of his would-be benefactor.

Kindness was dangerous. But kindness was also a form of resistance. On Saturdays, the Gentiles didn't have to work and Romek did odd jobs around the munitions factory. A truck arrived on Saturdays to haul away the newly-manufactured anti-aircraft parts. The Germans, of course, required paperwork, a bill of lading. Everything must be recorded. Every anti-aircraft part, every corpse. One of Romek's jobs was to go to an office and exchange some paperwork he had been given for a bill of lading to certify that the munitions equipment could be taken away by the truck. There was a secretary he went to see. He had no idea whether she was German or Polish. He would never dare to speak to her. She was not allowed to speak to him. On one particular Saturday, he presented the paperwork as usual, and she gave him the bill of lading as usual. He felt something was different. It was bulkier. When he got outside the office, he realized she had hidden a little package of some sort. "I took a look and it was a sandwich! Two pieces of bread with butter and jam on it. I can still taste it," he recalled, more than fifty years later. "I mean it was something absolutely fantastic. I mean, you didn't see butter and marmalade."

His sister was in the women's barracks, far away. That night he risked his life to take her half of that sandwich. He was so proud to provide it. "I knew how much she would appreciate it. Something like that could sustain you for a week. . . . She [the secretary] risked her life in doing this. If one of the SS men would say, "What are you doing here?" and he saw a piece of bread and butter . . . she'd be shot. I looked forward to this treat on a weekly basis because she did it for

Relatives listed at the Holocaust Memorial Monument in New Westminster, B.C.

weeks on end. Gave me her lunch. I don't know her name. To me, she was one of the righteous ones." Romek would continue to give portions of the sandwich to either his sister or father, whichever of the two he was able to find.

Different camps served the business enterprises of different companies, some of which have remained active. From 1943 to 1945, Romek was sent to various camps, where conditions varied. He and his father witnessed the brutal murder of his brother, Avram. The unpredictability of these years took a toll. Because his frame was slender, and he was still just a young boy, known to be a diligent worker, Romek was frequently valuable as someone who could crawl into cramped spaces, sometimes to fix faulty machinery. This joyless diligence was ultimately exhausting. He came down with typhoid. There were no medications. He was covered up with straw. He was hidden. His father could only visit him briefly, every twelve hours. He lay alone for eight days. If they found him, if the camp guards knew he was sick, he would have been murdered.

After eight days, as soon as he could stand, he forced himself to come back to work. It was the only possible way to survive. But he was noticeably weak. It was too soon. The guards pulled him out. "I was spotted you know [put on the truck for elimination]. I knew that when I got on the truck, my fate would be the same as that of my brother. . . . We mounted the trucks and I was right on the edge and I remember seeing from the truck my father speaking to one of the guards." It was a mystery as to how his father saved him. He was too ill to be happy. In fact, he felt so exhausted that he was not entirely sure he appreciated being rescued. His father urged him to live. A few months later, they were separated by different shifts in a factory. They barely glimpsed one another, except on Sundays. His father's hair had turned completely white. "We just crossed one another. And, very simply, one day I looked for him and he wasn't there. He was moved to another section and that was the last I saw him."

Only his sister might be left alive. But he had lost track of her. To endure, Romek befriended Abram Czapnik, who was eleven months younger. They risked their lives to steal potatoes. They became inseparable. "Without his friendship, I would have lost my bearings and perished." In 1944, they were relocated to Buchenwald. Oddly, both were placed in Block 8, mostly reserved for political prisoners. He had no idea that the vast majority of teenage youths were kept in Block 66. They thought they were the only two children in all of Buchenwald. On April 11, 1945, he heard that his sister, Leah, might still be alive. He would not get to meet Elie Wiesel until 426 of the approximately one thousand children liberated from Buchenwald were relocated by the Red Cross, en masse, as *les enfants terribles*, to France.

"It took a year before I cried."

Romek and Elie Wiesel arrived at the village of Ecouis, managed by a children's rescue society, with "a horde of suspicious, distrusting, rebellious and hostile children—as if from some other planet. They tried to give us salad to eat. Did we survive to be fed like rabbits? Then they gave us smelly Camembert cheese. Why were we given food that smelled foul to us, as if it should thrown away."

The first time he was asked his name, he blurted out his concentration camp number. The refugee children were mostly cold and indifferent. The social workers and other experts assumed they would be irredeemable. Naturally, many Holocaust survivors have questioned the existence of God. The children were no different. They divided themselves between the socialists (those who believed God was an empty fantasy) and the traditionalists (those, led by Elie Wiesel, who could be scornful of God but felt there had to be meaning in the Holocaust).

The fascinating story of how these child survivors nearly all recovered to lead successful lives has been recounted in Judith Hemmendinger and Robert Krell's *The Children of Buchenwald* (2000), the memoirs of Elie Wiesel, Miriam Rouveyre's *Enfants de Buchenwald* (1995) and Romek's own memoir, co-written with a Torontonian, Susan McClelland, *Boy from Buchenwald* (Bloomsbury 2021), published under his Anglicized name, Robbie Waisman.

Romek was one of the last to leave France, in December of 1949. He had learned his sister had survived, married a fellow survivor, and was living in Palestine, but efforts to reach Palestine were stymied. Since France was too close to Germany, Canada and Australia became the best choices. In Montreal, he'd be able to speak French. But he was sent to western Canada, where he hoped to reach Vancouver but instead was billeted in the Calgary home of Harry and Rachel Goresht, where they were able to communicate in Yiddish. He befriended a young Edward Bronfman, learned English and became an accountant. There he met a girl from a prominent family, Gloria Lyons, and they married. "When I was dating Gloria, the family looked into my personal history. My wife was warned she was marrying someone with a completely different background who had gone through the war. So, there was discouragement. Not many of us were integrated to a degree where they were dating Canadian-born women. As far as I was concerned, I was simply looking for the right person."

After ten years in Calgary, Waisman moved to Saskatoon where he opened a clothing store and served as President of the B'nai B'rith and the Saskatoon Jewish Society. Few people other than his wife knew he was a Shoah survivor. They moved to Vancouver in 1978. He worked in the hotel industry and they raised two children, Howard and Arlaina. "I skied with them, I skated with them, I did everything possible with them. I took a lot of time with my children and I'm told that did me a lot of good. The childhood that I lost, and was robbed of, I recaptured with my children, and that was a wonderful feeling."

Following the trial of Holocaust-denier Jim Keegstra in 1983, Waisman became treasurer of the Vancouver Holocaust Centre Society (later known as VHEC), then Vice-President, then President. In 2003, Waisman joined Willie Abrahams, a residential school survivor, to lecture B.C. students about their shared experiences in the face of violence and persecution. In 2014, he received the Governor General's Caring Canadian Award for his voluntary service to consciousness raising. In 2018, Robbie Waisman received an honorary Doctorate of Law from the University of Victoria. His wife Gloria died in February of 2020.

Near the turn of the century, he wrote, "I have lived a normal adult life, married and raised two children. In my mind, normality and surviving the Holocaust are two different things. When you really think about what survivors experienced, how can we be normal? It is true. Some of the thoughts and some of the ways we think cannot be normal. And yet, no one should feel sorry for me. I do not need sympathy. No one should say, 'poor Robbie, what you must have been through.' I don't want this. We have proven to ourselves that we're normal human beings, that we have raised families and become responsible members of our community. We have made many productive contributions and now, later in life, can look back and say, the Holocaust occurred, this is what happened, and these are the things we must do so that it does not happen again."

KRELL, Robert

FOLLOWING THE DEATH of Rudi Vrba, Robert Krell became British Columbia's most significant activist and educator pertaining to the Holocaust. A child survivor of the Holocaust and a psychiatrist in Vancouver, he has organized and managed countless initiatives, such as the Vancouver Holocaust Education Centre, since the 1970s, while his own extensive publications, as well as his pioneering work as a psychiatrist, have largely remained under the radar.

Krell has recently condensed a 400–page memoir into a new autobiography, *Sounds from Silence: Reflections of a Child Holocaust Survivor, Psychiatrist and Teacher* (Amsterdam Publishers 2021). As a poignant story about the difficulties inherent in being the son of two

Viewed from inside Auschwitz-Birkenau, the "Gate of Death" was built in 1943. Before the rail spur was added in May of 1944, Holocaust captives arrived two kilometres away and were transported by trucks or forced to walk to the gas chambers. "In 1991, we went to Auschwitz–Birkenau and Treblinka. Passing under the sign Arbeit Macht Frei into Auschwitz I experienced a violent shaking, a convulsion of my entire being. I thought I was having an epileptic seizure except that it did not reveal itself externally. I did not fall to the ground nor foam at the mouth. I experienced a seizure of the soul and was relieved it did not show. My grief remained a personal matter. I believe every Jewish child who survived was imprinted with this indelible grief and bereavement and loss. But I was beginning to speak about it." — Robert Krell families, Krell's autobiography succeeds as a candid and careful confessional on behalf of haunted generations of Jews who have suffered from "an overdose of death."

Like Yosef Wosk, Robert remains deeply inspired by Elie Wiesel, the teacher they separately knew as a both a mentor and a friend. In September of 2012, Krell brought Wiesel to Vancouver in order to receive an honorary doctorate from UBC. Wiesel participated in fundraising activities, visited with Robbie Waisman, and Krell interviewed Wiesel before a sold-out audience at the Orpheum Theatre.

"Elie," Krell says, "has been a spiritual rock in my life." Krell spent two formative days with Wiesel, survivor of Auschwitz and Buchenwald, during Wiesel's visit to Vancouver in 1978. "I talked with him and heard him speak and noted his manner, his mastery of silence, and of listening. I had his book, *Souls on Fire: Portraits and Legends of Hasidic Masters*. He inscribed it, 'For Marilyn and Rob—Souls on Fire, with affection, November 7, 1978.' It was true. He confirmed for me that indeed my soul was on fire. My motivation was burnt into me from all I had learned and heard."

"I live because I was not murdered." — Robert Krell

ROBERT KRELL WAS BORN in The Hague, Holland, on August 5, 1940. He was hidden from 1942 to 1945 with the non-Jewish Munnik family. He reluctantly returned to his parents, who had survived in hiding in 1945. Other members of his parents' families had been murdered in Auschwitz and Sobibor and the forests of Poland.

When his family was told to report for "resettlement to the East" on August 19, 1942, his parents Leo and Emmy Krell were aware that none of their friends who had obeyed previous directives had returned. Trains were leaving for Auschwitz and Sobibor every Tuesday packed with 1,000 Dutch Jews, though their destination was not yet known. His obstinate and brave father decided the family should flee rather than report. Robert's birth parents took care to take absolutely nothing with them that could identify them as Jews.

Robert, at age two, was hastily handed over to a Dutch neighbour, Mrs. Mulder, who agreed to give him shelter for just a few days. "My mother had packed me a little suitcase," Krell recalls. "When she left, I apparently tried to follow her, dragging my suitcase behind me. When she told me this story fifty years later, she said that I looked at her in a way suggesting that I would never forgive her. Of course, I denied that, but she was right. She was much smarter than I was. Although she would save my life by having the courage to leave me with virtual strangers, I never forgave her for leaving me." A child who cannot yet understand circumstances experiences only abandonment.

Because older Dutch people such as Mrs. Mulder and her father were being moved out of the city by the Germans, Robert was transferred to the care of Violette Munnik, again with the understanding that this arrangement would be temporary. Violette and her husband Albert Munnik had no idea those few days would turn into three years.

In countries under German occupation, an estimated 93 percent of Jewish children were slain in hideous ways or starved to death. Robert's parents went into hiding, then split up, causing a painful schism of distrust that would ruin their marriage decades later. They nonetheless had to simultaneously view themselves as the lucky ones because about 80 percent of Holland's Jews were murdered.

The Munnik's teenage daughter, Nora, once dared to take little Robert out in a buggy, seemingly for a forbidden visit to his birth mother in hiding. "Except for that lapse," he recalls, "she proved to be a wonderful older sister, hiding my existence from her school friends and coming home early to teach me how to read and write."

As a small child, Robert Krell did not know he was a Jew. Excessively quiet, co-operative and obedient, Robert never complained of pain or illness. He did not cry. With his dark-brown hair "in a sea of blondes," he was warned to stay away from the front window.

When he was reunited with his parents, Robert Krell's first post-war school was a Catholic kindergarten where he was the Mother

Leo and Emmy Krell outside their home in The Hague, 1940, with Robert.

Superior's prize pupil, always mindful and well-behaved.

"My parents survived the war," he writes. "How lucky. And they came to take me back. How unlucky."

Very simply, he loved the Munniks and he did not know the Krells. Leo and Emmy Krell struggled to convince their son he belonged with them. A dual family identity would never quite abate: The cover image of Krell's first personal memoir shows Krell alongside his adoptive mother, Violette Munnik, following a tree-planting ceremony at the Avenue of the Righteous at Yad Vashem Memorial Museum in Jerusalem in 1981. His birth mother appears on the back cover.

Robert Krell immigrated with his birth parents to Canada in 1951. Professionally, he graduated in medicine at UBC in 1965. He interned at the Philadelphia General Hospital and continued in psychiatric training at Temple University Hospital in Philadelphia, Stanford University Hospital in Palo Alto and then returned to the University of British Columbia. In 1970 he became F.R.C.P. (C) and in 1971 a Diplomat of the American Boards of Psychiatry and Neurology. He was appointed Assistant Professor in Psychiatry in January 1971 and served as Professor of Psychiatry until 1995, when he became Professor Emeritus. In his professional career, he was Director of Residency Training for ten years and for twenty-five years Director of Child and Family Psychiatry at the UBC Health Sciences Centre and B.C.'s Children's Hospital.

Krell took six months to recover from open heart surgery in 2009 but it was not his most alarming experience. In 1969, at age twenty-nine, he was aboard TWA Flight 840 from Rome to Athens, en route to Israel, when the plane was hijacked by Palestinian terrorists. Passengers feared there were explosives aboard and their plane would be crashed into Tel Aviv.

"My first reaction was rage," he writes. "My second was fear. The rage was instant, a primitive response to my having been hidden as a child in Nazi-occupied Holland. As far as I was concerned, the Arabs were about to finish the job that the Germans had failed to complete, my murder."

In a chilling chapter, Krell describes how and why he was once again successful in hiding his Jewish identity, concealing his passport as well as a gold ring made in Holland featuring his initials inside a Star of David. Passengers were advised to prepare for a crash landing. Instead, they landed in the new and yet-to-be officially opened Damascus International Airport.

Krell's chapter in his autobiography on Jewish hero Rudi Vrba is especially important. Outspoken, angry and intensely private, Vrba had frequently been ostracized because he repeatedly criticized Jewish leadership of complicity for their failures. Krell respected Vrba for remaining one of the world's most important and potent voices to counteract Holocaust deniers. Krell first arranged for the publication of Rudi Vrba's book in both English and Hebrew via Gefen Publishing, only to have Vrba kibosh arrangements and publish via the University of Haifa, instead, with the added bonus of an honorary doctorate.

Krell's subsequent friendship made him a rare confidante for Vrba who agreed to appear on the same Vancouver stage with Sir Martin Gilbert in 1999, one of countless events coordinated with Krell, as a mainstay of the Vancouver Holocaust Education Centre. Stricken with a terminal illness, Vrba initially asked Krell to make his funeral arrangements but plans for a distinctly Jewish burial site went awry when family wishes intervened. "I cherished my relationship with Rudi," Krell writes, "rocky though it was at times." He still hopes that someday Vrba will be reburied nearer to the majority of Jews in Vancouver.

Krell was also privileged to become acquainted with Miep Gies, the woman who looked after the Frank family in hiding in Amsterdam, bringing them food, news and encouragement until late 1944. It was Miep Gies who found and safeguarded Anne Frank's diary. In 2018, Robert acquired a first edition of the diary and donated it to the VHEC where it is on permanent display.

AS AN AUTHOR, Robert Krell remains hiding in plain sight. His "window-evasive" personality has seemingly prevented him from finding a mainstream Canadian publisher for important works such as *Child Holocaust Survivors: Memories and Reflections* (Trafford 2007). With Czech-born, Norwegian psychiatrist and Auschwitz survivor Leo Eitinger and his research assistant Miriam Rieck, Krell has also expanded on their initially small bibliography of medical and psychological research pertaining to Holocaust survivors and their children and produced a work with 1,400 references dating from 1945 to 1985 for *The Psychological and Medical Effects of Concentration Camps and Related Persecutions on Survivors of the Holocaust: A Research Bibliography* (UBC Press 1985). Hoping to produce an even more expansive work to be titled *The Eitinger Bibliography*, with a foreword by Elie Wiesel in honour of Dr. Eitinger, Krell was disappointed when this volume, co-edited with Marc I. Sherman, was re-titled. The collection of 2,461 bibliographic references, rather than being identified as a bibliography, was renamed *Medical and Psychological Effects of Concentration Camps on Holocaust Survivors.*

Retaining Elie Wiesel's introduction, Krell also re-wrote an English translation of Judith Hemmendinger's *The Children of Buchenwald: Child Survivors of the Holocaust and Their Postwar Lives* (Jerusalem: Gefen 2000). It describes the rehabilitation process for 426 boys (out of 1,000 children liberated from Buchenwald on April 11, 1945) who were considered too irrevocably damaged by most physicians and psychologists at the time to be reintegrated into society. Of those Jewish male children and adolescents who arrived at Ecouis, France, on June 8, 1945, there were 210 Poles, 118 Romanians, 49 Czechs, 43

Hungarians, four Lithuanians and two Germans. They included Elie Wiesel, Chief Rabbi Israel Meir Lau and Robert Waisman.

IN ORDER TO CONVEY why this book is dedicated to Robert Krell, it is necessary to note some of his other activities.

Robert Krell is one of the world's leading psychiatrists in treating traumatized survivors of the Holocaust or other prisoner-of-war circumstances. In his private psychiatric practice, Dr. Krell has treated Holocaust survivors and their families as well as Dutch survivors of Japanese concentration camps.

He has built friendships with Sarah Moskovitz, Sir Martin Gilbert and other educators while serving his community whenever and wherever possible.

He served on the Board of Directors of the Canadian Jewish Congress: Pacific Region from 1972, as Chair (1986–1989) and National Vice-President (1989–1992).

In 1975, he co-founded, with Dr. Graham Forst of Capilano College as co-Chair, and Professor William Nicholls, head of Religious Studies at UBC, the Standing Committee on Holocaust Education. They commenced a Holocaust education program for high school students in 1976, reaching more than 1,000 British Columbia high school students annually to this day.

In 1978, long before the Spielberg Archives was started, he created an audiovisual documentation program for recording hundreds of survivor testimonies.

In 1980 he urged the Canadian Jewish Congress to establish a national program, which resulted in a nationwide audiovisual project taping seventy survivors.

Being a child survivor of the Holocaust, he assisted with the formation of child survivor groups, first in Los Angeles between 1982 and 1984 and then in Vancouver.

He expanded audiovisual documentation of Holocaust survivors in the Vancouver area in 1983 and 1984 to tape 120 eyewitness accounts.

TWIGG PHOTO

Robert Krell and friend Yosef Wosk both received the Order of Canada in 2020.

He was fundamental in the creation of a memorial for Holocaust survivors, unveiled in 1987, at the Schara Tzedeck Cemetery.

He served on the International Advisory Council of the Hidden Child Conference that organized a gathering in New York in 1991 for approximately 1,500 child survivors who came from many countries to meet for the first time and have met annually ever since.

He also co-founded the Vancouver Holocaust Education Centre which opened on November 7th, 1994 in order to provide educational programs for high school children to warn them of the consequences of unchecked racism and intolerance. The Centre serves 20,000 students annually.

He has been awarded the Israel Bonds International Elie Wiesel Holocaust Remembrance Award (2008) and the Boston University Hillel Lifetime Achievement Award for "bringing solace and understanding to generations of Holocaust Survivors" (2011).

He was keynote speaker at the International Day of Commemoration ceremony in memory of victims of the Holocaust, at the United Nations, New York, January 27, 2012.

The Holocaust Educational Foundation at Northwestern University recognized his "distinguished contributions to Holocaust education" in 2012 and on December 5, 2012, he was awarded the Queen Elizabeth Diamond Jubilee Medal, "as an outstanding human rights educator."

He received an award from The World Federation of Jewish Child Survivors of the Holocaust and Descendants at its Gathering in Berlin (2014).

He received the B.C. Community Award (2015) for "dedicating his life to anti-racism, anti-Semitism and Holocaust education" for pioneering audiovisual testimony in conjunction with the VHEC and helping in the formation of Child Survivor Groups. He was recognized with a Governor General's Caring Canadian Award for the creation of the Vancouver Holocaust Education Centre and for his lifelong work promoting human rights and social justice (2016).

On September 27, 2017, Krell was the keynote speaker at the Jewish Federation of Ottawa's evening event marking the Inauguration of the Holocaust National Monument.

Krell served as co-chair for the 31st World Federation of Jewish Child Holocaust Survivors and Descendants annual Gathering in Vancouver, November 1–4, 2019. It was the first time the event was ever held on the West Coast and only the second time in Canada. Over 400 survivors and their descendants attended from around the world.

He received the Order of Canada (2020) "for his contributions to our understanding of mass ethnopolitical violence and for his advocacy on behalf of Holocaust survivors."

ROBERT KRELL IS MARRIED and has three children and nine grandchildren. He has authored six books, co-edited three and written twenty-one book chapters and over fifty journal articles. His prose can be plainspoken and redolent with uncomfortable truths.

> When I think of David Ben-Gurion or Golda Meir, Menachem Begin or Yitzhak Rabin, I am aware of how little of consequence Canada's prime ministers really face. Their issues are serious where the daily lives of Canadian citizens are concerned, in matters of health and education, the status of First Nations, and the ever-present concerns about Quebec. But never, in all my years in Canada, has our government been faced with major threats to its security and the personal safety of its citizens, as has Israel. It is disconcerting how nations relatively free from immediate danger have so much to say about what Israel can or cannot do in order to defend itself.

His writing is always clear, rarely drawing attention to itself. In a rare deviation from prose, here is an excerpt from notes he made for a never-published poem in 1979, called simply "god."

god has not been a friend of mine
since I have known
the truth of Auschwitz
nevertheless I drift occasionally
toward a synagogue
sometimes to pray
sometimes to curse
but mostly to wait
for him to ask
to be forgiven

Perhaps Robert Krell's writing has yet to attract any attention from mainstream media because overtly Jewish writing is too easily ghettoized by contemporary tastemakers. An argument can be made that readers and critics in Canada who are conventionally concerned with trumpeting the merits of writing from other minorities are now missing a great deal.

"I know that my life was scarred irrevocably by the Shoah," he writes. "I am not drawn to it like a moth to a flame. The flames are drawn to me. They pursue me. They will seek to engulf me. I ward off the flames through confrontation, through Holocaust education, through recording testimony, for ultimately there is no escape. I live because I was not murdered. Other two-year-olds were thrown alive into burning pits.

"One survivor acquaintance once took me aside: 'Robert, I must tell, but I can't . . . tell anyone. And I cannot write it down. I was a teenager. The Germans came. One went to the mother of a three-year-old, a blonde girl, a little angel, and asked if he could take the child's picture. He gave her an apple and posed her beside a tree. She was so pretty. Then he shot her in the head, picked up the apple, and ate it. I saw it.'"

PART TWO

Chorus

ADDERSON, Caroline

AFTER READING AN article in *The New Yorker* about the hair that was taken from Jews and later displayed in the Auschwitz museum, Caroline Adderson began imagining her debut novel about two unlikely travelling companions who make a pilgrimage to the Auschwitz museum specifically to see the hair.

She knew right away she didn't want to presume to write from a survivor's point of view or even from the perspective of children of survivors. "The subject of the novel had to be compassion, why some people are able to feel the suffering of others, even people they have no connection to, while others can't."

A History of Forgetting is therefore about Malcolm Firth, an aging, gay man who is losing his lifelong partner to Alzheimer's disease, and his naive, 20-year-old apprentice, Allison, who is traumatized by the recent murder of a co-worker. Unable to escape from their private pains, the pair instinctively move towards the even greater pain of the Holocaust.

Beyond the pair's relatively minor predicaments there is an overriding, philosophical question. How can we hope to make sense of

Caroline Adderson

a world that is so rife with so much cruelty? Adderson initially resisted visiting Auschwitz herself but realized it was necessary. "I was overwhelmed by what I'd seen and had no idea how to incorporate the trip into the novel. Since I had to start somewhere, I simply typed out the sign posted at the entrance to the Auschwitz Museum."

The sign says: *You are entering a place of exceptional horror and tragedy. Please show your respect for those who suffered and died here by behaving in a manner suitable to the dignity of their memory.*

"Because the sign is in second person," she says, "I continued on in that voice, describing the scene through the eyes of a neutral narrator who comes into the salon to have his hair cut." It would take her six years to complete the novel after her trip to Poland in 1994. "It wasn't until I reached the end of the book, however, that I understood that these second-person sections had a thematic as well as a functional purpose in the book.

"Compassion involves a feat of imagination. It asks you to get inside another person and feel what he or she feels. It occurred to me that by writing in the second person, I was forcing the reader to step into the shoes of these different characters and even witness a murder. In other words, the act of reading the book becomes an act of compassion."

A History of Forgetting was nominated for the 2000 Rogers Trust Fiction Prize and the Ethel Wilson Fiction Prize. "Her damaged and struggling people," commented reviewer Robert Harlow, "become your own to deal with as if they were relatives, and you follow them through the trivia of a hairdressing salon and eventually all the way to Auschwitz, the most relevant site in the 20th century."

ALMA, Ann

"The Nazis can only kill us once." — Mies Braal

BORN IN 1946 IN the small town of Uit-huiz-er-meeden (which translates into English as out-houses in the meadows), Ann Alma of Nelson, B.C. grew up knowing that many of her neighbours had died of exposure and starvation when the Nazis severely limited the transportation of food and fuel.

That's partly the impetus for Ann Alma's young adult novel, *Brave Deeds: How One Family Saved Many From the Nazis* (Groundwood 2008), written from the perspective of a fictional child but otherwise a true story.

After she moved to B.C. in 1970, Ann Alma learned that her Dutch-speaking neighbours Frans and Mies Braal had hidden, clothed and fed twenty-six people in an unused vacation camp called *Het Buitenhuis* on the island of Voorne during the winter of 1944–45. Along with those Jews in hiding was a downed Canadian airman named Philip Pochailo, as well as starving children.

Having parachuted into a field of Holstein cows, Pochailo was hidden by Dutch farmers and taken to the home of Frans Braal, who was the leader of the Dutch resistance in Oostvoorne. Unable to utilize escape routes due to his burns and an injured ankle, Pochailo spent seven months in hiding with 25 Jews, children and resistance fighters who were sheltered by Braal.

After World War II, Philip Pochailo came to B.C. where he married a St. Paul's Hospital nurse and raised a family in Vancouver from 1948 to 1958. Pochailo, who twice returned to Holland to celebrate the liberation, died in Ottawa at age ninety-five in 2016, exactly 72 years to the day his plane was shot down.

"They had a lot of rooms with dorms," writes Alma, "and they realized that the Nazis could only execute them once for hiding people, so they took in a lot of others. Peter Oppenheimer, for instance, was a thirteen-year-old Jew who stayed with the Braals until the end of the war, because his parents were sent to a concentration camp." During World War II, twice the hideaway was searched by Nazis soldiers and everyone remained undetected in an underground shelter.

President Dwight Eisenhower and Sir Winston Churchill sent certificates of appreciation to Frans and Mies Braal who first immigrated, with their children, to the USA in 1957. In 1969, they moved to the West Kootenays and built a house in the mountains where Ann Alma became their neighbour. Ann and Mies talked in Dutch every week while her husband Frans was in a seniors' home with dementia. "Their story came out little by little," says Alma, "and finally, after getting permission from Mies, I wrote the book."

Canadian airman Philip Pochailo, who became a Vancouverite, was hidden for seven months by the Braal family on the island of Voorne, west of Rotterdam, after his Lancaster bomber was shot down near the Dutch coast, returning from a mission over Germany.

The Dutch government sent the brave couple a bronze cross in 1982, and George Hees, Minister of Veterans Affairs, presented them with a certificate of gratitude in 1987 for sheltering the Canadian aviator. Frans Braal died at age eighty-nine in Nelson in 2004; Mies Baal died at age ninety in 2007.

The Jewish War Veterans of the Shalom Legion Branch in Vancouver planted fifty trees in Israel to honour the Braals in 1988. The Shalom branch of the Royal Canadian Legion was established in October of 1944 to assist returning Jewish service men and women from World War II.

BIRNIE, Lisa Hobbs

"Except for the usual suspects—such as photographer Leni Riefenstahl, Hitler's girlfriend Eva Braun or the wives of Goebbels and Goering—most war stories tend to be about men. The role of women in the Third Reich has been mostly overlooked."
— Maureen Kelleher, filmmaker

AT AGE EIGHT, a Polish Jew named Mania Fishel Kroll had dreams of becoming Poland's Shirley Temple. At age nine, she was taken to Auschwitz. At age eleven, the Nazis murdered Mania's mother. At age twelve, she found herself in the Reichenbach concentration camp. There she was protected by a German Christian prison guard named Johanne who gave her special food and enabled her to survive. Johanne offered to adopt Mania but this did not happen at war's end. They went their separate ways.

"She gave me proof that goodness exists everywhere," Mania recalled, "even when evil dominates. She always walked beside me when we went to work in the dark, just in case I fell, so I wouldn't be shot."

More than thirty years later, Mania was living in Toronto in 1977 when she hired a cleaning woman named Muller who struck her as strangely familiar. Mania became convinced her cleaning lady was the former SS Corporal Johanne Clausen, the beautiful German woman at Reichenbach who had been passionately in love with an officer of the Third Reich.

The cleaning lady steadfastly denied she was Johanne. "*Es ist ganz unmoglich.*" (It is completely impossible.) Before Muller returned to Germany, Mania took her out to dinner. They laughed like old friends. They exchanged letters. In her final letter, Johanne wrote, "*Sie weissen nicht wasfur ein Leben ich hatte.*" (You can't imagine the life I've had.)

Still, decades later, in 2002, Lisa Hobbs Birnie, one of Canada's most respected journalists, accompanied both these women on a visit

Lisa Hobbs Birnie

to the abandoned site of Reichenbach near the German-Polish border, hoping to unravel the truth. It proved to be a moving experience for all three women. "I'd sailed through life like a tourist," Birnie recalls, "and now unknown currents had pulled me into new territory."

Birnie herself had to admit she was not comfortable with Germans. "It's not a matter of choosing to like or dislike. It's a feeling that arises automatically whenever I meet a German." Her twenty-one-year-old brother, Robert, a bomber pilot in the Royal Australian Air Force, was killed on a raid over Magdeburg in 1945. Within her Australian family there had been no discussion, no grieving, no hugs, no funeral service, no details, no body.

The bizarre reunion between Mania and Johanne was recorded for the NFB documentary film, *Return to Reichenbach*, directed and produced by Vancouverite Maureen Kelleher, supported by BC Film. At age eighty-two, Lisa Hobbs Birnie subsequently published her tenth and final book, *In Mania's Memory* (Read Leaf 2010), a non-fiction investigation of an extraordinary Holocaust relationship.

"At first Mania's story seemed too strange to be true," Birnie told an audience at the Jewish Book Festival in Vancouver in 2010. "Were they fragments of a terrorized child's imagination? How often did this happen in the world that former prisoners met their tormentors years later? How many secrets are there in peoples' lives? And if this German housekeeper was the guard who saved Mania, why would she not admit it? What secret was she hiding?"

Ultimately, Birnie would unravel the mystery as to why Johanne had to always deny the truth.

"There was one other element that drew me close to Mania's life," Birnie continued. "I am and had been raised as a Christian. Much of Europe was Christian. In the face of extreme silence as children, whole families were terrorized and murdered. I felt outrage and shame. The Vatican knew. Yet no voice was raised. Now the present Pope wishes to take the first steps towards declaring Pope Pius a saint. I find this, as a Catholic, an unspeakable outrage."

The town of Reichenbach was transferred from Germany to Poland in 1945 and re-named Dzierzoniow. In World War II, Reichenbach was part of the Gross-Rosen system of approximately 100 camps in eastern Germany, Poland and Czechoslovakia. This system included approximately 500 female camp guards such as Johanne.

Female SS were also used at a number of camps: Brubblitz, Graeben, Grunberg, Gruschwitz Neusalz, Hundsfeld, Kratzau II, Oberaltstadt and Schlesiersee Schanzenbau. The most notorious guard Irma Ida Ilse Grese was stationed at Auschwitz and Ravensbruck before her appointment as warden for the women's section of Bergen-Belsen. When the murderess and torturer was sentenced to death at age twenty-two by a military court, she was the youngest woman to die under British Law in the twentieth century.

Mania Kroll and guard Johanne Clausen returned to Reichenbach in 2002.

Born in 1928, Lisa Hobbs Birnie married the Vancouver artist John Koerner in her early seventies. He died at age 100 in 2014. Born in Czechoslovakia in 1913, he had studied law and art in Prague and Paris, then moved to Canada with other family members in 1939, just prior to the Nazi takeover. During her writing career spanning seven decades, Lisa Hobbs Birnie published ten books, most notably

Uncommon Will: The Death and Life of Sue Rodriguez, to investigate the societal stigma of suicide and the need for medical assistance in dying in Canada.

"Writing Mania's story allowed me a chance to create a picture of an ordinary woman who lost everything but still was full of love and forgiveness," Birnie told her Festival audience. "Mania had one legacy from her mother. That legacy was just a handful of words. Bewildered, terrified in Auschwitz, Mania, nine years old, begged her mother to go on the wire [to electrocute themselves]. She said to her mother, 'Take my hand, Mama. We'll run onto it together. It'll only take a minute.' Mania's mother said, 'Listen, my child. As long as we breathe, we have life. As long as we have life, we have love.' That was Mania's treasured legacy."

BLUMAN, Barbara

"In my family, there is one great hero we always carry in our hearts and to whom we will be forever grateful: Chiune Sugihara."
— George Bluman

RAOUL WALLENBERG (sent to Budapest by the U.S.) was one of several foreigners who saved Hungarian Jews with a visa scheme developed by his predecessor, Per Anger, who attended the unveiling of a plaque to honour Wallenberg at Queen Elizabeth Park in Vancouver.

Far less known is a Japanese vice-consul who saved between 6,000 and 10,000 Jews by providing travel visas to Japan from an embassy in Kaunas, Lithuania, whereupon many reached Shanghai, via the Soviet Union, and some carried on to Canada after the war.

Among the latter were the parents of Vancouver siblings George, Barbara and Robert Bluman. It was Chiune Sugihara who gave Nathan and Susan Bluman their precious transit visas to reach Japan, via the Trans-Siberian Railway, after they had fled from Poland to Lithuania. The couple's suspenseful exodus ended happily when they boarded the last ship sailing from Japan to Vancouver prior to the attack on Pearl Harbor. At least 23 members of the Bluman family owe their lives to the Japanese diplomat Chiune Sugihara.

To tell the full story, Barbara Bluman eventually published *I Have My Mother's Eyes: A Holocaust Memoir Across Generations* (Ronsdale 2009).

Her brother George Bluman provided a briefer summary when he was keynote speaker for the 15th Annual Raoul Wallenberg Day gathering in Vancouver in 2020, an event organized by the Wallenberg-Sugihara Civil Courage Society. [For a condensed version of his speech, consult the Bluman entry on ABCBookWorld.com]

BORN ON JANUARY 1, 1900, in the remote Japanese village of Yaotsu, Chiune Sugihara studied foreign languages in Harbin, China, converted to Christianity and married a Russian woman. Divorced in 1935, he remarried in the same year to his Japanese wife, Yukiko, and received a diplomatic posting to Helsinki, Finland. They left Yokohama and arrived in Vancouver on August 30, 1937.

The Sugiharas next took a train from Seattle to the East Coast in order to reach Europe. He was re-posted to a new consulate in Kaunas, Lithuania, reporting to ambassadors in Riga and Berlin. The Japanese foreign minister, Matsuoka, had known Sugihara in Harbin. Essentially, Sugihara was a Japanese spy, monitoring Soviet and German movements. He arrived just four days prior to the Nazi invasion of Poland on September 1, 1939, accompanied by his wife, three sons and his wife's sister.

Wallenberg plaque in Queen Elizabeth Park, dedicated by Per Anger.

Sugihara put his family at risk

while he was saving Jewish lives. By September of 1940, he had to leave Lithuania for postings in Prague, Konigsberg, Germany and Bucharest. In Prague, he submitted the so-called Sugihara List to Matsuoka containing 2,141 names of those who had received the travel visas, of which ninety percent were Jews. His own family was later imprisoned in Bucharest by the Soviets in a POW camp for 18 months.

At the time, Sugihara's radical individualism was not appreciated and he was dismissed from the diplomatic corps in 1947. Back in Japan he survived by taking odd jobs. For sixteen years he represented Japanese companies in Moscow, visiting his family in Japan on an annual basis. He was not aware of how many Jewish lives he had saved until 1968. In 1985, Chiune Sugihara received the Righteous Among the Nations award from Yad Vashem in Israel and his descendants were given perpetual Israeli citizenship. He died in Japan the following year at age eighty-six.

The Dutch diplomat who worked in league with Sugihara's efforts, Jan Zwartendijk, was likewise honoured in 1997. By all accounts a modest man, Sugihara was rated Japan's most important citizen in a 2017 Tokyo poll because he had the strength of mind to act independently, without authorization from superiors. There are museums in his honour in Kaunas, Lithuania, Tsuruga and Yaotsu. A Chiune Sugihara Sempo Museum opened in Tokyo in 2019. On the 79th anniversary of the day he started issuing transit visas, he was celebrated globally with a Google Doodle on July 29, 2019. He is also the subject for Cellin Glick's feature film, *Persona Non Grata: The Story of Chiune Sugihara.*

BARBARA BLUMAN'S *I Have My Mother's Eyes: A Holocaust Memoir Across Generations* was completed by her daughter Danielle Schroeder, the grand-daughter of Susan (Zosia) and Nathan (Natek) Bluman. It describes how Zosia Hoffenberg, the daughter of a successful businessman, had a comfortable life in Warsaw and fell in love with eighteen-year-old Natek Bluman before the outbreak of World War

Persona Non Grata: The Story of Chiune Sugihara (2005), a feature film by Cellin Glick, depicts the life of diplomat Chiune Sugihara whose efforts to save Jews were largely overlooked during his lifetime until he was honoured by Yad Vashem in 1985, one year before he died. He was later hailed as Japan's most important citizen in a Tokyo poll in 2017.

II. While learning business skills in New York, Natek heard U.S. media reports and understood the enormity of the threat to European Jews, but when Natek returned to Poland, Zosia's father dismissed his warnings.

Three months after the German bombs fell on Warsaw, Zosia joined Natek in the countryside. There they were married and embarked on a long journey to freedom. On June 26, 1941, the Blumans sailed from Yokohama for Vancouver on an aging freighter, the *Hie Maru*, completing a journey to freedom of almost two years. A year later, Natek enlisted in the Canadian army, telling his pregnant wife, "I will never forgive myself if I don't fight against the Nazis."

Zosia's daughter Barbara Ruth Bluman graduated from UBC Law School in 1975. A commitment to human rights was demonstrated in all of her pursuits. She served as a member of the Medical Services Commission, the Vancouver Public Library Board, the Board of the Contemporary Art Gallery and the B.C. Paramedics Licensing Board. Her legal practice focussed on workers' rights and she served as a member of the Workers Compensation Board. She was among the first women arbitrators, primarily in public sector disputes.

Barbara Bluman contributed to the Gesher Project at the VHEC, a second-generation cultural exploration of the Holocaust, and helped to organize an important symposium on the Nuremberg trials. She was in the last stages of cancer when she set down her mother Zosia's story, interweaving it with her own, before she died on September 8, 2001. An afterword was written by Danielle Schroeder, making this memoir into a three-generational family project.

BORAKS-NEMETZ, Lillian

BORN IN 1933, Lillian Boraks-Nemetz survived the Warsaw Ghetto as a young girl after 18 months of fear, starvation, loss and quarantine for typhus. She escaped with a paper of false identity, with a different name and a certificate that said she was a baptized Christian. As arranged by her father, Stanislaw Boraks (1903–1949), a prominent lawyer, she escaped by walking through a checkpoint guarded by German soldiers pointing their rifles at anyone who dared to cross to the Aryan side of Warsaw. The soldiers were bribed and let her through. They were known for taking bribes and not keeping their word, but in this case they did.

Once on the other side, a Polish woman took her to the village of Zalesie where her grandmother lived under false papers with a Catholic man from Krakow. As a survivor/mentor, Lillian revisited that house in 2014 with 80 students from Western Canada. For the very first time in all her talks with students in many schools, she told them about how the man with whom she was hiding had abused her, offering her a piece of bread in exchange for refuge. She took several groups of six or eight young people through the little house, each time repeating her story.

"He was both good and bad. How does a child of eight take that? that, on the one hand, he saved our lives, and, on the other hand, he was a drunk who could have given us away but somehow didn't." Because the students were so kind and compassionate upon hearing her story, she felt that never again would she have to hide this truth from the world.

In 2009, Boraks-Nemetz also recalled the house on Spokojna Street in a speech to the Janusz Korczak Association of Canada, an organization of which she is a board member: "It was near the outhouse that I was once hidden inside a hole in the ground to avoid being noticed by the visiting Nazi delegation, who came to investigate the murder of the village *Volksdeutscher*. Luckily, they didn't find me. One night, standing by the fence, I recalled with a chill in my heart the unforgettable night when my grandmother and I stood by the same fence. We were facing Warsaw, staring at the blood-red sky over the burning Ghetto and wondering with despair about the fate of our family."

Lillian Boraks-Nemetz immigrated with her family to Montreal, Quebec, in 1947, moving to Vancouver in 1949, then onto Victoria where she attended St. Margaret's School for girls. She attended UBC in 1965, gaining her Bachelor and Masters degrees in Comparative

Literature. She is now best-known as the author of young adult novels that include *The Old Brown Suitcase*, a true-to-life account that is written as the story of a 14-year-old immigrant girl, Slava Lenski, who comes to Canada from Poland after World War II. Her suitcase is filled with memories of the Warsaw Ghetto where she left behind her parents and sister. Slava's problems of adjustment to her new life in Canada as a teenaged, immigrant Jew are juxtaposed with her heart-wrenching memories of her lost childhood in Poland. This book won the Sheila A. Egoff Chuildren's Literature Prize and other awards.

In a sequel, *The Sunflower Diary*, we follow Slava's experiences in the form of a personal journal which she begins in the summer of 1949, soon after her mother's remarriage. It is two years since her arrival in Canada and her father has recently died of cancer. She must reluctantly leave Montreal to attend a private boarding school for girls on Vancouver Island where she is told by the mistress of the school it would be better if she conceals her Jewish background. As "Elizabeth," she tries to conform while confiding in her diary: "To be a 'new girl' as well as an 'immigrant,' not to mention a 'Jew in hiding here in Canada', is a triple horror."

Ultimately, however, the chronicler concludes: "If I forget my memories, who will remember and act on them?"

In the final book in the trilogy, *The Lenski File*, Slava, at eighteen, returns to Poland to search for her missing sister and soon attracts the attention of the secret police. Lillian lost her own five-year-old sister in 1942 when she was brutally murdered, on the order of a Nazi officer, simply because her sister was Jewish. Boraks-Nemetz subsequently published her autobiographical story as an adult novel, *Mouth of Truth: Buried Secrets*. It recounts the ways the trauma and child abuse she experienced during the war affected her adult life: her relationships with her children, husband and mother, and her life in the community. Such struggles can result in a family break-up and intergenerational transference of trauma; they can also generate a resolve to begin again on a journey for truth and healing. Hence, *Mouth of Truth* has been used in university courses.

The Old Brown Suitcase
LILLIAN BORAKS-NEMETZ
BC BOOK PRIZE WINNER
CANADIAN JEWISH Winner BOOK AWARD
THE CANADIAN CHILDRENS BOOK CENTRE CHOICE

Boraks-Nemetz has taught Creative Writing at UBC and co-founded the Holocaust Child Survivor Group of Vancouver in 1989, serving as its Chair for four years. She frequently gives talks on the Holocaust and racism to elementary and secondary school students within the Outreach Program of the Vancouver Holocaust Centre for Education (VHEC).

She has also translated volumes of poetry by two Polish emigre poets living in Canada, Waclaw Iwaniuk (*Dark Times*, Houslow Press) and Andrzej Busza (*Astrologer in the Underground*, Ohio University Press, with Michael Bullock), and she has appeared in documentary projects concerning the Holocaust including a 2013 PBS Frontline documentary about Polish child survivors, *Never Forget to Lie*, as well as *My Holocaust Survival and Hidden in Poland*.

The killing of George Floyd in May of 2020 by a Minneapolis police officer prompted her to write a poem about racism, 'The Arm,' that begins: "Today I am George Floyd / I am a Jew / so I know how it feels / To be stifled / By the arm of hate / That extends toward anyone / Who is different in colour / Culture or creed."

BUCKMAN, Alex

IT WAS COMMON FOR THE EXHAUSTED and famished inmates in concentration camps to fantasize about food. In his presentations to young audiences, Vancouver survivor Alex Buckman often refers to a recipe book made by his Aunt Becky and other inmates during her 16 months in the Ravensbruck camp for women. Her little cookbook, constructed by stealth, contained instructions for making her specialty, *Gateau a l'orange* (Orange Cake).

While forced to work in a German factory, Rebecca "Becky" Teitelbaum stole a swath of brown paper, a pencil and a pair of scissors and hid them in her clothes. Back in her barracks, Becky cut out squares of paper and recorded her recipes from memory.

"If caught with all these stolen goods—no questions asked—they would have hanged her in front of all the prisoners for stealing," Alex

Buckman often tells his young audiences in schools.

Once Becky's precious bible, her recipe book of hopeful memories, was lost when a transport truck she was riding in was bombed after she was liberated from the camp. Becky Teitelbaum had jumped into a ditch for safety, severely injuring her arm, and the recipe book was left on the roadside. Miraculously, it was found and returned to her four years later.

For the rest of her life, she kept it, as a prized possession, in a special bag, but she never spoke of it. Eventually, Alex Buckman found it and asked his aunt, "Why didn't you show it to us?" She didn't know why. She couldn't say. Buckman could only surmise that keeping the book out of sight, unmentioned, was part of an unconscious strategy to help her forget what she had endured.

ALEX BUCKMAN was born in Brussels, Belgium, on October 31, 1939. He was seven months old when the Nazis invaded Belgium. He last saw his birth mother at age two. The sister of his father Isaac Buckman, his aunt Rebecca, would serve as his primary caregiver, raising him as her own child. His father also paid a Catholic family to keep him safe. At age four, after Alex had been hidden successfully in various homes, he was sent to a Catholic orphanage in Namur, located two hours away from Brussels. His father made arrangements for Alex's little cousin, Annie, to be hidden there, too.

"Our last names were changed," Buckman recalls, "so that Annie and I would be known as brother and sister instead of cousins. That way, if anything would happen to our parents, at least the two of us could stay together."

Several times, when Nazi inspectors visited the orphanage, the boys were sent to hide in the cellar, where there was total darkness, and they were told to remain silent. He was given some material to stuff in his mouth to prevent him from crying out. At first, they were confused. Had they done something wrong? Cold and confused, the boys peed their pants. "We saw large things running around us. They told us later they were rats." When at last it was safe to re-emerge, they were afraid to do so because they had peed their pants. "From four to five-and-a-half, it happened too many times. So many years after, I still can't sleep without lights throughout the house."

Hence the title for Buckman's 60-page memoir is *Afraid of the Dark: The Memoir of Alex Buckman*, produced as part of the Langara College English Department's Writing Lives project, with the recording, transcribing and editing assistance of Paulina Bustamante, Katelyn Ralph and Joey Law. CBC made a radio documentary on the Writing Lives course taught by Rachel Mines that featured the orange cake recipe. [Buckman's publication is cited herein as being representative of the Writing Lives series undertaken by the Vancouver Holocaust Education Centre, Langara College and the Azrieli Foundation of Quebec. Contact VHEC for more information on this series.]

When most of the concentration camps were liberated, Buckman's circumstances were not much improved. "At six-and-a-half in an orphanage, nothing was that rosy," he said, during a UBC panel moderated by Dr. Ilona Shulman Spaar seventy-five years later. "We saw parents come and pick up their children and take them home, but nobody came for us. Annie was crying and wondering why our parents weren't coming and I tried to tell her that I was sure that they will come. But, like her, I didn't know why they weren't coming."

Eventually, they were sent by the Red Cross to Brussels where the names of unclaimed children were posted throughout the city. A paternal uncle found them and took them to a family that Alex assumed must be his. Annie's parents pretended to be his parents, supposedly for his benefit, until another cousin cruelly blurted out the terrible truth: Annie's parents were alive; his were dead. His parents had been turned in to the Gestapo and sent to Auschwitz where they were murdered at ages thirty-one (father) and thirty-two (mother). "I took a step back and, for the first time, I realized I was alone."

Buckman came to Canada at age eleven with his cousin, his uncle and his aunt, Rebecca Buckman Teitelbaum, in 1951. She had spent seventeen months in Ravensbruck. She barely survived her first four months as an outdoor labourer, hauling wood and stones in heavy carts. Having worked in a department store in Belgium, she was able to gain a life-saving transfer to work in the office of the Siemens Factory, affording far more liveable conditions at the Siemenslager subcamp. There, as was mentioned earlier, she was able to steal a roll of brown paper, a pencil and scissors. Her recipes were read over and over by the other women in the camp, dreaming of life before and after the Holocaust. She went on to produce two more recipe books as gifts for other women, as well as a thin volume of poems and resistance songs (on display at the Vancouver Holocaust Education Centre) and two sets of playing cards that were used by Roma in the camp to tell fortunes. She died in December of 1998.

Alex Buckman left Montreal and came to Vancouver in his early '20s. In April of 2010, as a survivor-participant in the March of the Living program that brings Jewish youth to Poland and Israel, Buckman entered Auschwitz, having learned that both of his parents were murdered there. "We finally walked in a shower room," he later told journalist Pat Johnson, "and I closed my eyes. I was thinking of my mother and her sister. We were told that the women panicked when they did not see water come down from the showers. They ran towards the walls and scratched them with their fingernails. When I heard this, I turned and caressed the wall, feeling the scratches made by Jewish women prisoners. I wondered, were those scratches made by my mother? I would never know. In that room, I finally said, au revoir, Maman."

A strong advocate for child survivors, Buckman has served as president of the Vancouver Child Survivors Group and has served as a frequent speaker for the Vancouver Holocaust Education Centre and also as Treasurer of the World Federation of Jewish Child Holocaust Survivors.

Orange cake is often shared when he gives his classroom presentations.

CORNWALL, Claudia

Baptized as an Anglican, Claudia Cornwall did not find out that three of her grandparents were Jewish until she was in her forties. She was born as Claudia Maria Wiener, in Shanghai, in 1948.

Shanghai was a place of refuge for approximately 17,000 to 18,000 German and Austrian Jews during World War II because it was one of the few places on earth that did not require a visa. By comparison, Britain took in 70,000 Jews prior to September 1, 1939, and another 10,000 during the war. Pre-war, Australia took 8,200; South Africa, 3,500; Canada, 4,000; India, 5,000. When the flow of refugees to Commonwealth countries became a trickle during the war, the significance of Shanghai as a sanctuary was further enhanced.

Jews made the journey to Shanghai in 1938 and 1939, either via Poland and Russia or by sea on German and Italian liners. The seldom-cited diplomat-rescuer, Dr. Feng-Shan Ho, issued life-saving visas to nearly 2,000 Jews who requested them from the Chinese Consulate in Vienna, facilitating their escape without permission from either the Chinese Ambassador in Berlin or his superiors in the Chinese government. In 1990, Dr. Feng-Shan Ho finally wrote his memoirs, *Forty Years of my Diplomatic Life*. Born in 1901, he died in 1997.

Not all the Jews who made it to Shanghai had Ho-issued visas. Cornwall's parents did not. She was baptized in Shanghai and immigrated to Canada in 1949 with her parents. She attended UBC and the University of Calgary, completed her doctorate in philosophy and became a journalist under her married name, Claudia Cornwall.

In 1988, Claudia wrote to her uncle in Austria, asking for a photo of her father, Walter Wiener, who had left Vienna in October of 1938, to escape Nazism. Walter sailed from Italy on the *Conte Rosso* to Shanghai where he found work as a financial journalist. A Christmas card arrived for Claudia in January of 1989. In it, was a photo taken in a garden, showing her father at the age of three or four.

"I took the picture out of the card and laid it down, thinking I would frame it and hang it on my bedroom wall." There were also two women in the garden. Claudia began to read her uncle's message offering warm wishes and news about his family. But he also had some more startling information. "The lady standing up was our mother," her uncle wrote, "who died in a concentration camp." Claudia called her mother, Lore, to ask whether this could be true.

"Yes," she answered.

"Why didn't you tell me?" Claudia asked.

"If I have to choose between my loyalty to Daddy and my loyalty to you," her mother told her, "Daddy comes first. He never wants to talk about it. But now the Pandora's box is open."

The trauma of those years has ebbed and Claudia found that her parents were willing to speak about what happened. Her paternal grandparents, who were Jewish, perished in the Holocaust, and her father and his brother escaped to Shanghai. The Wieners had kept diaries, letters, and other documents in a large black trunk. Though Claudia spoke some German, she had never read the contents because the old German script was difficult to understand. Her mother helped her to translate them. One of the most exciting "finds" was the diary of her maternal grandfather, Willy Frensdorff. Claudia proceeded to piece together her family's origins, making research trips to Germany and Austria to interview remaining family members and visit archives.

Willy Frensdorff, a naval engineer from Bremen, had been incarcerated in Sachsenhausen for three weeks, after he had converted to Lutheranism and married a non-Jewish wife, Melitta. Six months after his release from the camp, he fled to Shanghai, sailing on the *Sharnhorst*. In 1940, his wife and daughter joined him. But Melitta was unable to handle the heat and foreign environment of Shanghai. She returned to Germany, survived the war and eventually reunited with her daughter in Canada.

In Shanghai, Lore, a trained dressmaker, met Walter Wiener in March of 1941. In December, sixteen days after the Japanese had taken control of the International Settlement in Shanghai, Lore Frensdorff married Walter Wiener. Details of that era can be found in David

Kranzler's *Japanese, Nazis and Jews: The Jewish Refugee Community of Shanghai* (1938–1945).

The end result of Claudia Cornwall's curiosity and research was *Letter from Vienna: A Daughter Uncovers Her Family's Jewish Past* (Douglas & McIntyre 1995) which received the Hubert Evans Prize for best non-fiction book in B.C. Cornwall's comments in a review she wrote about Barbara Kessel's book *Suddenly Jewish* (Brandeis University Press, 2000) express her awareness that her own story is far from unusual:

> At first, I thought that I was the only person in the world who had made such a discovery. But I quickly found out this was not the case. I kept meeting people who had a similar experience or who knew someone who did. Once when I was interviewed on TV about my 'finding', a cameraman, quite literally, was jumping up and down with excitement. As I left the studio, he told me that he had just learned that his father was Jewish. I fell into conversation with a Jehovah's Witness who came to my door and found out that her mother had uncovered Jewish roots. Madeleine Albright rather famously discovered her Jewish family in the Czech Republic several years ago. And recently I read that Elvis Presley may have been Jewish. Sometimes I wonder, is everyone Jewish?

DRABEK, Jan

IN 1985, Vancouver novelist Jan Drabek travelled to Poland with his father Jaroslav Drabek to film *Father's Return to Auschwitz* (1990), a twenty-minute documentary directed by Czech-born Ivan Horsky. As an Auschwitz survivor and a lawyer for Jews, Drabek's father was invited to serve on President Jimmy Carter's 34-member President's Commission, chaired by Elie Wiesel, for the creation of the United States Holocaust Museum at 100 Raoul Wallenberg Place in Washington, D.C. This work will be published in English, for the first time, in a proposed sequel, *Bearing Witness, Holocaust Literature of B.C., Vol. II,* or else provided as an adjunct for a website at rudolfvrba.com, a site envisioned by Alan Twigg and Yosef Wosk.

When Jaroslav Drabek died in 1943, *The New York Times* ran an obituary in its national edition, Section 1, page 31, on December 29, 1996, entitled "Jaroslav Drabek, Lawyer and Voice of Czechs, 95" in which he is cited for his resistance to "German occupiers and Communists" and his successful prosecution of Karl Frank, Nazi Governor of Bohemia and Moravia. There is no mention of Auschwitz.

BORN IN 1901, in Chrudim (the "Athens of Eastern Bohemia"), formerly part of the Austro-Hungarian empire, Jaroslav Drabek gained his law degree in Prague, and served in the Czechoslovak Army against the forces of Hungarian Communist Bela Kun. Married with two sons, Drabek Sr. practised law and wrote for newspapers until the 1938 Munich Pact doomed Czechoslovakia as a sovereign country. In 1938, en route to London to report to the exiled President Eduard Benes on behalf of the Czech resistance movement, Drabek Sr. and his wife witnessed the aftermath of Kristallnacht in Germany and reported the plight of German Jews to London.

While under surveillance by the Gestapo, Jaroslav Drabek worked with other Czech court officials to arrange for Jewish mothers to swear false affidavits that stated their children were fathered by Aryan men, out of wedlock. " . . . some people tried to prove they were only half Jews," he wrote, "in other words that they really had a non-Jewish father, a fact which could possibly save one from the gas chambers. Of course, it was necessary to prove that the mother had relations with some non-Jew and not with her husband who was Jewish.

"To this day," he wrote, "I remember the unpleasant feeling these memorized testimonies of Jewish mothers who, out of love for their children, allowed themselves to give it. Such invented testimony in court meant horror and degradation for them. All of us knew—the

Jan Drabek with his father Jaroslav on Bowen Island,1985.

tribunal as well as the attorneys—that the mother by her lie is trying to save her children; none of us dared to look into her eye or to ask her a question.

"We felt the magnitude as well as the monstrosity of this motherly sacrifice. It was really terrible to look at an elderly exhausted mother who had to publicly and under an oath claim that she had committed adultery. It was obvious how she was suffering, how difficult it was for her to recite the lie she had learned by heart.

"The perjury didn't disturb us. We knew for certain that the Lord would forgive these mothers. I must attest that the Czech judges understood fully this grotesque situation and tried to make such cases as easy as possible for us. At times it was they who advised me how to arrange it so that the case would proceed as smoothly as possible.

"There was, however, one unfortunate part of the thing. It became well known that I was successfully concluding such cases and my practice grew by leaps and bounds until I became quite worried about it."

Jaroslav Drabek was arrested by the Gestapo for resistance activities and sent by train to Auschwitz with his documents stamped RETURN UNWANTED. He was incarcerated on January 9, 1943. His tattoo number was 94692.

His son, Jan Drabek, has explained how a leader of the Czech Resistance, Vladimir Krajina, a family friend, contrived his father's release.

"When [Vladimir] Krajina heard that he was in Auschwitz, he told the Gestapo that my father played a much larger role than he actually did in the Resistance, so that way the Gestapo would want to keep him alive and bring him back for interrogation. But just at that time typhus broke out in the camp and father's return was delayed by a few months due to the quarantine. By the time he returned, the Germans were on the run on the eastern front and the invasion was about to happen in the West. There was an active underground cell at the Prague prison and father, with the help of the Czech prison doctor, faked a leg injury. But then the Gestapo placed him on another transport to Auschwitz. Again, his prison doctor friend and others helped and, in the summer of 1944, he was released and placed in care of the Prague insane asylum. Father always said that those days in the asylum were the calmest days for him and without them he couldn't have survived the war and postwar turmoil."

Upon his release from prison in 1944, with the complicity of a turncoat Gestapo agent, Jaroslav Drabek learned that Reichsprotektor Heydrich, before his assassination, had used his veto power to cancel the validity of civil verdicts brought out by Czech courts and so many of Drabek Sr.'s carefully planned and executed cases were annulled. "For many of my clients," he later wrote, "this, of course, meant the verdict of death."

At war's end, Drabek Sr. was made chief prosecutor of the People's Court, bringing successful cases against collaborators and Nazi war criminals that included Karl H. Frank, the Nazi governor of Bohemia, against whom he obtained a death sentence. During these investigations, Drabek Sr. simultaneously uncovered nefarious Communist activities and published a collection of Auschwitz stories, *Povídky o*

Drabek greeting Hillary Clinton and Madeleine Albright in Prague, 1996.

krutém umírání (Stories of Cruel Dying), in Prague in 1947. When the Communists took full control of Czechoslovakia in 1948, there arose Communist suspicions and phoney allegations that Drabek Sr. had been too lenient in prosecuting Nazis. Consequently, the Drabek family, preceded by Vladimir Krajina by one day, escaped on skis from Communist-controlled Czechoslovakia, into Bavaria, in 1948.

The Drabeks were processed for immigration in Frankfurt. After the family had passed several months in Germany and France, Czech-American Jewish friends who had been advised by Drabek to leave Europe back in 1939, facilitated their resettlement in New York. There, Drabek Sr. became a commentator and announcer for Voice of America.

After retiring from Voice of America in 1971, Drabek Sr. was named to the President's Commission on the Holocaust. This was on the advice of Madeleine Albright, who was the daughter of the Drabek family friend, Professor Josef Korbel. Eventually, President Jimmy Carter decreed by an executive order to build the U.S. Holocaust Memorial Museum on October 26, 1979. Congress unanimously endorsed the initiative in 1980 and the Museum was dedicated on April 22, 1993. The researchers at that facility proceeded to document 42,000 ghettos and concentration camps erected by the Nazis.

President Vaclav Havel appointed Jan Drabek, his erstwhile schoolmate, as an ambassador to Kenya. Jan Drabek later became Chief of the Czech Diplomatic Protocol Department. There was also a literary connection. Some of Drabek's novels had been published in Czech, and Havel was himself an established playwright.

When Madeleine Albright was serving as the U.S. Ambassador to the United Nations, it was Jan Drabek who welcomed her to Prague on behalf of the government. It was also during this period, in Prague, that Hillary Clinton and Albright befriended one another. Hillary Clinton would subsequently prevail upon her husband President Bill Clinton to appoint Albright as the first female Secretary of State.

Also, in 1996, Jan Drabek was the first official to welcome Queen Elizabeth II and Pope John Paul II to Prague.

Jaroslav Drabek's wife, Jarmila Kucerova Drabek, who had been instrumental in his release from Auschwitz, died in Washington in 1983. Jaroslav Drabek died there in December of 1996 at age ninety-five.

JAN DRABEK immigrated to Canada in 1965 after he had served in the U.S. Navy (1956-1958), on the editorial staff of the *Washington Evening Star* (1958-1960), as a refugee settlement officer in Vienna (1961), a broadcaster in Munich (1961-1963) and as a travel clerk for American Express in New York. His wife's family was already in Vancouver, as was the Czech botanist, Vladimir Krajina, who had headed his father's underground group.

Although little-known in his adopted country, Vladimir Krajina, a UBC-based botany professor, was personally thanked for his wartime resistance by Winston Churchill and was accorded some of the highest honours provided by both Canada and Czechoslovakia (before it was divided into the Czech Republic and Slovakia). Jan Drabek eventually published a biography of Krajina, the founder of B.C.'s Ecological Reserve Program, that was published in Prague in 2016 and re-issued in English as *Vladimir Krajina, World War II Hero and Ecology Pioneer* (Ronsdale 2012). It was then re-launched in a new Czech version at the Canadian Embassy in Prague as *Dva Zivoty Vladimira Krajiny* (*Two Lives of Vladimir Krajina*).

Jan Drabek recalled the Nazi invasion of Czechoslovakia and his family's flight through the Alps in the first of his three memoirs, *Thirteen: A Childhood in Wartime Prague* (Caitlin 1991).

In 2005, Drabek Jr. returned to the Czech Republic for the launch of one of his own books as well as Jaroslav Drabek's posthumous novel, *Podzemi* (*The Underground*), in Czech. In 2013, Jan Drabek received the Masaryk Prize awarded annually by the Czech and Slovak Association of Canada to a Canadian of Czech or Slovak origin who has played a role in bringing freedom to Czechoslovakia, or enriched the lives of Czechs and Slovaks in Canada.

FLORIS, Steve

PRECIOUS FEW PEOPLE who have ever dined at the upscale Teahouse Restaurant in Vancouver's Stanley Park can tell you that its origins are Yugoslavian, Hungarian and Jewish. The original proprietors were displaced persons, Eva and Steve Floris, whose own story would likely have remained untold were it not for the bizarre and tragic death of Eva Floris on the city's Granville Island in 2000.

Grief-stricken and guilt-ridden when the family car plunged into the waters of False Creek, causing Eva to drown, Steve Floris, an agnostic Jew, resolved to pay tribute to their lives two years later with his memoir, *Escape from Pannonia: A Tale of Two Survivors* (Creative Connections, an imprint of Granville Island Publishing, 2002).

"I wanted to express our gratitude to Canada for giving us refuge," he wrote, "and now that my wife is gone, killed tragically through my own mistake, I want more than ever to tell our story which I have kept hidden in my heart for so many years."

BORN IN BUDAPEST on September 21, 1920, Steve Floris was sent as a youth by the fascist-leaning Hungarian government at the time to visit Mussolini's Italy but as a schoolboy he was unimpressed. With few career paths available to Jews upon graduation from high school, he trained as an apprentice in his uncle's pastry shop and candy factory. In 1943, when Floris was conscripted for a Hungarian labour battalion, his culinary skills kept him alive and fed. He was transferred the day before his battalion was overwhelmed by Russian soldiers. Those who weren't killed were sent to Siberia. Floris was eventually sent to a work camp in Austria in 1944.

As Allied forces advanced, Floris was loaded onto a cattle car but the train was forced to stop because the tracks had been bombed at the town of Krems. Parallel to the tracks was a road crowded with refugees on foot. Floris was able to escape and infiltrate the throng of refugees. Through a series of deceptions and disguises, he made his

This Holocaust statue on the banks of the Danube evokes the 1942 massacre at Novi Sad.

way back to Budapest where he would be eventually re-united with his mother and his beloved Eva.

Eva had been living in the Yugoslavian city of Novi Sad (now the second-largest city in Serbia) in 1941 when Nazi-affiliated gendarmes murdered Jews, Gypsies and Serbs in the early days of January, 1942. Variously known as the Novi Sad massacre or the Ujvidek massacre, the raid in southern Backa was a campaign of terror undertaken by forces from Hungary, commanded by Kiralyi Honvedseg, ostensibly to vanquish partisans after Hungary had annexed Yugoslav territories. In fact, citizens were detained at random. The Danube was strewn with corpses when an estimated 3,000 to 4,000 civilians were slaughtered in the Backa (or Bacska) region, approximately 1,000 in Eva's hometown. Tragically, victims were forced to march across the frozen Danube, only to drown in the icy waters when the ice sheet was shelled from the shore. Others were pushed into the gaping holes or simply gunned down in the streets.

Officially, the Hungarian government condemned the mass killings and four perpetrators were executed in 1943, but deep resentments have lingered. One of the alleged perpetrators, Sandor Kepiro, was tried in 2011 for murdering 30 civilians in the Novi Sad massacre but he was acquitted. In 2013, Hungary's president formally apologized to Serbia. That apology came too late for Eva Floris.

After surviving World War II, the couple soon discovered the new yoke of Communism was nearly as stifling and prejudicial as that of the Nazis. Seeking better prospects in Austria, they found jobs working for the American Joint Distribution Committee, which was the primary North American agency helping Jewish survivors in Europe. When they were allowed to immigrate to Canada from Salzburg, they arrived in Halifax on September 23, 1948, and were sent to Winnipeg, with its harsh climate.

"One day, my wife told me of a conversation she overheard between a hairdresser and a customer at the beauty parlor," Floris writes. "The customer said, 'I listed my house for sale a year ago because we want to move to B.C. and not a bite yet!' The hairdresser replied, 'If I could sell this crummy business wouldn't I be in Vancouver in an instant!' It was that overheard conversation that prompted Eva and Steve Floris to save all their money for two bus tickets to Vancouver."

Escaping the prairie winter, they arrived on January 4, 1949. Life on the West Coast seemed idyllic. The couple obtained a lease from the Vancouver Park Board to operate the then-named Art Gallery Tea Room in Stanley Park. The building had been a garrison and officer's mess during World War II. Under their management the operation became the iconic Ferguson Point Tea House until they sold the restaurant in 1964 and went into real estate. While the couple succeeded in the Vancouver real estate market, the so-called tea room fell into disrepair until it was re-opened in 1978 as The Teahouse restaurant. The Florises made numerous trips back to Europe where they were alarmed to find that anti-Semitism was still much entrenched.

"On numerous occasions in the course of this story I refer to my Jewish heritage, yet I am not really a religious man at all. You could call me an agnostic. When I was a young man, I considered myself, first and foremost, not a Jew but a Hungarian. I studied the country's history, loved its literature, its music and its arts. I felt sorry for its great poets and novelists, who were unknown outside the borders of the country merely because they wrote in a language so removed from other living languages that few were ever translated. Bit by bit, however, I became aware that Hungarians were anti-Semitic. My fellow countrymen, I learned, considered Jews to be despicable usurers, exploiters of decent working men, con artists, Christ killers, bolsheviks, capitalists, cheats, seducers of virtuous Christian virgins.

"The great Hungarian novelist Kalman Mikszath summed up the Hungarian attitude when he described an anti-Semite as a person who despises Jews more than absolutely necessary. Eventually, this anti-Semitism produced the Holocaust, which I had the good fortune to survive. Compared to those millions who perished in the Nazi murder camps, my suffering may seem trivial. Yet to me and the other Hungarian Jews who survived, such suffering was very real, and those of us who did survive have a responsibility to bear witness, especially since there are some who try to deny that the Holocaust ever happened."

FRIE, Roger

THE SON OF NON-JEWISH Germans who were children during World War II, Roger Frie was born shortly after his parents arrived in Canada and grew up bi-culturally with frequent trips to Germany. He learned about the Holocaust at a young age at home, but the history of his grandparents, whom he knew as a child, remained unspoken. "It was as though one door to the Nazi past was opened," he recalls, "while the other remained closed."

On one of his trips to Germany, the discovery of a photograph of his young grandfather in uniform led Frie to confront the obligations of memory and what it means to be the grandson of a Nazi party member. While Germans today generally acknowledge a collective responsibility for the crimes of the Nazi regime, they often know little about the actions of their own family members.

In his memoir *Not in My Family: German Memory and Responsibility After the Holocaust* (Oxford University Press 2017), Frie explored what it means to be caught in a web of history and be part of a traumatic past over which people have no control. He sheds light on the threads that connect us and reveals the impact of perpetrators' histories across generations.

"The silence surrounding family participation in the Nazi past leaves traces, hauntings that are transferred from one generation to the next."

For *Not in My Family*, Frie was awarded the 2017 Canadian Jewish Literary Award in the category of history, a 2018 Western Canada Jewish Book Award and was a finalist for the 2018 Vine Award for Canadian Jewish Literature. The Foreword is by Anna Ornstein, a survivor of Auschwitz. According to Erna Paris, "Roger Frie's riveting exploration of inter-generational war memory and submerged guilt will be read as an instant classic."

Frie has also edited *History Flows Through Us: Germany, the Holocaust and the Importance of Empathy* (Routledge 2018) in which historians of the Holocaust, German historians and psychoanalysts address the synergy between history and psychoanalysis. This volume was a nominee for the Gradiva Award and includes an extended dialogue with Thomas Kohut, a historian and son of a Holocaust survivor, in which they reflect on the Holocaust at the intersection of German history and psychoanalysis.

A psychologist, historian and philosopher, Frie was educated in London and Cambridge and is professor of Education at Simon Fraser University and Adjunct Professor of Psychiatry at UBC. He is also Faculty and Supervisor at the William Alanson White Institute of Psychiatry, Psychoanalysis and Psychology in New York and associate member of the Columbia University Seminar on Cultural Memory.

FRINTON, Ernst

BORN OF JEWISH PARENTS in 1917, Ernst Frinton (formerly Arnost Frischler) grew up in Ostrava, an industrial town in the Czechoslovakian Republic, with a mixture of Czech, German, Polish and Jewish residents. His father was a cobbler and his mother repaired and altered clothing. With much sacrifice from the family, he entered Medical School at the German University in Prague in 1935. When Frinton was in his third year of studies, the Nuremberg laws were applied and Jews were no longer allowed to study at universities.

He remembers vividly the roar of German aircraft and the rumbling of tanks on the morning of March 15 when he hurriedly dressed and went to Wenceslaus Square. Sleet was driven by a fierce wind. Citizens were immediately shot if they dared to raise their fists or shout insults. On the fourth day, Hitler came to Hradcany Castle to accept surrender. Suddenly, Frinton was living in The Protectorate of Bohemia and Moravia.

"Our only hope was emigration," he recalls.

For two desperate weeks Frinton went into hiding and started to learn English. His country's president had already gone into exile in London with the foreign minister, Jan Masaryk, son of the liberator Thomas Masaryk. A right wing politician served as a puppet dictator. "Our mutual defence pacts with France, Britain and the Soviet Union had proved to be useless," Frinton writes in *Memories, An Autobiography* (Deckside 1994). "Britain believed that Herr Hitler was a gentleman and would keep to his promise that after the Sudetenland he had no further claims against Czechoslovakia."

Towards the end of the month, Frinton learned that the soundproof vaults of the Pecek Bank were used as torture chambers and for executions; political prisoners were hanged on meat hooks. With great difficulty and a lot of luck, he managed to get a refugee train ticket to London via the Dutch border town of Oldenzaal. Upon Frinton's arrival in England, the British Committee for Refugees from Czechoslovakia placed him with a family in the countryside until he found

Ernst and Lili Frinton

a way to carry on his medical studies at St. Mungo's College, one of the oldest medical schools in Glasgow. In 1942, while still in school, he married Lili, herself a refugee from Berlin. She was looking after refugee children from Germany and Austria, a program financially supported by the Glasgow Jewish Community. Dr. Frinton started in General Practice in the slums of Glasgow.

In 1945, a few months after the war was over, the news came that his mother and sister had died in Auschwitz; his father never returned from a labour camp. After Lili and Ernst's first child was born in 1946, they moved to Liverpool where Frinton was offered an assistantship in a general practice. After two years, unable to find a medical practice with a future, they immigrated to Canada where Frinton accepted a coal miners' union-funded medical position in the foothills of the Rocky Mountains in Alberta. In 1950, the Frintons' second child was born. Despite having loved their time in Coal Valley, it was time to move on.

Frinton and some partners developed a busy general practice in the Cloverdale and Surrey area of the Lower Mainland before he opted to specialize in radiology in 1957. The family moved back to England, where Frinton started his two-year specialty studies at the Institute of Radiology in London. After a year, Lili was expecting their third child, so they returned to Vancouver before the baby was due. Frinton completed his specialty training at St. Paul's Hospital in Vancouver and settled into a busy radiology practice in New Westminster for the next twenty years, retiring in 1982.

"A good wife, three loving children, two beautiful granddaughters, many good friends, financial security . . . . I often feel guilty to have all this while my parents and in particular, my younger sister, who was probably a much better human being than I am, had to perish in misery. Life is not fair."

GALLANT, Mary J.

"Human greatness does not lie in wealth or power but in character and goodness." — Anne Frank

ONE OF THE LEAST-KNOWN Holocaust books to originate from British Columbia is also one of the best. The American Holocaust scholar Mary J. Gallant's 323-page presentation of profiles in the field of psychotherapy, *Coming of Age in the Holocaust: The Last Survivors Remember* (Lanham, Maryland: University Press of America 2002), highlights the caring and ingenuity of eighteen survivors while enduring captivity and abuse. Possibly by coincidence, the number 18 represents "Chai," the Hebrew word for life.

Ostensibly, Gallant does not reveal the identities of the Holocaust informants or where they reside. Each of the eighteen interviewees is identified by their real first names along with a fictitious surname. This veil of anonymity arguably stimulated candour. However, once one knows all these interviews were conducted in British Columbia, it takes very little detective work to deduce the sources. Each fictitious surname commences with the actual first letter of that person's real surname.

Gallant fails to make clear whether or not she herself conducted the interviews that frequently contain alarming and disturbing contents. At least six of the interviewees have since proceeded to publish books under their own names. Robert Krell reviewed Gallant's book for the *American Journal of Psychotherapy* in 2003 and respected the privacy of the informants. Following suit, here are just a few excerpts from a female informant born in Hungary in 1928.

K. WAS SIXTEEN when Hungarian police knocked on the door of the family home on a Sunday morning at 5 a.m. and gave them all twenty minutes to prepare for transport. K. had a brother and a sister. All five family members hastily prepared to give up their freedom at gunpoint as police waited at the door.

K. and her family stayed overnight in a school, then they boarded a train. The days that followed were a descent into hell. At a second railway station, SS officials politely told them they were being sent to work on a Hungarian farm, and could return at war's end. Locked into a cattle car with 84 people and no food or water, and just one tiny window, no bathroom facilities, nearly suffocating in terror, they survived on meagre rations of hope as the train moved relentlessly beyond Hungary's borders, arriving in a barbed wire compound at Birkenau where K. and her family were greeted by Dr. Josef Mengele.

"... And there were all these old people who couldn't move at all and so they just fell, everybody on top of each other, and the small children and the babies and these young mothers holding their babies. And everybody was screaming and everybody was just terrified.

The most hated and notorious Nazi who was never captured, killed or convicted was Dr. Josef Mengele who was renowned not only for selecting who was to live, and who was to die, on the train platform when Jews arrived at Auschwitz-Birkenau, but also for his hideous experiments on helpless victims, particularly twins, among them Vancouverites Leo and Miriam Lowy.

They were asking for water and, of course, there was none. All of a sudden we were surrounded by dogs, you know, the German shepherds. They never walked without a dog. Before we knew (it), my father and brother were gone. I never said goodbye to them.

"We were walking and my mother was in the middle. I was on one side and my sister on the other. He [Mengele] was there, standing, and he just put his arm between my mother and myself. They went the other way and that was it.

"The dogs were barking and there was blinding light. There were hundreds of light bulbs and it was night and it was terribly cold and everything happened so fast. It was so frightening because of all the screaming, and people were shouting to one another. And so by the time Mengele put out his arm between my mother, sister and myself . . . . They were lost in the crowd."

K. and other women were forced to stand in the icy cold all night, waiting to be processed. All their clothing was taken from them and they were forced to undergo a disinfectant bath. Then all of their body hair, in all places, was brusquely shaved in the presence of many SS men who appeared indifferent. She was given a light summer dress, four or five sizes too big for her. She recounts:

"So, we got out of the bath and with my shaved head which was bleeding because they were terribly, terribly rough, and there was no time to just gracefully and gently shave our hair off. So, we got out and I had a short-sleeved sort of little summer dress down to the ground and no underwear and I was freezing and it was pouring outside. There was an icy rain and we had to go out and line up! Probably the worst part of it was the SS were all around–men! And we had to get undressed. And they were standing there while we were shaved everywhere. And we were completely naked and, you know, for a sixteen-year-old girl to stand there in front of men and be shaved. And my head. I had long hair, heavy, wavy hair [She gives up trying to find the right words.]"

On that first night in Birkenau there was one blanket for twelve women. They squeezed together, twelve to each of the three levels of bunk beds. Early the next morning, they were commanded to reassemble outdoors. It was still pouring. "The SS came with a dog and a whip. With his whip he would point at 'You . . . You . . . You . . . ' and so on. Whoever he pointed to had to come out and get on the truck. We didn't know what was going on, but, as he came close to me [she sighs deeply] he pointed to a girl who would have to come out. But her mother came out, too, and was holding on to her daughter. We didn't know yet that it was a no-no, that we should never let them know that we were sisters, mother-daughters, or even close friends, because they made sure that those would be separated.

"So, the mother was kicked by the SS man and was told that she had to get back into the line and the girl had to get up onto the truck.

But the mother wouldn't go. And so he kicked her again, and she fell. It was raining and there was a big puddle. She spoke German, this woman. She asked the SS to let her daughter go with her. She said, 'This is my daughter and I want to go with her.' He started to beat her with his whip and kick her and finally the dog . . . . He was holding the dog on a leash and he gave the order to the dog, and the dog just took her. The dog just tore her apart, right in front of us, right in front of her daughter. The girl had to get onto the truck. I don't know if the mother was dead by the time we were allowed to go back into the building. She was left there in the puddle. We were all splattered with blood."

Gallant incorrectly states that K. was in Auschwitz-Birkenau for almost precisely one year, from April 16, 1944 to April 15, 1945. In fact, she was in Birkenau for four months, then forced into labour because her small, flexible hands were well suited for fine, tedious work. K. laboured at the camps in Mahrisch Weisswasser (subcamp of Gross-Rosen) and Horneberg (sub-camp of Neuengamme in northern Germany) making small machinery and lightbulbs for airplanes. Five days before K. was liberated, her work group was marched from a [unspecified] work camp [likely Horneberg] to Bergen-Belsen.

"There was one room. We were practically on top of each other, and in the morning, when I woke up, I seemed to be the only one alive. . . . Bergen-Belsen was the place where at liberation the dead were piled up like mountains. When the British came in, they caught the SS, whoever stayed, and they were put to work. They would have to put their very long ladder on this mountain of corpses, and they would carry up the corpses and put one on top of the other. And later on they had a mass grave. Fifteen thousand in one grave. This was in the Germans' own records."

K. was taken to a hospital. Depressed, she married a fellow survivor in 1953, in Hungary. He was one of the few Jews allowed to obtain a doctorate in Law. Despite being forewarned that she might never have children due to her camp experiences, she had a daughter and they fled from Hungary in 1957 with only the items they could carry.

A peasant guided them across the border to Austria. K. and her new family left Vienna and immigrated to Vancouver in 1955 or 1956. Along with other Jews who survived, she would help to establish a monument to those who were murdered at Bergen-Belsen.

AS HER FAMILY'S SOLE SURVIVOR, K. recorded her story within a program for historical interviews that was initiated by Robert Krell and others. Krell began a program of conducting such in-depth interviews on film with Holocaust survivors in 1978 under the auspices of the Vancouver Holocaust Education Committee. His first videotaped interview was with Vera Slyomovics (1978) after she had spoken publicly for the first time a Holocaust symposium in 1977. She was emboldened by speeches made by fellow Holocaust educators Peter Parker, Niki Wisniewski and Leo Lowy at a seminal and inaugural symposium on the Holocaust, held in Vancouver on April 27, 1976. Lowy spoke publicly for the first time about how he and his sister had survived the infamous Dr. Mengele's experiments on twins. Other survivors who spoke with Lowy and Slyomovics at that event were Rudolf Vrba and Leon Kahn.

GOLD, Joe

AFTER THREE DAYS and two nights in a cattle car crammed with 100 people sharing a single bucket for waste and a single pail of water, David Goldberger arrived at Auschwitz on April 20, 1944. Dr. Josef Mengele directed him to the right. He could live.

All his possessions were confiscated. Goldberger stood naked with the other lucky ones while their heads were shaved and the crevices of their bodies were searched for valuables.

It wasn't until David Goldberg's Vancouver-raised son Joe was himself in his seventies that his father's story of faith, perseverance and family love made its way into print as a book, *Two Pieces of Cloth, One Family's Story of the Holocaust* (Page Two, 2021).

Much of the text that Joe Gold prepared to honour his family's story was gleaned from interviews conducted with David Goldberger decades before by Robert Krell.

IN REMEMBRANCE lies the secret of redemption. That idea is from the teachings of the Polish mystic Rabbi Israel ben Eliezer who is regarded as the founder of Hasidic Judaism. Vancouver businessman David Goldberger always knew he had a story to remember and tell. He just never found a voice for it.

After the home and the textile business of the Goldberger family in Spisske Vlachy was confiscated because they were Jews, the Slovak government proceeded to solve its so-called unemployment problem that ensued by deporting Jews in the spring of 1942.

In keeping with the philosophy of so-called Aryanization, the first train to Auschwitz from the Poprad transit camp in Slovakia departed on March 25, 1942 carrying 1,000 unmarried Jewish women between the ages of sixteen and forty-five in cattle cars.

U.S. HOLOCAUST MEMORIAL MUSEUM. PHOTOGRAPH NUMBER: 77396

Among the Jews sent from Slovakia to Auschwitz in March of 1942 was Linda Reich (centre), seen sorting belongings confiscated from Carpathian Ruthenian Jews in 1944 as a member of the *Aufraumungskommando*.

Family transports commenced on April 11. Jewish males were dispatched to labour battalions in 1943. After German troops occupied Hungary in March of 1944, bribes were less viable to avoid detention. Almost half a million Hungarians were transported to Auschwitz-Birkenau between May 15 and July 9.

"The speed with which the Hungarian authorities cast out Jews from society, and robbed, segregated and deported them, was unprecedented in the entire history of the Holocaust," Joe Gold claims.

David Goldberger first worked as a slave labourer in 1944 in one of the 32 factories of the Manfred Weiss Steel and Metal Works. (The wealthy Weiss family had been allowed to immigrate to Portugal but their enormous art collection was confiscated.)

David Goldberger was ultimately transferred from Auschwitz to Bergen-Belsen on February 17, 1945. Exactly 303 days after he had boarded the cattle car, he was liberated from Bergen-Belsen among 60,000 ghostly inmates. By then, David Goldberger—who was known as Deszer, or Deszy—weighed sixty-five pounds.

Yugoslavia was the only government that came swiftly to rescue its Jews. Seemingly too skeletal to travel, Goldberger was told by the camp's liberators to wait for the arrival of Slovakian troops. The concentration camp was rife with typhus. The risks of remaining were lethal. He opted to take flight with a group of men to reach Hanover, 50 kilometres away, in northwestern Germany. It was there he was given two pieces of woollen cloth that would enable him to begin anew.

"My father noticed a large building which housed a textile company," Joe Gold writes. "He recognized the name of the company as one of his woollen fabric suppliers before the war. He walked inside and introduced himself to the owners. When asked how they might be able to help him, my father replied 'If you are able to give me two pieces of cloth—two times three metres—I will be able to start my life again.' Three metres of fabric would be sufficient to make a suit. It was with these two pieces of cloth that my father was able to barter for other merchandise and necessities and to move on and support his family once again."

In *Two Pieces of Cloth, One Family's Story of the Holocaust* (Page Two 2021), we learn that several thousand Jews fled from Czechoslovakia to Hungary aided by Rabbi Shmuel Dovid Ungar. In the voice of David Goldberger, his son Joe Gold recounts his father's successful return to Budapest after the Holocaust to find his wife, Aurelia, and their first-born son, Andrew, who had been in hiding with false Christian identities.

Andrew was disguised as a girl.

"Andrew's hair was long and beautiful. It was imperative that Andrew be dressed as a girl in case we were ever stopped by the gendarme. They would check any suspicious boys for circumcisions."

Although the story is mainly told from the perspectives of the separated couple, it opens with Joe Gold, as child, discovering a book of concentration camp photographs hidden in his father's fabric store. "It made sense that my father, upon arrival in Canada in 1948, would open a fabric store," Gold says. "Having successfully managed and owned textile businesses twice (both before and after the war) in his native country of Czechoslovakia, it was the natural way for him to make a new start once again." This precious and rare album that Joe Gold first saw in 1952 went missing for seventy years until Joe Gold traced its origins just before *Two Pieces of Cloth* went to press.

In the camps, David Goldberg, formerly a salesman from Bratislava, vowed to God that if he survived he would arrange to be buried in Jerusalem. He made many trips to Israel, including this visit to the Wailing Wall in 1975.

"For as long as I can remember," Joe Gold says, "I have thought of the Holocaust every day."

Joe Gold's mother Aurelia was

born in the Czech lands of the Austro-Hungarian empire in 1915. The independent state of Czechoslovakia was not established until 1918. Born in Benedikovce one year earlier, David Goldberger, the youngest of eight children, apprenticed in the textile business and much later became highly successful in Canada's clothing sector with a prominent store for Gold's Fashion Fabrics on Granville Street in Vancouver. Born in Czechoslovakia in 1947, Joe Gold worked in the family business and also found time to play keyboards in an R&B group. He says the inspiration to complete his family story arose from a poem written by Rabbi Harold M. Schulweis in the High Holy Day prayer book, *Backwards and Forwards*:

> Looking backward, we recall our ancestry.
> Looking forward, we confront our destiny.
> Looking backward, we reflect on our origins.
> Looking forward, we choose our path.
> Remembering that we are a tree of life, not letting go,
> holding on, and holding to, we walk into an unknown
> beckoning future, with our past beside us.

Joe Gold's grandfather perished in Sobibor. The uncle he was named after died in Majdanek. Joe Gold's father survived Auschwitz-Birkenau, Gross-Rosen, Chelmno and Bergen-Belsen.

In his tribute to his father, Joe Gold notes that Dachau was the first concentration camp, established in 1933, and that Bergen-Belsen had the lowest survival rate "from which not five percent came home alive."

Initially, as of 1941, Bergen-Belsen held thousands of Soviet prisoners; then in 1943 it was also used for Jewish hostages who were kept in case international agreements could be made to exchange them for German prisoners of war being held overseas.

Overcrowding and lack of food led to outbreaks of typhus, as well as tuberculosis, typhoid and deadly dysentery. Prior to liberation, more than 35,000 prisoners died before the British 11th Armoured Division arrived on April 15, 1945, and discovered the ghoulish pres-

A British Army bulldozer cleans up after the Nazis at Bergen-Belsen, April 19, 1945. Photo by H. Oakes, (Sgt), No 5 Army Film and amp; Photographic Unit.

ence of 60,000 starving prisoners.

It is seldom cited that Canadian troops were also among the liberators. In Bergen-Belsen, British and Canadian troops found approximately 13,000 unburied corpses.

In 1944, a new part of Bergen-Belsen had been established as a "women's camp" accommodating around 9,000 women and young girls, beginning with Poles from the failed Warsaw Uprising. Among the last women to arrive at Bergen-Belsen were two sisters, Margot and Anne Frank, who died in either February or March of 1945.

Anne Frank had the misfortune of being allotted a sleeping stall near the main door. During the bitterly cold winter months, each time the door was opened, it was impossible to stay warm. Even though there were no gas chambers at Bergen-Belsen and it was supposedly designed as a centre for recovery and the bartering of souls, it is estimated that the cumulative death toll for Jews, Czechs, Poles, intellectuals, homosexuals and Roma at Bergen-Belsen exceeded 50,000.

Newsreel footage of British Army bulldozers pushing piles of naked, emaciated bodies into mass graves has been seared into the minds of millions as one of the most enduring images of the Holocaust. [Such footage was fundamental for the existence of this book. Home alone, at age 13, the author of this book was introduced to the Holocaust by such footage. There was no mention of the Holocaust from grades seven to twelve at West Vancouver High School.]

GOLDBERG, Adara

ON JUNE 7, 1939, a total of 907 Jewish refugees who had fled Nazi Germany aboard the MS *St. Louis* were denied entry to Canada, having been previously denied entry to Cuba, other Latin American countries and the United States. During the twelve-year control of Germany by the Nazi regime, only about 5,000 Jewish refugees were allowed to enter Canada.

The racist policies of the true north, strong and free, were in keeping with what Prime Minister Mackenzie King wrote in his diary in 1938: "We must nevertheless seek to keep this part of the Continent free from unrest and from too great an inter-mixture of foreign strains of blood. . . . I fear we would have riots if we agreed to a policy that admitted numbers of Jews."

Canadian school children for many decades were never told that Canada was one of the most restrictive western states in terms of admitting Jews fleeing the so-called "Final Solution" policies of Nazi Germany, before, during and soon after World War II.

Canada's racist policies were made clear in Irving Abella and Harold Troper's *None is Too Many: Canada and the Jews of Europe 1933–1948* (Lester & Orpen Dennys 1983).

According to researcher Adara Goldberg, despite the anti-Semitic policies in Canada, "Approximately 17,000 Jews—roughly one-fifth of the country's Jewish male population—enlisted in the Canadian armed forces. This figure was disproportionately higher than any other minority ethnic group. Of those who served, 421 Canadian

Jewish personnel died in service; and 1,971 received military awards."

To trace the influx of 35,000 Jewish survivors of Nazi persecution who came to Canada in the decade after the war, Adara Goldberg published *Holocaust Survivors in Canada: Exclusion, Inclusion, Transformation, 1947–1955* (University of Manitoba Press 2015) when she was Education Director at the Vancouver Holocaust Education Centre.

Based on research conducted at Holocaust survivors' kitchen tables as well as in traditional archives, Goldberg's groundbreaking study was largely based on her Ph.D dissertation at Clark University in Worcester, Massachusetts, where Goldberg received her Ph.D from the Strassler Center for Holocaust and Genocide Studies.

Goldberg's book received the Marsid Foundation Prize for Holocaust literature at the first Western Canada Jewish Book Awards held in Vancouver.

"Signs that read 'Gentiles Only' and 'No Jews or Dogs Allowed' were posted well into the 1930s and 1940s," she writes. "During this time, discriminatory immigration policies denied sponsorship requests to nearly all Jewish applicants. Canadians overwhelmingly supported government policy that classified Jews as foreigners who could not assimilate. They were seen as posing potential threats to the health of the nation."

In addition, prior to World War II, Jews had faced limits on enrolment in educational institutions. Their participation in various fields, such as medicine and law, was also restricted, and Jews were prohibited from accessing some property and vacation sites.

Jews were especially vulnerable in French-speaking Quebec where Roman Catholic priest Lionel Groulx, the so-called "father of French Canadian nationalism," espoused racist and anti-refugee rhetoric. He did so from the pulpit, on the radio, and in such journals as *L'Action Nationale* and *Le Goglu*.

Meanwhile, journalist and Nazi sympathizer Adrien Arcand founded the anti-Communist and anti-Jewish *Parti National Social Chretien* (Christian National Socialist Party) and led the National

Crude images made by the Swastika Cub featured on the front of the *Toronto Evening Telegram*, 1933. Club membership numbered 400.

Unity Party of Canada, an offshoot of the anti-Semitic fascist groups that were organized in many towns and cities across the country.

"During the Great Depression in Alberta," Goldberg has noted, "the governing Social Credit Party spread anti-Semitic beliefs through radio broadcasts and racist literature. Chief among this racist literature was *The Protocols of the Elders of Zion*. It was a fabricated text first published in Russia in 1905. It claimed to outline a plan for Jewish world domination."

So-called "swastika clubs" in Ontario were formed mainly to intimidate Jews and keep them from visiting the city's public beaches on the shore of Lake Ontario. On the night of August 16, 1933, a six-hour, violent street brawl known as the Christie Pits riots took place on the streets of Toronto between swastika-brandishing Anglo Protestants and Jewish and Italian Catholic immigrants.

After three years, Goldberg left her job as Education Director at the Vancouver Holocaust Education Centre where she produced various teaching guides, such as *Enemy Aliens: The Internment of Jewish Refugees in Canada, 1940–1943 Teachers Guide* (with Nina Krieger) to become the 2016–17 Azrieli International Post-Doctoral Fellow in Israel.

Goldberg became Director of New Jersey's Kean's Holocaust Resource Center/Council on Global Education and Citizenship in 2018. She has been a member of the Yad Vashem Working Group on Child Holocaust Survivors and the Canadian advisory committee for the International Holocaust Remembrance Alliance.

GOLDMAN, René

RENÉ GOLDMAN HAD A LONG CAREER teaching Chinese history at UBC before he retired to Summerland and self-published *Childhood on the Move: Memoirs of a child-survivor of the Holocaust* (2014). It was republished and edited by the Azriel Foundation as *A Childhood Adrift* (Second Story 2016). The French version is *Une enfance a la derive*. More than half of it is devoted to his time in France, from 1942 to 1950, where government and police collaborated zealously with the Nazi pogroms and he experienced his closest brush with death.

"French cooperation led to the death of so many Jews from France," he told Pat Johnson of *Zachor* in 2017. "The deportation to the camps—over 75,000 Jews from France were deported to Auschwitz and other camps—was basically the work of the French. All the roundups were done by the French police, and the Jews were denounced or reported to the authorities by French people."

As a small child, Goldman survived in the shadow of terror across three countries in succession: Luxembourg, where he was born in 1934; Belgium, where his parents thought they had found refuge in 1940; and France. He remembers the introduction of the wearing of the yellow star in Brussels in 1942, when he was eight years old, and seeing signs going up in front of cinemas and parks saying that Jews and dogs were not allowed. "That's when I was beginning to feel fear and dread."

When the family fled for a second time, as the Nazis advanced into the Benelux countries, the Goldmans planned to leave France and sail to safety in South America from France's so-called "free zone" in the south governed by the German-puppet Vichy regime. His father was fortunately absent during an unexpected round-up of Jews. During this period, they were temporarily housed in a hotel with other migrants in the town of Lons-Le-Saunier in eastern France. At around 8 a.m. his mother tried to get him to cry, hoping that might move the heart of the police who were collecting him, but he could not summon any tears.

"The entire station was a scene of bedlam, with men, women and children being pulled, shoved and hurled into the train," he recalled. "Just as the commissar was about to throw me into the train as well, two gendarmes in khaki uniforms appeared in the nick of time to stop him. Without a word he let go of me. . . . That was the last time I saw my Mama."

Goldman was spared due to the intervention of his mother's older sister who had become a French citizen. At the time, that distinction still mattered. After hiding in a series of rural villages, René Goldman found refuge in a Catholic institution where Jewish children were assigned new identities. He was warned never to allow anyone to see his private parts "since in France only Jews were circumcised."

At war's end, Goldman was placed under the care of the left-leaning Commission Centrale de l'Enfance (CCE), a committee of the Jewish resistance movement. Instead of immigrating to Canada with an uncle and aunt, he remained in Europe, hoping to hear some news of his father. Relatives had chosen to withhold the grim truth from him. He eventually went to Poland for three years where he worked for the Polish national radio network and became aware of the anti-Semitic purges in Czechoslovakia and Moscow.

Goldman searched for evidence of his parents and discovered his mother had been on a convoy sent to Auschwitz-Birkenau. His mother had first been taken south from Lons-Le-Saunier to a detention camp at Rivesaltes in the Pyrenees, then north to another collection depot at Drancy, a suburb of Paris.

"Of the 407 women who arrived at Birkenau on that train," he writes, "only 147 were registered and had a number tattooed on their forearm; the others were sent directly to the gas chambers. I can only assume that my mother, being small and frail, was among the latter, unless she died because of the atrocious conditions in which the doomed passengers of that train travelled. I never learned for certain what happened to her; there will never be closure for me."

In 1953, he accepted an opportunity to study in China for five years but soon came to the realization that the communism of Mao

René with parents Mira and Wolf Goldman

Zedong was also dangerous and despicable. By 1958, with the onset of the Great Leap Forward, famine would soon result in the deaths of between 30 and 40 million Chinese. Goldman received a scholarship to Columbia University and arrived in the United States in 1960. He came to Canada in 1963 and pursued his distinguished academic career in Vancouver at UBC.

In 1965, Goldman was able to speak to a man who described the death of Goldman's father in his arms in 1945, during a death march twenty years earlier from Auschwitz.

In his memoir, Goldman writes, "I bear witness to a tragedy unprecedented in history, during which six million Jews, including my entire family in Poland, with the single exception of one uncle, were murdered in cold blood. I seek here to offer my modest contribution to the perpetuation of the memory of that tragedy in the fervent hope that it will neither be forgotten, nor denied.

"May present and future readers find in these memoirs matter for reflection, and perhaps some will discover in them an avenue of research.

"I belong to the generation of survivors who in the 1980s received recognition as a class different from that of adult survivors of the Shoah. We are known as the 'child-survivors,' who were too young to comprehend why the Nazis and their collaborators across Europe waged a war of extermination against us. We are also known as the 'hidden children,' since we survived by hiding in various ways, mainly under the protection of caring Gentiles.

"Like many of my peers, I have over the decades written and spoken publicly in schools, universities, churches, about my personal experience as a child-survivor of the Shoah. My family and people of various walks of life have encouraged me to write my story. Thus motivated, I put pen to paper in the late evening of my life.... I deem it nothing short of miraculous that I survived all those times of anguish and pain."

In an interview for the Azrieli Foundation, René Goldman soberly concluded, "I know how low human nature can descend... how very terrible people can become. I have no illusions. I don't believe in a good nature of people. I know that Anne Frank in her diary wrote that she still believed in the goodness of people. But I wonder. I think that once she got to Bergen-Belsen, she no longer had that idea. That's my educated guess."

GRANIRER, Pnina

PNINA GRANIRER and her mother escaped from Romania when they were ransomed for $100. This was done without the knowledge of the Jewish community at large and was kept secret from the world.

Pnina Granirer was born of Jewish parents in the Danube port-city of Braila, Romania, in 1935. Her childhood was lived under the brutal fascism of the Iron Guard, an ultra-nationalist, anti-Semitic movement, fueled by Orthodox Christian zealousness, under the dictatorial direction of Horia Sima.

When Ion Antonescu came to power in September 1940 and destroyed the Iron Guard, the Romanian Jewish community were seemingly less endangered than other Eastern European Jews. But freedoms were steadily eroded. Ownership of telephones and radios was forbidden; cars and homes and libraries were plundered.

Only much later, when she read I.C. Butnaru's *The Silent Holocaust: Romania and its Jews*, did Granirer understand the full extent of the devastation: half the Jewish population had been slaughtered. Cattle trucks had stood ready to deport the remaining Jews to the death camps, even as the country was "liberated" by the Russian army. This salvation, greeted rapturously at first, turned into another form of persecution.

With Romania under Communist rule, Granirer's father, a committed socialist, was forced into hiding until he could be smuggled out to Israel. The rest of the family eventually followed him; their emigration was made possible by Israel's willingness to pay a ransom for Romanian Jews, who constituted the largest number of European Holocaust survivors.

In her memoir, *Light Within the Shadows: A Painter's Memoir* (Granville Island 2017), Granirer recalls being assigned the task of producing a portrait of Stalin when she was a school girl. She was extremely fortunate in 1950 when she and her mother were allowed to emigrate to Israel to be reunited with her father who had fled Communist persecution via a Yugoslav freighter.

Named Paula in Romania, in Israel she adopted Pnina—meaning "pearl" in Hebrew—and describes her adolescent years as relatively happy ones, in spite of poverty and crowded conditions. As an immigrant to Israel who didn't know the language, she nevertheless worked hard to gain an education. She met a fellow Romanian émigré who became her husband in 1954 and, until marriage exempted her, she did the required military service. The Hebrew University had no position for her husband, who had earned his Ph.D in mathematics there, whereas the United States, propelled into the space race by the Russian success of Sputnik, was recruiting mathematicians. Her family therefore went to Illinois in 1962, then moved to Ithaca, New York, in 1964.

In Israel, after finishing her studies at the Bezalel School of Art, she had worked as an illustrator but, lacking a green card in the U.S., she was unable to work. Instead, she discovered a new freedom in drawing and painting, practising art for art's sake. During a year in Montreal, her camaraderie with artists living bohemian lives devoted exclusively to their art made her question the effect on her work of her own conventional life as a wife and a mother.

Her husband's career brought them finally to Vancouver, where Granirer began to find her way as an artist. It was in Vancouver in 1965 that she made her first association with a gallery, the small Danish Art Gallery in Point Grey. There, at the age of thirty, she made her debut exhibition. Granirer's paintings express her belief that "beauty has always existed side by side with violence, cruelty and war."

A triptych by Granirer from the 1988 international exhibition Fear of Others, Art Against Racism is now in the collection of the Yad Vashem Museum in Jerusalem and a second painting is in the collection of the United Nations Human Rights Commission in New York. A forty-year retrospective of 120 of her paintings at the Richmond Art Gallery in January of 1998 showed her artistic development over her long career. Published in conjunction with a 40-year retrospective of her art at the Richmond Art Gallery, Ted Lindberg's lavishly illustrated *Pnina Granirer: Portrait of an Artist* was launched at the opening of the exhibition. In 2015, Granirer returned to her hometown of Braila and reunited with school friends and a close friend of her mother, Marcela Dermer.

Pnina Granirer: "Only now do I understand how lucky we had been to escape the camps and death trains." [Inset] Pnina Granirer in 1937.

HARVEY, Stella Leventoyannis

"Therefore, it is not said that Greeks fought like heroes, but heroes fight like Greeks." — Winston Churchill

ALONG WITH describing his consummated love affair with a female inmate, Rudi Vrba's illuminating memoir, *I Escaped From Auschwitz* recalls a rare attempt to organize an uprising in Auschwitz.

At the last minute, the planned rebellion was cancelled because the person chosen to unite the various factions—a widely-respected German Jew named Fredy Hirsch—committed suicide.

There was, however, a quixotic, hour-long uprising at Auschwitz on October 7, 1944. According to the United States Holocaust Museum, it occurred among the *Sonderkommando*—the name used to describe Jewish prisoners who prolonged their lives by guiding new arrivals into the gas chambers. There were usually about 400 men in each *Sonderkommando* group, divided equally into two shifts. They were required to remove the corpses, shave and preserve hair, remove teeth containing gold, sort through possessions for valuables, cremate the bodies and finally dispose of the ashes.

Whenever a new batch of *Sonderkommando* was selected (usually around every four months), their predecessors became fully aware that their horrific knowledge of the extent of the genocide and its methodology had marked them for death from the outset.

The story goes that when *Sonderkommandos* for Crematoria IV were forced into the gas chambers, there were Greek men en route to death who altered the lyrics to Greek songs in order to alert the remaining members of their *Sonderkomando* group what was likely in store for them. On Saturday, October 7, 1944, at around 2:30 in the afternoon, as German guards were preparing to send the second contingent of *Sonderkomandos* (mainly Greek and Hungarian Jews) to the gas chambers, a voice, assumed to be that of a Greek army officer from Ionnina, Josif Barouch, reportedly shouted out in Greek,

"We will make our attack, or not?" And so that fought back.

Equipped only with the element of surprise, die-hard courage and makeshift weapons, the predominantly Greek prisoners used their superior numbers to overpower and kill some of their German guards. The rebels took refuge inside Crematorium III and attempted to blow up Crematorium IV with dynamite. This show of defiance, they hoped, could foment massive unrest and possibly enable them to escape into nearby woods. The dynamite had been gradually accumulated for months by Ester Wajcblum and her sister, Hana, along with Ela Gertner and Regina Safirsztain. They had risked their lives to smuggle small amounts of gunpowder from the Weichsel-Union-Metallwerke, a munitions factory within the Auschwitz complex, and deliver it to Roza Robota, a member of the camp underground who worked in the clothing detail at Birkenau. Small amounts of dynamite were wrapped in bits of cloth or paper and hidden on their bodies. Roza Robota passed it along to co-conspirators in the *Sonderkommando*. In this way, it was hoped that the uprising would destroy gas chambers and crematoria.

The Germans troops easily crushed the revolt, but Crematorium IV was destroyed and never used again. Nearly 250 prisoners died during the fighting. Guards shot another 200 after the mutiny was suppressed. Several days later, the SS identified the four Jewish female prisoners who had been involved in supplying explosives. The four were not hanged in front of the assembled women's camp until January 5, 1945. Roza Robota is said to have shouted, "Be strong and be brave." According to *Greeks in Auschwitz-Birkenau*, a 2009 publication from by the Greek foreign ministry, an estimated 300 Greek Jews died in the uprising and 26 survived. It alleges that the Greek anthem was heard being sung as their rebellion was being crushed.

EVEN THOUGH IT IS commonly estimated that approximately 85 percent of the Jews in Greece were killed during the Holocaust, public awareness of the Holocaust tends to focus on events in Poland,

Czechoslovakia, Hungary, Austria, The Netherlands, etc. The only British Columbia novelist whose work has incorporated the persecution and murder of Greek Jews is Stella Leventoyannis Harvey, who also manages the Whistler Writers Festival. One of the chapter headings in her third novel, *Finding Callidora* (Signature 2019), reads "Jews in Salonika Registering at Liberty Square, Salonika." It's an actual headline that appeared in a Greek newspaper on July 1, 1942. One of the characters in *Finding Callidora* is heard to complain, "What does any of this have to do with us? We're farmers trying to survive." Harvey writes:

> "They are your neighbours," Katarina shot back before she knew she'd opened her mouth. "You have no problem drinking coffee with them, or selling our melons to them, but you won't lift a finger to stop the Nazi pigs from taking them away to God knows what end."

Anti-Jewish measures were introduced in Greece in April of 1941 when German troops entered Salonika. After properties were confiscated, prominent Jews were arrested and cultural treasures were destroyed. In July of 1942, all Jewish men in Salonika between the ages of eighteen and forty-five were assembled in Plateia Eleftherias at 8 a.m. In public view, as Christian Greeks watched the spectacle, they were flogged, forced to do gymnastics and doused with water until late afternoon.

Forced labour and ghettoization followed. Eichmann's deputy R. Gunther and Himmler's assistant D. Wisliceny arrived in Salonika in January 1943 to oversee the implementation of the "Final Solution." On March 14, Rabbi Koretz announced that a series of convoys would take Jews for resettlement in Krakow. The next day 2,500 Jews were herded onto forty freight cars to Auschwitz-Birkenau.

More convoys left March 17, 19, 23, 27; April 3, 5, 7, 10, 13, 16, 20, 22, 28; May 3, 9 (two). The 19th and last convoy left Salonika, now more commonly known as Thessaloniki, on August 19. In three months, 45,649 people were sent from Thessaloniki to Auschwitz.

Directed by David Antoniuk, the 20-minute film called *Eleftheromania* was first shown at various film festivals in 2018, starring Olympia Dukakis. It was made freely available on Vimeo on Holocaust Day, 2021.

The total number of Greek Jews sent to their death in the murder camps has been estimated at 60,000.

In this way the great centre of Sephardic Jewry in Europe, Thessaloniki, known also as Malkhah Israel—La Madre de Israel—for five centuries, was decimated and relegated to the history books. More than 90 percent of its Jews were killed.

Due largely to the efforts of Greek Archbishop Damaskinos with the assistance of an extensive Greek underground movement, only 1,300 Jews were deported from Athens. Meanwhile, approximately 1,300 Jews joined the Greek partisans and took part in guerilla warfare.

Stella Leventoyannis Harvey didn't know how much about how resistance fighters would fit into her first novel, *Nicolai's Daughters* (Signature 2012), until she visited Kalavryta, north of Athens, near

Diakofto. There, on December 13, 1943, German forces massacred all the males in Kalavryta over the age of thirteen. They also attempted to lock women and children in a school and set it on fire. Many of the women and children were able to escape the blaze, but only thirteen males over the age of thirteen survived. Operation Kalavryta resulted in the destruction of homes and monasteries in twenty-eight communities. Approximately 1,000 houses were looted and burned. Some 700 civilians were killed. With dual narratives from a father and a daughter, *Nicolai's Daughters* profiles the tragedy-ridden Sarinopoulous family in the village of Diakofto, on the Gulf of Corinth. It was translated and released in Greece in 2014 by Psichogios Press.

"The novel found its soul in that tiny mountain village," Harvey says. "I listened to the testimonials of the victims recorded in the Kalavryta museum, which had once been the village school, and I climbed Kappi Hill (The Place of Sacrifice) where the massacre happened and it was then I realized I wanted to tell the Kalavryta story. It's considered the worst atrocity perpetrated by the Nazis in Greece during World War II."

One of the testimonials Harvey listened to in Kalavryta was by a man in his eighties. "He talked about being lined up with the other men and boys that bright December day and being asked by a German soldier how old he was. He lied about his age. He didn't know what made him lie because he had no idea what was to come. He lied almost as an act of defiance. It saved his life. He broke down during his testimonial, saying he'd felt guilty his whole life for surviving while all his friends died. I've often thought about that man and what the impact would be on a survivor with so much guilt to bear."

One of Harvey's protagonists in her novel *Finding Callidora* is Georges Psychoundakis, the Greek resistance fighter on Crete who served as a dispatch runner behind German lines. Immediately following World War II, he was mistakenly imprisoned for sixteen months as a deserter even though he had the Medal of the Order of the British Empire for Meritorious Service. In prison he wrote his acclaimed memoir, *The Cretan Runner*, and he later completed Cretan translations of the *Iliad* and the *Odyssey*.

"Crete and Greece were greatly desired by Hitler," says Harvey, "because of their strategic location. Occupying Greece would have given the Nazis an advantage while they forged ahead to Russia. Although Crete eventually fell, Hitler's troops suffered many casualties and this threw off Hitler's war plan. It is believed this was one of the reasons Hitler was forced to delay invading Russia. This delay caused the German troops to try to invade Russia during winter, a task they were ill-equipped for and one that ultimately sealed their defeat."

IN MID-1944, when Auschwitz-Birkenau was deluged with trainloads of Hungarian Jews, the Nazis required more workers in the *Sonderkommando* units to process the influx of Jews through the gas chambers. The story goes that 400 Greek male prisoners were given the opportunity to spare their own lives if they agreed to work as a *Sonderkommando* unit and escort Hungarian Jews to their deaths in the gas chambers. Their task would be to reassure their fellow Jews, before they were stripped of their clothing, that everything would be fine. They were merely being prepared to be given a shower. Then the Greeks would have to gather and dispose of the corpses.

Jewish physician Otto Wolken provided proof at Nuremberg that a phalanx of Greek Jews chose death rather than serve as a *Sonderkommando* unit and escort Hungarian Jews to the gas chambers.

On the night before they were sent to serve the Nazis as *Sonderkommandos*, the Greek Jews unanimously decided their own deaths with dignity were a better choice.

Seventy years later, a would-be film producer named Gregory Pappas visited Auschwitz for four days to undertake research for a film project to represent how the Greeks had enacted their "Freedom or Death" philosophy (*Eleftheria i Thanatos*) at the prison camp.

With the persistence and expertise of Piotr Malarek, a Polish native, semi-fluent in German, who regularly helps families re-connect with the fate of their relatives in Krakow, Pappas found the verification of this event in Holocaust history within the memoirs of Dr. Otto Wolken, a Jewish physician from Vienna who was deported to Auschwitz. After the camp's liberation in 1945, Wolken immediately wrote a chronicle of his knowledge and experiences.

When the International Military Tribunal at Nuremberg opened in November of 1945, Dr. Wolken was selected as the first of more than 300 witnesses to testify. For two hours he provided harrowing details of camp life and German atrocities in Auschwitz-Birkenau. Here is a part of Wolken's written narrative that provides the context for the 20-minute film, *Eleftheromania*, written by Joanna Tsanis and produced by Chuck Scott, Tsanis and Pappas. This section proves the dramatization is not wishful thinking:

> At the time of my arrival in Birkenau, crematoria I and II were already in operation, crematorium IV was being finished, and crematorium V was just being built. The people employed at building the latter two crematoria were housed in block 18 of camp sector BIId. The gassing and burning in the crematoria was the task of the *Sonderkommando*. The people placed in that kommando were chosen by the camp doctor or the Rapportfuhrer from among the prisoners arriving in transports to the BIIa quarantine camp. Usually, entire transports were marked for the *Sonderkommando*. And so, from 446 Greek Jews arriving in the quarantine camp on 30 June 1944 in transport no. 49, Thilo chose 434 prisoners on 21 July 1944 and sent them to camp BIId. Once there, 400 prisoners were chosen and sent to the *Sonderkommando* for the crematorium.

> The next day, that *Sonderkommando* was taken to the crematoria to work, and when they refused to work, the entire commando—400 prisoners strong—was gassed and burned. I learned that from the corpse counter, a Slovak Jew named Neumann, who worked in camp sector BIId and kept a registry of corpses of people who died in the hospital and in other sectors. That Neumann told me about it in person; he had found out about the gassing of those Greek Jews on the spot in the crematorium, where he was to ensure the right count.
>
> Besides, the SS made no secret of it, the entire camp knew about that action. The SS men would spread the story to scare others from refusing the work they were ordered to perform—it was a frequent occurrence that people would refuse to work in the crematorium *Sonderkommando*. Such *Sonderkommandos* were all gassed in their entirety.

Also, in 1944, a 26-year-old Greek Jew from Thessaloniki, Marcel Nadjari, buried another 13-page manuscript in a thermos flask, in a leather pouch, near Crematorium III at Auschwitz. He detailed the process for mass murder of a least one million people. "The gas canisters were always delivered in a German Red Cross vehicle with two SS men. They then dropped the gas through openings—and half an hour later our work began. We dragged the bodies of those innocent women and children to the lift, which took them to the ovens."

Thirty-six years later his account was unearthed at a depth of 16 inches by a Polish forestry student who was hired to dig at the site. It took a year of work by Russian expert, Alexander Nikityaev, to restore the faded text in Nadjari's thermos to make it legible. As reported by BBC News in 2017, four other *Sonderkommando* members also left written records, most importantly a Polish Jew named Salmen Gradowski.

HAY, Peter

"Her life is an offering, her words a poem, her story an inspiration."
— Elie Wiesel

FROM 1980 TO 2007, Peter Hay of Summerland, B.C. lived and worked in Los Angeles where he wrote *Ordinary Heroes: Chana Szenes and the Dream of Zion* (Putnam 1986). Hungarian-born Chana Szenes is famous as a national hero of Israel, a Joan of Arc figure, due to her daring mission as a paratrooper behind German lines that led to her death at age twenty-three during World War II.

"Anna" Szenes (anglicized as Hannah Senesh) was born on July 17, 1921, the daughter of a well-regarded Hungarian playwright. In 1939, leaving her widowed mother in Budapest, she went to Palestine "to realize the dream of Zion." With a group of young pioneers Chana helped found Kibbutz Sdot Yam in the Haifa district near the site of ancient Caesarea. While making plans to bring her mother and her brother Gyuri (George) to Palestine, she secretly joined the Palmach, the paramilitary group that was the precursor of the Israeli Defense Forces. In 1943, she enlisted in the British Women's Auxiliary Air Force as an Aircraftwoman 2nd Class. This enabled her to train as a paratrooper in Egypt. She eventually was selected to parachute behind German lines on a spy mission.

On March 14, 1944, she and colleagues Yoel Palgi and Peretz Goldstein were parachuted into Yugoslavia and joined a partisan group. A few days later the Germans occupied Hungary, their erstwhile ally, and Chana was racked with anxiety about her mother and friends trapped in Budapest. Frustrated with waiting for action among the partisans, she decided to act alone, crossing the Hungarian border on June 7, 1944, the same day that Adolf Eichmann began the deportation of Hungarian Jews to Auschwitz. Chana was captured by Hungarian border guards and brutally interrogated for five days. Some of her teeth were knocked out. She refused to divulge who might have helped her, or give the codes for the radio transmitter found on her.

Transferred to a Budapest prison, she was confronted with her mother, Katherine, who had no idea that her daughter had left the safety of Palestine. Chana remained defiant, even when the Nazis threatened to murder her mother. Her resistance infuriated her captors and raised the morale of her fellow captives. Then, as the Soviet army was closing in on Budapest, Chana was hastily dragged before a military court and sentenced to death. Her mother, who had been freed, made desperate attempts to save her. Her daughter was executed by a firing squad on November 7, 1944.

Chana Szenes 1939.

From age thirteen, Chana kept a diary, wrote poetry first in Hungarian and then in Hebrew, and had ambitions to become a writer like her father. Parts of her diary were published as early as 1946, the year that a ship named the *S.S. Hannah Szenes* brought Jewish survivors of the Holocaust through the British blockade of Palestine. Her diary and letters, first published in England in 1971, have been reprinted numerous times. After the founding of the State of Israel, several schools, streets and community centres were named after Chana Szenes. In 1950, her remains were taken from Budapest and given a state funeral in the National Military Cemetery on Mount Herzl in Jerusalem, where she rests with six other fallen parachutists. Former Israeli Foreign Affairs Minister, Deputy Prime Minister and U.N. Ambassador Abba Eban concluded, "All the definitions of great courage come together in Chana's life."

PETER HAY WAS BORN in Budapest to a Jewish family as Peter Majoros on February 9, 1944, the same year that Chana Szenes died there. Her parents and his grandparents were neighbours and friends. Peter survived his first year as a hidden child. His father, Istvan Majoros, was a writer who was saved by Raoul Wallenberg while his mother was in hiding. In May of 1945, Hay's mother met the Hungarian playwright Gyula Hay. She eventually married him and Peter became adopted by him. In 1957, Peter was sent to England, where his maternal grandparents had fled in 1939. Two weeks later Gyula Hay was arrested and later tried for treason.

While attending English boarding schools, Peter won a scholarship to Merton College, Oxford, where he first read classics and became interested in the theatre. He was instrumental in producing the English premiere of his father's play, *The Horse*, at the Oxford Playhouse, in 1965. At Oxford, Peter Hay was asked by Katherine Szenes to translate Chana's poems from Hungarian for the first English-language edition of her diary.

Peter Hay emigrated to BC in 1967 to teach theatre at Simon Fraser University and concurrently he became the first dramaturge (literary manager) of the Vancouver Playhouse Theatre Company and the founding drama editor of Talonbooks. John Juliani directed a production of Gyula Hay's *The Horse* and started rehearsing his play *Have* until The Playhouse kiboshed the production as too radical. It was finally produced in 1995 at UBC's Frederic Wood Theatre. Hay also worked for the Justice Development Commission in Dave Barrett's government. In Vancouver, Peter Hay published *Have*, followed by Beverley Simons' *Crabdance*—which led to his partnership with David Robinson and Talonbooks.

Peter Hay retired to Summerland, B.C. in 2007, a place he knew from his long association and friendship with the playwright George Ryga, whose plays he published with Talonbooks in the 1970s. After Ryga died in 1987, Hay became active to preserve Ryga's legacy. He co-founded and guided the Ryga Arts Festival in its first five years and he is currently working on a Ryga Archive at the Summerland Museum.

Hay has been involved with the Simon Wiesenthal Centre and worked on plays and documentaries about Chana Szenes, including a film by Roberta Grossman, *Blessed is the Match* (2008). In his biography of Szenes, Hay uses the diminutive of Anna, which is Aniko, for the Hungarian parts, and then Chana after she went to Palestine.

EVA HOFFMAN

IN PREPARING TO speak at the Annual Kristallnacht Commemorative Program as the Beth Israel Synagogue in Vancouver in 2002, Eva Hoffman said, "For those of us who are direct descendants of Holocaust survivors, that historical tragedy constituted our first childhood knowledge, and it has deeply informed our biographies and psyches. Yet we did not experience it ourselves. What can we know of the past, and what kind of knowledge do we want to pass on?

"The second generation after any atrocity stands in a particular relationship to events: it is the hinge generation within which living memory can be transmuted into either history or myth. I am going to suggest that our task in the second generation is to move from personal and familial knowledge to a morally informed understanding of history."

Born in Krakow on July 1, 1945 (as Ewa Wydra), Eva Hoffman moved from Poland to Vancouver with her Jewish parents at age thirteen. Her parents had survived the Holocaust by hiding in a forest bunker and being hidden by Polish and Ukrainian neighbors. Her mother, Maria, finished high school but was not allowed to go to college by her Orthodox parents, despite being offered a scholarship. Her father finished only fourth grade—but his fearless resourcefulness was largely responsible for their survival. They both knew several languages: Polish, Yiddish, Hebrew, Ukrainian and later English. Their knowledge of world literature was extensive.

She describes their move to Canada as the formative experience of her life. "My parents had just emerged from the Holocaust when I was born. They came from a small town in the Ukraine. They had a strong sense of Jewish identity. A sense of suffering was very palpable in them. At the same time there was a sense of a tremendous will to live which I imbibed from them. They were largely self-educated but

Eva Hoffman with her parents in Krakow, 1945: "A sense of suffering was very palpable in them."

great readers. They passed along a very natural and intimate love of books . . . The assumption was that we would never go back. There was a great deal of a sense of rupture about it. The differences between Krakow and Vancouver were enormous. There was a cultural trauma, let us say, during those first stages of immigration."

Ewa changed her named to Eva in Canada. Initially, writing in English as a second language was a major hurdle. "Nothing fully exists until it is articulated," she writes in *Lost in Translation*. She has said, "This was really the main impact of immigration for me. My sense of the enormous importance of language. It is something that truly shapes us and truly shapes our perception of the world. . . . My struggle was for English to inhabit me."

She won the struggle and received a scholarship to study English literature at Rice University in Houston, later studying at the Yale School of Music and then received her Ph.D in English and American literature from Harvard in 1975. Having married fellow Harvard student Barry Hoffman in 1971, they divorced in 1976. A gifted pianist, she chose literature over music with much difficulty. "The Vancouver to which I came did not have a rich musical life."

After she worked for the *New York Times* from 1979 to 1990, serving as deputy editor of Arts and Leisure, and as a senior book editor, she was a visiting professor at Columbia (New York), University of Minnesota and CUNY's Hunter College. Her first book, *Lost in Translation: Life in a New Language* (E.P. Dutton 1989), describes her experiences in Poland and Vancouver. Her other books include *Exit into History: A Journey Through the New Eastern Europe* (Penguin 1993), *Shtetl: The Life and Death of a Small Town and the World of Polish Jews* (Houghton Mifflin 1997) and *After Such Knowledge: Memory, History and the Legacy of the Holocaust* (2004).

Hoffman has received the Jean Stein Award (1990), a Guggenheim Fellowship (1992), the Whiting Award and an honorary D.Litt from Warwick University (2008). She is a Fellow of the Royal Society of Literature and lives in London, England.

KAELLIS, Rhoda

IN 1987, RABBI VICTOR REINSTEIN of the congregation Temple Emanu-El in Victoria suggested recording recollections of the Holocaust. Rhoda Kaellis located survivors and recorded their histories over a period of nine months for *The Last Enemy* (Arsenal Pulp, 1989).

"The Holocaust holds such a weird fascination that it is difficult to analyze," she wrote. "There is such a sense of profound unreality about these experiences, that accepting them became, for me, almost a feat of will. The survivors seemed to have a similar problem. Again and again they told me, 'It happened to me but it's still hard for me to believe.'

"I have mulled and puzzled over why this should be so, as I shook my head in disbelief, not about the truth of what I was told, but over the fact that one human being could do these things to another. I finally decided that no sane person is capable of understanding how men and women could methodically and repeatedly—even within the context of a program of annihilation—gratuitously engage in such prolonged cruelty towards defenceless men, women, old people, infants and children. There is no way a rational mind can ever understand why or how the "Final Solution" could be carried out.

"In spite of this, or because of it, the fear remains that it could happen again."

Kaellis gathered the experiences of 15 Holocaust survivors before completing the fictional, composite story of 12-year-old Sarah Carozo, the only child of a post-World War II, Jewish family in New York City, and Lilly, her Belgian cousin, who came to live with her after her Belgian parents died in a concentration camp. A dramatized reading of the work was presented at the Jewish Community Centre in Vancouver in 1990. Rhoda Kaellis' only novel, *A Question of Values* (Lulu 2009), also concerns two women in New York in the aftermath of World War II.

Kaellis was the editor for *Keeping the Memory: Fifteen Eyewitness Accounts of Victoria Holocaust Survivors* (Vancouver Holocaust Centre Society for Education and Remembrance, 1991). With a foreword by Robert Krell and a teaching guide by Kit Krieger, it provides thirteen Jewish accounts (two of them by couples) of Holocaust experiences, including slave labour, in Germany, Poland, France, Holland, Belgium and Indonesia.

Born in 1928, Rhoda Kaellis came to Western Canada in 1967 with her husband Eugene Kaellis, who was born in New York City. While living in Burnaby, the couple co-wrote an advice column for seniors, *Primetime*, and co-authored *Satisfy: A Relationship Repair Manual* (Braemar, 1985). They lived in New Westminster for sixteen years and she became a tireless advocate for affordable housing for all until her death in 2006.

Opened in 2011, the Rhoda Kaellis Lookout Society House is a four-storey, residential building in New Westminster, built as part of BC Housing's Homelessness initiative. With thirteen permanent one-bedroom units and eleven units of transitional housing for adults, it serves as a transitional centre for those who have been homeless.

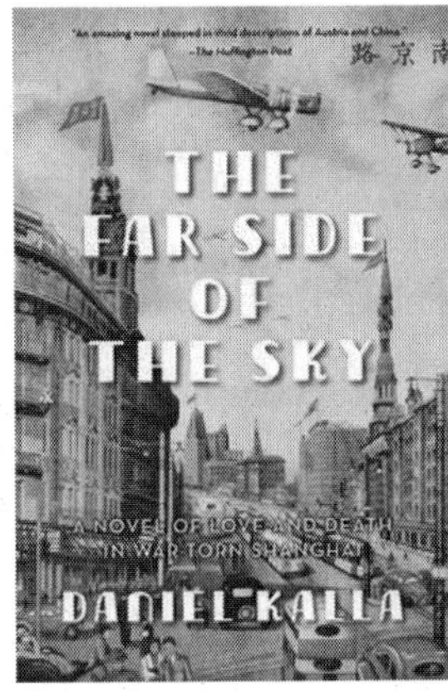

KALLA, Daniel

DANIEL KALLA'S GRANDFATHER was a Jewish family doctor from Prague who left Czechoslovakia, with family in tow, weeks before the Nazis arrived. Daniel's father, a surgeon, spent much of his teen years evading Fascists and Nazis in Budapest, and fled the Soviets during the Hungarian Revolution. As a third-generation physician who is also married to a pediatrician, Daniel Kalla now practises as an emergency physician in Vancouver when he is not writing medical bestsellers, several of which have been optioned for films.

Part love story, part medical drama, and part wartime saga, Daniel Kalla's seventh novel *The Far Side of the Sky* (HarperCollins 2011) begins with Kristallnacht in Austria. A secular Jewish surgeon named Franz Adler flees the Nazis with his daughter to operate a refugee hospital in Shanghai where he falls in love with an enigmatic nurse, Soon Yi "Sunny" Mah. The story marks the start of a trilogy about German and Austrians Jews in Shanghai.

Rising Sun, Falling Shadow (Forge 2013) continues the story of Dr. Franz and Soon Yi Adler through 1943, the bleakest year of the war in Shanghai, when Allied citizens were interned and sixteen-to-eighteen thousand mostly German Jews were crammed into a ghetto already teeming with impoverished locals. The Adlers risk their lives to support the cause of the Chinese Resistance while staring down a threat from local Nazis. The story delves into both the heroism and the treachery that can result when ordinary people find themselves facing extraordinary dangers.

Nightfall over Shanghai (HarperCollins 2015) completes Kalla's Shanghai trilogy, opening in 1944 as the Japanese are losing the war. Dr. Adler and his daughter, Hannah, are imprisoned in the Shanghai Ghetto with other Jews. He is forced to perform surgery for his Japanese captors while his beloved Eurasian wife delivers an unwanted baby that she decides they must raise. In 1945, as American B-52s begin strategic bombing raids on Shanghai, they also become involved in the Zionist movement to create a Jewish homeland.

KAHN, Leon

"It is the duty of the survivor to speak of his experience and share it with his friends and contemporaries. Leon Kahn's story is poignant and its message eloquent."
— Elie Wiesel

LEON KAHN'S LIFE STORY reads more like Jerzy Kosinski's harrowing 1965 novel *The Painted Bird* than an autobiography. Of all the various memoirs in book format from British Columbia-based survivors, few come anywhere near to being as consistently riveting and alarming.

As a boy growing up in the village or "shtetl" of Eisiskes, near the Lithuanian/Polish border, Liebke Kaganowicz—later known as Leon Kahn in Vancouver—was a straight-A student who gorged himself on Tarzan comic books when the reality of the German occupation became too horrible to accept. "I was sure that if I believed hard enough and willed it to be happen with every ounce of concentration I could muster, I could transport myself to Tarzan's jungle paradise." Possibly this devotion to fantastical feats and death-defying actions in a fantasy world explains, as much as anything else, why Kahn survived his serial escapades from 1939 to 1948.

Eisiskes was in Poland in 1939 when Russian Communists successfully took control. In June of 1941, the Nazis invaded, abetted by Lithuanians who welcomed the Germans as allies. Soon the Polish Jews could not walk on the sidewalks; they could only walk in the gutters. Yellow stars of David had to be worn, belongings were confiscated and ultimately most of the 5,000 people in the village were murdered by Lithuanian collaborators of the Einsatzgruppen (paramilitary mobile killing units).

BORN IN 1925 INTO an Orthodox Jewish family, Liebke (Leon) Kaganowicz (Kahn) took refuge with his family in the nearby Radun Ghetto until it was liquidated in May of 1942. Most of Leon's family hid in an attic but were soon discovered. His father escaped, while his mother stayed behind with his grandmother. Later, his mother would disappear, probably deported to Treblinka and murdered by gas.

At age sixteen, when Leon was forced into hiding with his brother Benjamin, they found a place to sleep in a tangle of bushes, close to a wall, in the oldest part of the cemetery, next to the gravel pit. They heard a rumble of field wagons approaching. Concealed in the bushes, they peered over the wall and watched an unbelievable parade as the women and children of Eisiskes were herded along the road by Lithuanian police, whipped and beaten to move them faster.

When the cavalcade arrived at the gravel pit, and the police barked orders, separating the women from the children, they saw an aunt, a cousin and a neighbour. They were much relieved not to see their mother, grandmother and sister. Kahn recalls:

Leon Kahn

> The women were taken in groups of a hundred or so down the path into the gravel pit. When they reached the point where the bushes that grew there would hide them from the sight of the others,

Kahn (right) with Jewish partisans, forest near Bransk, Poland, circa 1943

the women were made to strip naked, and pile their clothing nearby. Then many of those who were young were separated from the others and dragged into the bushes to be raped and raped again by soldier after soldier and policeman after policeman. At last, they were dragged off to join the others, marched to the bottom of the gravel pit, lined up and coldly shot to death by the Lithuanian killers.

I clung to the edge of the cemetery wall, as horror welled up within me. I wanted to hide, to run screaming from the cemetery, to make this hideous thing end. Didn't they know what they were doing? These were human lives! These were people, not animals to be slaughtered!

My mouth opened to scream, but I could not. I wanted to close my eyes, but they wouldn't close.

"Don't look, Leibkie! Don't look," Benjamin sobbed, and pulled at me to make me leave the wall.

I didn't want to look, but I couldn't stop looking. I saw the

> Lithuanians shoot the breasts off some of the women, and shoot others in the genitals, saw them leave others with arms and legs mutilated to die in agony, and some to smother as the next load of bodies fell upon them. I saw my aunt die in a volley of gunfire. I saw my beautiful cousin raped and raped until death must have been the only thing she longed for.
>
> My fingers slipped from the wall and I fell beside my brother, retching and sobbing. He clung to me.

Leon Kahn then describes how the Lithuanians proceeded to slaughter the children that remained, all of them. Some were shot. Many others were dashed to pieces by smashing their heads on granite boulders, one by one.

Horrors persisted. These included forced labour in the ghetto of Radun, collecting and burying corpses, sorting the clothing of murder victims he knew, cleaning up after massacres. Chopping wood and cleaning toilets for the Germans. "In my heart, I was still convinced that the only refuge for us was the forest. Throughout the nightmares of Eisiskes and Radun, I had longed to flee to its safety, feeling that there at least I could find some means of defence. Even if I lived as the animals lived, I could die there with the dignity of a man. Part of this feeling that the forest was the right place to go came from my boyhood idolization of Tarzan, of course."

It is an odd experience for a reader to be told by a good man how and why he was obliged to commit two murders, killing two German guards silently with a knife, in order to flee terror of imminent deportment to a concentration camp. He vomits after each murder but proceeds to lead his weakening father and brother and little sister on a nightmarish journey through the winter forests and snow-laden fields, through a bizarre litany of traumas.

To give their lives meaning, the boys eventually fought with the partisans against the Nazis. As a teenager, Liebke Kaganowicz became an expert at blowing up trains. His brother was killed by Lithuanian collaborators; his father and sister were killed by members of the Polish Home Army. When the Soviet Army eventually liberated the area,

Liebke/Leon spent two months catching Germans and sending them to POW camps or else killing them on the spot.

Both Russian and American forces detained Kaganowicz until they could verify that he was not an enemy alien. In September, he returned to Eisiskes but found no one from his family. He was enrolled in a KGB school in Vilnius but after three months he ran away and managed to get over the border to Lodz, Poland. From there he went to a Displaced Persons camp in Salzburg, Austria. In the fall of 1948, he was among 1,800 refugee immigrants who sailed on the American troopship S.S. *Stewart* to Halifax. He could not comprehend how it could possibly take five nights and six days to reach his destination by train. Managing to pose as a tailor, he immigrated to Vancouver and started a new life as Leon Kahn. There his memoir ends.

He later recalled: "I spoke no English, but this didn't worry me because I already spoke Polish, Lithuanian and Yiddish, and could make myself understood in Russian and German. I knew I could learn one more language. I was told that the best place to learn English was the movie theatre, so night after night I sat listening and watching as the famous lips of Hollywood moved and formed words for me to copy. It's surprising how well this system worked.

"One evening, after the last show was over, I came out the back door of the Capitol Theatre onto Seymour Street. The street was quite deserted, except for two drunks coming noisily along the sidewalk toward me. For a moment I watched them approach; then I crossed the sidewalk and stood in the gutter, hoping they wouldn't notice me. But they did.

"Still arguing drunkenly, they paused to look at me, obviously surprised at what I had done. Then off they went again down the street, shouting and shoving one another. I didn't know whether to laugh or cry! Neither of them had made a move to strike me. They hadn't called me names. They hadn't even understood why I was standing in the gutter! Where I had come from, no drunk ever forgot—even when he forgot his own name—that Jews were there to be beaten, abused and thrown in the gutter!"

Leon Kahn eventually worked successfully in real estate. Originally self-published in 1979 under his imprint of Laurelton Press, Kahn's posthumous memoir *No Time To Mourn: The True Story of a Jewish Partisan Fighter* (Ronsdale, 2004), as told to Marjorie Morris, was edited by Betty Keller. It was dedicated to his 24 relatives (including his mother, father, sister, brother and grandmother) who were killed by the Nazis. All are listed at the outset.

"I remember Kahn telling me that when he was in that DP camp in Salzburg," Keller recalls, "he worked the Black Market and amassed a small fortune, but when he was accepted for Canada, he gave it all away because he was told the streets here were paved with gold. He arrived with just a few dollars in his pocket and was a little disappointed to find that Vancouver's streets were just the ordinary kind. When I met him, he had a huge office in the building that is kitty-cornered to Christ Church Cathedral at Georgia and Burrard."

The *Jewish Independent* once provided a synopsis as to how he rose from poverty:

> In 1952, Leon Kahn travelled to New York to meet some relatives for the first time and, while there, attended a dance for Jewish newcomers, where he met Evelyn Landsman, a Bronx girl with Eishishkes roots. They married, Evelyn moved to Vancouver with Leon, and they had four children, Mark, Charlene, Hodie and Saul. (Charlene, who was born with severe developmental disabilities, passed away in 1966.) After they married, Leon Kahn scoped out an unlikely business niche for a Jew—Christmas trees—but his entrepreneurial spirit made a go of it and the business flourished. It was on a Christmas tree lot in 1957 that Kahn met a man who would change his life forever.
>
> Henry Block was a partner in the emerging local real estate giant Block Brothers. Spotting a talent for sales, Block asked Kahn to come and work for him. Beginning as an entry-level commercial real estate agent, Kahn finally met his match. He wasn't very good at it. Block refused to acknowledge defeat,

> however, and pushed Kahn over to the construction wing of the company, offering the advice that, to cover up Kahn's initial ignorance of the construction industry, he should walk around confidently opening and shutting a tape measure.
>
> Block Brothers became Western Canada's largest real estate firm and Kahn would become president of its construction division before parting amicably to start his own firm. Among Kahn's most notable projects were the Vancouver Show Mart Building and the Seattle Trade Centre. Leon Kahn's son, Saul, told the *Bulletin* that being his family's sole survivor of the Holocaust gave Leon a special purpose and perspective in life. 'He always felt that he survived the war because he was meant to give of himself to the community,' Saul Kahn explained.
>
> Infused by a deep sense of obligation mixed with an overwhelming guilt at surviving while the rest of his family did not, Leon Kahn's outlook was unique, said his son. He avoided the trappings of wealth that many of his station exhibited and devoted himself to community service and providing for his own family.

In old age, Kahn recounted some of his experiences as a Holocaust survivor for the documentary film, *Unlikely Heroes: Stories of Jewish Resistance* (2004), produced by Moriah Films, the media wing of the Simon Wiesenthal Center in Los Angeles.

Leon Kahn died on June 8, 2003. His beneficiaries included Jewish causes devoted to Holocaust education and secular causes for medical research and health care, as well as the Jewish Family Service Agency, the B.C. Lung Foundation, the B.C. Cancer Foundation and the Jewish Federation of Greater Vancouver.

Leon Kahn was forever haunted by the question, "Why me? Why did I survive when so many others died?" Long torn by guilt and anguish, he took some solace from what Golda Meir once told a group of survivors. "You can get used to anything if you have to. Even to feeling perpetually guilty. It is a small price to pay for being alive."

In a moving Epilogue, Kahn described the many ways the Holocaust could haunt him—such as stopping his car at a railway crossing, waiting for a freight train to pass, unable not to think of his mother and grandmother inside a cattle car to Treblinka.

"I remember lying in the tall rye grass near the forest in the summer of 1943," he writes, "waiting for the night to come. A skylark soared up into the heavens, dived down, and soared up again, and I prayed to be transformed into a bird like that.

"How marvellous to have wings and fly straight into the heavens leaving all my miseries and terrors behind! I lay there willing myself into that bird's form, just as I had tried to will myself far from Eisiskes long before.

"But the bird flew away and night came again."

KARWOWSKA, Bozena

EVERY SPRING, for five years, from 2014 to 2019, undergraduate students from UBC travelled to Poland for a month of lectures and study tours on subjects pertaining to pre-war Jewish life and the Holocaust in Poland. Students spent two weeks at the Auschwitz-Birkenau State Museum where they worked and studied with the Museum's historians, collections specialists and members of its publishing house and education centre. They spent another two weeks studying in Warsaw, Krakow and Bialystok.

Bozena Karwowska

[Auschwitz was the laboratory for the experiments undertaken on twins by Dr. Josef Mengele. In 1985, for three days, witnesses supplied testimonies at a Yad Vashem Holocaust memorial event to record his atrocities. These included keeping hundreds of human eyes pinned to his lab wall "like a collection of butterflies" and tearing an infant from a mother's uterus and throwing it into an oven, disappointed it wasn't a twin. Mengele had impregnated the girl with the sperm of another twin, pampered her during her pregnancy and attended the birth himself, only to be enraged by the result. Vera Kriegel, at age sixty, described watching the Auschwitz guards crush the skulls of babies with rifle butts.]

By the end of the visitation program, UBC students wrote essays pertaining to the Holocaust and Poland. They were guided by UBC professor Bozena Karwowska, Chair of UBC's Modern European Studies department, who edited their collaborative anthology of selected articles and essays for *The More I Know, The Less I Understand. Young Researchers' Essays on Witnessing Auschwitz* (Osweicim: Auschwitz Birkenau State Museum Publishing House 2017).

This program called Conflicting Stories and Memories was in-

USHMM/BELARUSIAN STATE ARCHIVE OF DOCUMENTARY FILM & PHOTOGRAPHY.

Kept alive for medical experiments by physician Josef Mengele, twins Eva and Miriam Mozes, on the far right, both wearing knitted hats, were liberated from Auschwitz-Birkenau on January 27, 1945. This photo has been attributed to Alexander Voronzow or else others who worked with him under the direction of Mikhael Oschurkow, head of the photography unit for Soviet army liberators. Eighteen minutes of a film they made was later introduced as evidence at the International Military Tribunal in Nuremberg. Another segment of the film disappeared for forty years before resurfacing in Moscow in 1986.

terrupted by the onset of Covid-19. This partnership with the Auschwitz-Birkenau State Museum and the Emanuel Ringelblum Jewish Historical Institute was formulated by UBC's Department of Central, Eastern and Northern European Studies (CENES) in partnership with the Vancouver Holocaust Educational Center, the University of Warsaw, the Jewish Historical Institute and the Polish Consulate in Vancouver.

Bozena Karwowska (MA, Warsaw, 1977; MA, Ph.D, UBC, 1989, 1995) is also the author of a study of Polish literature of the Holocaust, with a particular focus on the first-hand testimonies written immediately after the war, *Gender, Sexuality, Concentration Camps* (Krakow University, 2009). This is a brave work that investigates matters of gender, body, sex and sexuality. According to one review, Karwowska places an emphasis on feminist discourses, "especially those approaches that recognize the ways in which even non-gender related persecutions have an effect on genders and their cultural formations" and she "tests the relevance of various feminist and post-colonial approaches for studies concerned with the concentration camps, limitations of humanity, morality and ethics."

Karwowska received the UBC Killam Prize of Excellence in Teaching (1999) and the UBC AMS Just Desserts Award (2000). Her book, *Second Sex in Exile. Migration in Narratives by Polish Postwar Female Writers* (Krakow University 2013) was nominated for the Jan Kochanowski Prize for the best book on Polish literature and culture.

KIRK, H. David

TO COUNTERACT the revisionist books of David Irving falsifying matters regarding the Holocaust, H. David Kirk translated and published two essays by the German historian Eberhard Jackel, and provided his own commentary in *David Irving's Hitler: A Faulty History Dissected* (Ben-Simon, 1993), with a foreword by Robert Fulford.

In particular, Jackel disproved Irving's absurd claim that Hitler was unaware of the Shoah. In doing so, Jackel quoted a prophecy made by

Hitler in a Reichstag speech in January of 1939 when he said: "I shall once again be your prophet: if international Jewry with its financial power in and outside of Europe should manage once more to draw the peoples of the world into world war, then the result will not be the Bolshevization of the world, and thus the victory of Jewry, but rather the total destruction of the Jewish race in Europe." Hitler's wartime speeches repeatedly cited this prophecy.

Born into a Jewish family in the Rhineland, West Germany, in 1918, Dr. H. David Kirk was a B.C. publisher based in Brentwood Bay. His small operation specializing in children's books and Judaica was created in 1984 after Kirk retired from teaching in the University of Waterloo's sociology department. He and his wife Beverley ("Beve") Tansey set up their own press in order to re-publish Kirk's own previously published book *Shared Fate*, after the title had gone out of print.

Having adopted four children, Kirk examined the social and psychological meanings of adoption since the 1950s. His seminal work on adopted persons' civil rights, *Shared Fate* (first published in 1964), remained available in hardcover for eighteen years and became available in paperback, as did *Adoptive Kinship: A Modern Institution in Need of Reform*. Kirk's *Exploring Adoptive Family Life* was re-published when he was aged seventy as *Exploring Adoptive Family Life: The Collected Adoption Papers of H. David Kirk* (Ben-Simon 1988).

Arguably, the most noteworthy book published by the Ben-Simon imprint was Lillian Boraks-Nemetz's Holocaust novel for young readers, *The Old Brown Suitcase: A Teenager's Story of War and Peace*, in 1994. H. David Kirk died in Kitchener, Ontario, on December 14, 2019, at the age of 101 years.

KOMAR, Leon

PHYSICIAN LEON KOMAR was one of the interview subjects for *Primary Voices*, the series of reminiscences recorded by the Vancouver Holocaust Education Centre in Vancouver. He also translated *A Re-*

"An Extra Portion," a painting by Noemi Judkowski. The text, in Polish: "You got too little soup? This evening you'll get an extra portion." Thus promises Schultz, the forced-labor boss. "Here's what the extra portion looks like."

quiem for Two Families (1990), a self-published memoir of his family and the family of its author, Noemi Judkowski, with whom he had corresponded in order to learn that his entire family had perished in the Holocaust. His own story was self-published in *Memoirs* (1995).

Born in Warsaw, Poland, on January 30, 1915, Komar fled with his parents Moses and Sara Komar to Moscow when he was only six weeks old. They returned at war's end in 1918. Unable to find work, his father went back to Moscow on his own where he died of typhus. His mother managed a small factory that imported and re-sold sofas and other furniture. An aunt looked after Leon and his younger brother, Iza. In Warsaw he studied both Polish and Jewish subjects in a secular Jewish school and faced increasing anti-Semitism. After high school, he opted to study in England with funding from his uncle and the Jewish community. He was accepted into medical school in Glasgow in 1939 and graduated in 1944. He promptly volunteered to work as a doctor on a British Royal Navy vessel.

An uncle who had escaped to Tangier, Morocco, had managed to locate Leon's family in Poland, but only briefly, during World War II. While corresponding with Noemi Judkowski in Warsaw, he learned his mother and brother were likely sent to Auschwitz. His aunt was sent to Treblinka. He met his future wife, Liselott (nee Frey), a German-born Jew, in 1945, while working as a surgeon at a hospital in the Midlands.

In 1947, Leon immigrated to Edmonton. His wife followed three months later. The couple moved to Fort St. John after Komar found work as a civilian medical practitioner on an air force base, then briefly lived in Hazelton, Kemano and Philadelphia before moving to Vancouver, where Komar had a private medical practice for over forty years. When he had a private practice in Kemano, he looked after the Indigenous residents of Kemano Bay. "They needed attention and medical equipment," he said. "They were really neglected." Leon and his wife had two sons and also built a house in Israel, which they often visited.

In 1955, Komar visited Kibbutz Lohame HaGeta'ot where he met Noemi Judkowski and they commenced an ongoing correspondence for the rest of their lives. Along with biographical material relating to Komar, *A Requiem for Two Families* offers Judkowski's memoirs of the Warsaw Ghetto and the Majdanek and Auschwitz concentration camps.

"After studying at the Polytechnic in Warsaw and gaining practical experience designing and building bunkers in the Ghetto," writes Komar, "Noemi became a very successful architect. With work in her own kibbutz of Lohamei Hagetaot and elsewhere, she had very little time for writing. Finally, realizing that her memoirs might have historical and educational merit, she consented to publication."

This book reproduces some of her sketches of scenes from Majdanek and Auschwitz, some of which were exhibited in Israel. As well, it is noteworthy that drawings by five painters: Leo Haas, Ferdinand (Felix) Bloch, Frantisek Moric Nagel, Yehuda Bacon and Zofia Rosenstrauch (aka Noemi Judkowski) were presented at the Eichmann trial in Jerusalem in 1961–1962. These included an album of

20 images by Judkowski.

Upon his retirement from medicine, Leon Komar earned a BA in Anthropology and an MA in Arts and Religious Studies. His wife Liselott died in 1991. A booklet addendum to his *Memoirs* entitled "*Letters from the Warsaw Ghetto 1938 to 1942*" includes photocopies and translations of letters written by the Komar family in the Warsaw Ghetto. A copy is kept in the United States Holocaust Memorial Museum Collection.

KREMER. Roberta S.

WITH SCOTT ANDERSON, Roberta S. Kremer curated *Ravensbruck: The Forgotten Women of the Holocaust* (February to May, 2002), the first Vancouver Holocaust Education Centre exhibition to focus on the victimization of women during the Holocaust. Built exclusively to house female prisoners, this concentration camp in northern Germany, 90 kilometres north of Berlin, reputedly had one of the highest percentages of murdered prisoners of any concentration camp in Germany according to the VHEC exhibit.

Ordered built by Heinrich Himmler, Ravensbruck was not primarily for Jewish prisoners. Instead, it also included Jehovah Witnesses, Resistance fighters, lesbians, prostitutes and aristocrats (including the sister of New York's Mayor Fiorello La Guardia).

Named after the village of Ravensbruck, it opened in May of 1939 and was liberated by Soviet troops in April of 1945. More recently Sarah Helm has published *Ravensbruck: Life and Death in Hitler's Concentration Camp for Women*, also entitled *If This Is A Woman: Inside Ravensbruck: Hitler's Concentration Camp for Women* (Penguin Random House 2015). Ravensbruck was constructed on the banks of Lake Schwedt, near the town of Furstenberg an der Havel, where there is now a memorial site.

Jews dominated the profitable fashion industries in Berlin and Vienna, so those Jews who thrived within that business were quickly targeted by anti-Semites as outlined by the essays that Roberta S. Kre-

Ravensbruck, the concentration camp exclusively for female inmates

mer edited for *Broken Threads: The Destruction of the Jewish Fashion Industry in Germany and Austria* (Berg Publishing 2007). Her book developed from a Vancouver Holocaust Education Centre exhibition in partnership with the Original Costume Museum Society of Vancouver in 1999, for which Claus Jahnke assembled period clothing made or designed by Jewish designers. Jahnke and Ivan Sayers served as curators for this exhibition and publication was produced through the Morris & Yosef Wosk Family Publishing Fund with additional sponsorship from Dick Haft, Max Fugman, Sandy Hayden and Karen Simkin.

Essays by Chris Friedrichs, Charlotte Schallie and Gloria Sutano trace how and why the Jewish fashion industry was systematically "targeted with a campaign of propaganda, boycotts, humiliation and Aryanization" by the Nazis in the 1930s.

Broken Threads is one of eight books thus far directly supported with funds from The Morris J. & Yosef Wosk Publishing Endowment established in 2000.

Born on November 26, 1946, in Superior, Wisconsin, Roberta S. Kremer arrived in Canada in 1987 and earned her Doctorate of Philosophy in Art Education and Museum Studies in Vancouver from the University of British Columbia. She served as the Executive Director of the Vancouver Holocaust Education Centre from 1996-2006, then as the Acting Curator of Education and Public Programs at the Museum of Anthropology at UBC from 2007 to 2008. She curated VHEC exhibitions including "Faces of Loss" and has edited *Memory and Mastery: Primo Levi as Writer and Witness* (State University of New York Press 2001).

KUJUNDZIC, Zeljko

ZELJKO KUJUNDZIC's outdoor installation, "The Gate of Life," is a 135-ton sandstone archway at the Jewish Community Centre in Uniontown, Pennsylvania, dedicated to remembering those who died in the Holocaust. It was also used as a memorial gathering place for grieving after synagogue shootings killed eleven people in Pittsburgh in 2018.

Born in Subotica, Yugoslavia, on October 23, 1920, Zeljko Kujundzic published an autobiography, *Torn Canvas*, in 1957, in which he recalls his experiences in WW II, including escapes from both the Nazis and the Russians. "I have lived under the White and Red terror," he writes, "and I know that there is nothing at all to choose between them."

As young man, Kujundzic had resisted his father's advice to become a banker and instead travelled under a scholarship from the Hungarian Ministry of Education to study Folk Art in Transylvania. During WWII he was captured and held in prison twice, first by the Nazis and then by the Russians. The first time he was forced to work in a Nazi slave battalion on the Russian front until 1944. The second time he was bound for slave labour in Siberia until he made an underwater escape and trekked a thousand miles through Ukraine and Romania to reach post-war Yugoslavia.

Kujundzic briefly joined Tito's partisan force until he was horrified by mass executions and limited freedom in post-war Yugoslavia. Kujundzic returned to his art studies in Budapest and received a Masters of Fine Arts degree from the Institute of Fine Arts in Budapest.

TORN CANVAS
ZELJKO KUJUNDZIC

Disenchanted with socialism under Tito, he fled across the border of Hungary in 1946 to a Displaced Persons Camp in Austria. He was then able to immigrate to Scotland where he painted for ten years and married Ann Johnson in 1948. They had six children; five survived into adulthood. He wrote a manifesto, *Art in the Modern World*, which was published in 1956.

The family immigrated to Canada and settled in Cranbrook, B.C. in 1958. In 1959, they moved to Nelson, B.C. where he worked as an art instructor at L.V. Rogers High School. He became the first Principal of the Kootenay School of Art in 1960, remaining in that position until 1964. In Canada, as a fifth-generation craftsman of Turkish descent, he further developed his work in sculpture, clay, painting, printmaking, metal, stained glass & weaving. He was interested in First Nations culture and he painted in Indigenous settings, believing Indigenous artistic expression had an affinity to his own Byzantine roots. His explorations in this area were encouraged by a Koerner Foundation grant from the Anthropology Department of the University of British Columbia. In 1964, Kujundzic converted a church and established the Art Centre in Kelowna, B.C. near the juncture of Richter Street and Bernard Avenue. He also had a formative role in the creation of the Okanagan Summer Arts Festival, and he formed the Contemporary Okanagan Artists group with Weldon Munden, Des Loan, Leroy Jensen, Frank Poll and writer George Ryga.

In 1968, Kujundzic separated from his wife Ann and accepted a position in the United States where he served as the head of the new Arts Department at Pennsylvania State University's Fayette Campus. In 1971, he was elected as a full member of the International Academy of Ceramics in Switzerland, enabling him to travel in the U.S. and Europe to show his work. Also an inventor, he experimented for twenty years to ultimately build a working solar kiln in 1976. Divorced in 1982, he married his second wife, Elizabeth Campbell, an artist. Retiring from Penn State in 1982, he returned to the Okanagan Valley where he taught workshops and maintained studios in Entiat, Washington State and in Osoyoos, B.C.

Zeljko Kujundzic died of Alzheimer's disease at age eighty-two in Osoyoos in 2003. He was survived by his wife Elizabeth, his first wife Ann, his children Laszlo, Kate, Claire, Judy, Andrew and Natanis, and grandchildren Willow, Shane, Joshua, Chelan, Narisse & Jadzia. His daughter Claire Kujundzic is also a B.C. author.

Zeljko Kujundzic's art has been exhibited in public and private collections around the world, including Italy's Palazzo Medici-Ricardi, the Smithsonian in Washington D.C., Edinburgh University, Pennsylvania State University, the National Sculpture Collection, Toronto, and the Kyoto National Museum in Japan. In Vancouver, he was commissioned to create the Thunderbird sculptures at UBC's Thunderbird Stadium.

LESTER, David

EVER SINCE Art Spiegelman's *Maus* series (1980–1991) became the first graphic novel to win a Pulitzer Prize in 1992—by depicting the experiences of Spiegelman's father as a Shoah survivor, with Jews portrayed as mice, and Germans as cats, and Poles as pigs—graphic novels have become a serious medium for reflecting and sharing history.

David Lester's 312-page graphic novel *The Listener: Memory, Lies, Art, Power* (Winnipeg: Arbeiter Ring, 2011) deftly portrays how German society was complicit in the rise of Adolf Hitler. Seven years in the making, this unusually complex work of visual storytelling mixed with history quickly went into a second printing and was a finalist for a Book of the Year Award sponsored by the U.S. magazine *ForeWord Reviews* in the graphic novel category.

By reflecting the under-examined, formative era of Hitler's rise—when repressive police and propaganda tactics parlayed his party's narrow state election victory in Lippe on January 15, 1933 into an alleged "massive victory," whereupon his "fake news" triumph prompted President Hindenburg to appoint him as Chancellor of Germany on January 30—*The Listener* awakens contemporary readers to the fragility of democracy.

Mauthausen concentration camp, from *The Listener* by David Lester

The story starts with Louise—the "listener" of the title—as she takes a tour of the museums of Europe, trying to overcome guilt and sadness after a young Cambodian activist, inspired by one of Louise's sculptures, fell to his death while hanging a protest banner off the Woodward's W tower in Vancouver. She has received letters absurdly blaming her for the death of the activist. As an antidote, Louise decides to examine famous and favourite paintings and sculptures throughout Europe, seeking re-direction and possible inspiration.

In Austria, she meets Tomas, an intellectual who has a particular interest in artists who were monsters. She learns Stalin and Mao wanted to think of themselves as poets, and Hitler believed he was a serious painter. Tomas accompanies Louise to the Mauthausen concentration camp where Louise struggles to absorb the atmosphere. On a hill above the market town of Mauthausen, roughly 20 kilometres east of Linz, in Austria, was the main camp of a group with nearly 100 further subcamps located throughout Austria and southern Germany. Awestruck at Mauthausen, she mostly feels her inability to fully comprehend the magnitude of what occurred there.

In 1975, when Yosef Wosk visited the infamous rock quarries of Mauthausen, about 100 miles west of Vienna, in northern Austria, where close to 200,000 had been imprisoned and over 90,000 died tortuous deaths, he observed, "We saw wild Spring flowers blooming on the hills and wondered how anything could ever dare grow there again?" Wosk noted that Mauthausen was a camp like no other because it was where educated people and members of the higher social classes—the so-called intelligentsia—were sent to be worked to death. Therefore, it was a place to kill artists.

Louise and Tomas discuss the role of art and the responsibilities of artists. The question as to how self-centred an artist should be is discussed. We learn the brilliant and articulate Orson Welles considered running for the U.S. Senate but declined, whereupon Joseph McCarthy won that election. Eventually, Louise meets an older couple, Marie and Rudolph, who recall working for a newspaper in the conservative state of Lippe, in Germany, in the 1930s. The couple recall joining the DNVP (German National People's Party), hoping for the return of the monarchy. In a series of flashbacks, we revisit how attacks on Jews, and restrictions on their freedoms, were popular with the German people. When Paul von Hindenburg, the President of Germany, had to select a new Chancellor, the main choices were the DNVP's Alfred Hugenberg (who owned the paper where Marie and Rudolph worked) and Adolf Hitler. At the time, Hitler's stubborn desire to be autocratic was actually hurting the party's fortunes, but Hugenberg struck a self-interested deal with Hitler, hoping for a position of power in a Hitler-led government.

Marie and Rudolph describe how Hitler's party was in deep financial trouble. The Lippe election fight could have marked the end of Hitler, but Hugenberg ordered his newspaper's staff not to attack the Nazi Party. When Nazi party stormtroopers arrived in Lippe from across Germany, local rallies were manipulated and members of the opposition were brutally attacked. DNVP campaign posters were covered over with Nazi posters. The Nazis won the Lippe election in January of 1933 with only 39 percent of the vote. After Hitler had been appointed as Chancellor by Hindenburg, other political parties were banned. Opposition leaders were killed, Communists were killed, too. The persecution of Jews greatly escalated. With Trumpian vanity and insanity, Hitler presented himself as a national hero.

More of a listener than an activist, Louise feels incapable of mounting any meaningful response to evil when she returns to Canada. Then she meets someone who knew the Cambodian-born activist who plunged to his death near the outset of the story. He tells her the life story of Vann, a Cambodian doctor who survived genocide under the Pol Pot regime. Vann lost his parents and was never able to overcome his survivor's guilt. Because the Pol Pot regime targeted artists for execution, Vann took a great interest in art, wondering what made artists so dangerous that so many of them had to die. Louise learns Vann was inspired by her art and she was not responsible for his death. She is inspired to create a new sculpture that is the culmination of all she has learned on her journey through Europe.

All her "listenings" have not been for naught.

Much of the dialogue from Hitler (and other Nazi party leaders) in *The Listener* contain direct quotes from his speeches and writings. Lester details what are historical facts and what are his own inventions at the back of the book, which also includes an excellent timeline for the rise and fall of the Nazi party. There are also mini-biographies for pro-Nazi animators, filmmakers and cartoonists, detailing their specific involvement in Nazi propaganda, as well as what happened to them after World War II.

Born in Vancouver in 1958, David Lester is a graphic designer and a musician whose band, Mecca Normal, a venerable guitar-and-voice duo with Jean Smith, has garnered international acclaim, including a four-star album review in *Rolling Stone*. Lester is also the publisher of Get-to-the-Point Publishing, an imprint that has produced 20 titles since 1993 including Bud Osborn's *Keys to the Kingdoms*, winner of the City of Vancouver Book Prize. His book *1919: A Graphic History of the Winnipeg General Strike* (Between The Lines), authoured with the Graphic History Collective, was co-winner of the 2020 CAWLS Book Prize. Lester released *Prophet Against Slavery: Benjamin Lay, A Graphic Novel* (Beacon) in 2021.

LINN, Ruth

HAVING GROWN UP in Israel, Ruth Linn first became aware of Rudi Vrba's existence and his escape from Auschwitz when she saw Claude Lanzmann's monumental 1985 documentary *Shoah*.

"This was very strange to me," she later told Pat Johnson, of the *Jewish Independent*, in 2006. "I read a lot about the Holocaust but I never, ever read about Vrba in Israeli textbooks in the Hebrew language. Am I the only Israeli who fell asleep in class when we studied this in the Holocaust?" she asked. "Or maybe we never studied it."

She remained mystified by this ignorance and sought to locate Vrba for seven years until she arrived in Vancouver to teach at the University of British Columbia in 1994. She found him teaching pharmacology at the university. Having grown wary of researchers and journalists, Vrba gave her a copy of his book, *I Cannot Forgive*, but was initially hesitant to engage much further.

As Linn later told Johnson: "In terms of literature, it [*I Cannot Forgive*] is in the class of books by Primo Levi and Elie Wiesel. But then I turned the book back and forth and I saw on the cover, 'First published 1963.' And the year is 1994. I said to myself, 'Where has this book been for thirty-one years?' I had never read about it in Israel.

"Now I had an Agatha Christie mission to try and trace what happened to this book. It was published in London in 1963 . . . but it wasn't translated into Hebrew. What, there was no money? So many books have been translated and this is not a [story about a] tiny shtetl in Siberia. This is Auschwitz, centre of the Holocaust narrative. So, this became, accidentally, my mission: to do justice to history, to bring this guy to Israel and give him an honorary doctorate. We didn't know about him and I wanted to put him back into our history."

Returning to Israel, Linn was able to have *I Cannot Forgive* finally published in Hebrew in 1998, in a version translated by a Holocaust survivor of Slavic origin, Yehoshua Ben Ami, after its noteworthy rejection by Yad Vashem. A trusting relationship arose between Vrba and Linn after she also arranged for him to attend a conference in Israel where he signed copies of his book. In recognition of his courage and his contribution to Holocaust education, she arranged for the University of Haifa to award him an honorary doctorate. Linn also arranged for publication of the Vrba-Wetzler Report for the first time in Hebrew by the University of Haifa Press.

After Ruth Linn came to know Rudi Vrba (born Walter Rosenberg), she later published *Escaping Auschwitz: A Culture of Forgetting* (Cornell University 2004) to critically examine why news of the murder of Jews at the Auschwitz-Birkenau concentration camp, brought to the Jewish Council in 1944 by escapees Vrba and Alfred Wetzler, was mostly repressed, and why Hebrew readers around the world, especially in Israel, have continued to be mostly ignorant of the Vrba-Wetzler Report and the two escapees' memoirs.

Vrba and Wetzler escaped in April of 1944. Some contents of their unprecedented reportage were published by the BBC on June 15, 1944, and by the *New York Times* on June 20, 1944. In response to subsequent appeals made by world leaders to Hungarian leader Admiral Miklos Horthy, the deportations to Auschwitz-Birkenau were stopped on July 9, 1944.

Vrba always maintained that if Jewish authorities had not delayed making his report public knowledge, many of Hungary's Jews would not have been murdered. As previously stated: he believed many more would have been inclined to either attempt escape or fight rather than obediently board the trains under the guise of re-settlement.

The Vrba-Wetzler report continues to generate historical debate. Many, including Vrba himself, have questioned whether the report was disseminated and acted upon as rapidly and as forcefully as it should have been. In an unanswerable "what if," Vrba continued to question to his last day whether more victims could have been saved had the Allied and the Jewish leadership of the time pursued a more vigorous course of action in light of his report. The report was circulated to Allied countries, but winning the war as soon as possible was the Allies' answer to demands made for rescue of the Jewish victims. This line of thought has at times made his ideas somewhat at odds with the predominant Israeli historical narrative concerning the events of that time. Whereas the two escapees accurately predicted the fate of the Hungarian Jews, what they could not have foreseen was that their post-war memoirs and documented report would be kept from the Israeli Hebrew-reading public.

Ruth Linn is the former dean of the Faculty of Education at the University of Haifa (2001–2006). As the only Israeli researcher trusted by Dr. Vrba to record his escape from Auschwitz-Birkenau, she is an expert in the field of moral psychology and resistance to authority. Her major academic work focusses upon suppressed testimonies in times of war and peace. Ruth Linn has been studying Wikipedia's allegedly one-sided restaging of Vrba's narrative in Israeli historiography for a new book.

At age eighteen, Ruth Linn of Haifa was conscripted in 1968 into the Israel Defence Forces. She obtained her doctorate from Boston University in 1981. Linn has since been a visiting scholar at Harvard University, the University of Maryland, the National Institute of Mental Health and the University of British Columbia. In 1990, she received the Erikson Prize from the International Society of Political Psychology to recognize her pioneering studies on Israeli soldiers who were selective conscientious objectors during wartime. Linn has also examined how inappropriate reporting of Vrba's escape by some Jewish historians has been used as ammunition by some Holocaust-deniers. Her other books include *Not Shooting and Not Crying: A Psychological Inquiry into Moral Disobedience* (Praeger 1989), *Conscience at War: The Israeli Soldier as a Moral Critic* (SUNY Press 1996), *Mature Unwed Mothers: Narratives of Moral Resistance* (Springer 2002) and *How Did You Survive?* (Tel Aviv: Hakibuttz Hameuchad 2016).

While revisiting six grandchildren in Vancouver in 2020, Linn unexpectedly became a prolonged resident of British Columbia for a second time, during the Coronavirus pandemic.

MARTZ, Fraidie

ONE OF THE MOST famous of the 1,123 Jewish war orphans whom the Canadian government reluctantly allowed into Canada from 1947 to 1949 was John Hirsch who arrived in Winnipeg as a seventeen-year-old from Hungary, speaking no English. As the son of a shopkeeper, he had been raised in a home that had attracted theatre people, including Nijinsky, until he was forced to wander orphaned and penniless across Europe at age thirteen.

After only ten years in Canada, he co-founded Manitoba Theatre Centre. Hirsch proceeded to direct actors such as Martha Henry, Anthony Hopkins and Maggie Smith, while mounting productions in Los Angeles, New York, Stratford and Toronto, leading to four tempestuous years as CBC's head of TV drama in the 1970s. Hirsch was Stratford Festival director from 1981 to 1985. He died in 1989.

Refugees' arrival at Pier 21, Halifax. Between 1947 and 1949, 1,123 Jewish orphans came to Canada.

Fraidie Martz's co-authored biography, *A Fiery Soul: The Life and Theatrical Times of John Hirsch* (Vehicule Press 2011), was preceded by an arguably more essential book, *Open Your Hearts: The Story of the Jewish War Orphans in Canada* (Vehicule Press 1996), winner of the Joseph and Faye Tannenbaum Award for Canadian Jewish History.

In a radio interview about the Jewish war orphans for *Jewish Digest*, conducted by Leslie Lutsky in 1996, Martz said, "They had lost everything that is considered essential for human growth and development. And they did it at a time when the Jewish community of Canada was of modest means, spread out across the country."

First, the Jewish war orphans had to be gathered. On November 9, 1943, representatives of forty-four nations had met in the East Room of the White House and established the United Nations Relief and Rehabilitation Administration. Two of the primary organizers for assembling and organizing war orphans at the UNRRA's Children's Center in Germany were Lottie Levinson of Vancouver and Ethel Ostry from Winnipeg. Levinson became recognized worldwide for the next three decades for her service to displaced people in Europe before she retired to Vancouver in 1976 and died in 1989.

As a former UNRRA field worker in Europe, Marion Pennington of Vancouver told Martz her strongest memory of UNRRA training was being instructed in the use of a DDT spray gun: "Up women's skirts, down men's trousers. I shudder to think of the harm we might have done."

The Jewish orphans arrived in Canada in groups of fifteen or twenty, at random intervals. They were generally acclimatized in group facilities before they could be matched to families. It was pre-determined that no orphan was to be institutionalized.

"Nobody in Canada could *fathom* what they had been through," Martz recalled. "That's why group identity was very important for some. Some people depended upon their fellow refugees as their peer group, as their extended family. They helped one another, they loaned each other money. They understood one another. . . . But for some others, they wanted nothing to do with that refugee group. They wanted to become Canadianized as quickly as possible."

Having worked as a social worker in the psychiatric department of Montreal's Jewish General Hospital, Martz spoke to about fifty of the war orphans in Vancouver, Winnipeg, Toronto and Montreal decades later to write her book, *Open Your Hearts.*

"Many told me that for years nobody was interested in their story. The ones who came forth were very glad to talk to me but I was also fully aware that a lot of those people were very successful in life, they had done well in business, they had fine families and homes, and they were very proud of what they had accomplished and were very pleased to let it be known.

"At the same time, I was aware that there were a group of people who were living in the shadows, who were not doing so well, for whom life had been very difficult. The scars of the past had not healed enough for them to be able to carry on the kind of life that they had hoped to lead. I knew they were there but I didn't get to speak to them; they were much harder to reach.

"I began this project hoping to understand how is it possible for these young people to have gone on to lead such rich lives given what they had been through. That was an underlying question. And I must say I am no further ahead in understanding how that is possible. I am awed by what they did, and how they did it, and I don't know if I have an answer. When I asked that question, I was told, 'When you have lived in hell, and seen the worst, life's problems are often very pale by comparison.'"

Fraidie Martz (nee Peritz) has three daughters and lives in Vancouver. Her husband Sam Martz died on December 19, 2015.

MAZZEO, Tilar J.

IT'S NOT PROMINENT, but if you search in the cement concourse of the plaza outside the entrance to Yad Vashem in Jerusalem, you can find a tree with an inconspicuous marker that honours one of the most admirable defenders of decency and children who ever responded to Nazi barbarism: Irena Sendler.

Tilar J. Mazzeo's *Irena's Children* (Simon & Schuster 2016) is a biographical tribute to the heroic Polish social worker Irena Sendler who saved the lives of an estimated 2,000 Jewish children during World War II. Her life is typically over-shadowed by that of the children's author and pedagogue Dr. Janusz Korczak, the principal and fundraiser at their orphanage that provided sanctuary and schooling for Jewish orphans in the Warsaw Ghetto.

Born in Warsaw in 1878, Janusz Korczak was the pen name of Henryk Goldszmit. He had operated an orphanage in Warsaw prior to the Nazi invasion. Forced to relocate to within the walls of the ghetto, Korczak handled the complex politics and fundraising. Stefania Wilczynska managed the day-to-day affairs of education and hygiene. Irena Sendler is now revered for having masterminded the countless, death-defying escapes of orphans who were continuously being smuggled to freedom in safe houses beyond the ghetto.

In 1942, instead of saving his own life, Korczak famously opted to march side-by-side with the orphans from the Warsaw Ghetto

TWIGG PHOTO

Irena Sendler, remembered at Yad Vashem in Israel

to the deportation point from which they would all go to the Treblinka death camp to be murdered. Sendler was not with them. As they walked as a cavalcade, each child carried a blue knapsack and a favourite book or two. An eyewitness named Joshua Perle later recorded: "Janusz Korczak was marching, his head bent forward, holding the hand of a child, without a hat, a leather belt around his waist, and wearing high boots. A few nurses were followed by two hundred children, dressed in clean and meticulously cared for clothes, as if they were being carried to the altar."

Sendler was later dubbed "the female Oskar Schindler." As a Roman Catholic, she was tortured and sentenced to death for her child-smuggling but was released when a guard was bribed. Before she died at age ninety-eight in a Warsaw nursing home, she became one of the first Righteous Gentiles to be honoured at Yad Vashem in 1965. James D. Shipman, a lawyer who was born and raised in the Pacific Northwest, has also published an historical novel, *Irena's War* (Kensington Publishing 2020).

In 2017, The Belfry Theatre in Victoria presented a critically acclaimed production of Hannah Moscovitch's play about the orphanage, *The Children's Republic*, in which Kerry Sandomirsky brilliantly depicted the fortitude and wisdom of Korczak's lesser-known female cohort Stefania (Stefa) Wilczynska who first met Korczak in Warsaw in 1908 and remained his closest associate for thirty-four years. They worked together ever since he founded his first Jewish orphanage at 92 Krochmalna Street in 1911.

A believer in the Montessori education system, "Stefa" has been largely overlooked in the shadow of Sendler's reputation. Rather than accept papers that would have enabled her to leave Poland, she chose to stay with sick children and be the main comforter for the orphans until she, too, marched to her death with the orphans.

Anyone who looks very carefully in Yad Vashem will find a brief testimonial from someone named Yitzchak Belfer: "Stefa was with us 24 hours a day. We felt her presence even as we slept. We were also aware of how she worried about our every need." Her enduring selflessness remains overshadowed by Korczak and Sendler.

Tilar J. Mazzeo first gained *New York Times* bestseller status with *The Widow Clicquot* (HarperCollins 2008), her biography of Barbe-Nicole Clicquot Ponsardin, the eponymous founder of the champagne house Veuve Clicquot. As a cultural historian, Mazzeo proceeded with *The Secret of Chanel No. 5: The Biography of a Scent* (HC 2010) and *The Hotel on Place Vendome* (HC 2014), both bestsellers. The latter is significant in Holocaust history because it describes intrigues at the Ritz Hotel in Paris during the Nazi occupation.

As soon as the Nazis far too easily overtook Paris in 1940, Adolf Hitler ordered the Ritz Hotel to remain in its luxury mode, serving as headquarters for his highest-ranking officers, including Reichsmarschall Hermann Goring while also attracting rich patrons and artists like Coco Chanel who reputedly took a lover in Nazi military intelligence and allegedly used Nazi laws to vanquish Jewish business associates. It's a story of nasty, evil, ambitious people amid opulence. Arletty, star of *Les Enfants du Paradis*, had her head forcibly shaved after the war, for her affair with a Luftwaffe officer.

Having received her permanent residency papers in 2014, Tilar J. Mazzeo lives in Saanichton, B.C. with her husband, Dr. Robert Miles, a Canadian professor of English. As a wine writer, she doubles as the co-proprietor and winemaker at Parsell Vineyard.

MEDVEDEVA-NATHOO, Olga

THE JANUSZ KORCZAK Association of Canada was created in Vancouver in February of 2002 to assist the Vancouver Holocaust Education Centre in its presentation of a travelling exhibit called "Janusz Korczak and the Children of the Warsaw Ghetto." The opening at the Jewish Community Centre in October of 2002 featured a lecture by Korczak Association board member Lillian Boraks-Nemetz, "A Child in the Warsaw Ghetto," recalling her experiences as a child survivor of the Warsaw Ghetto. The friendship that arose within the organization between two other board members, Gina Dimant and editor

Olga Medvedeva-Nathoo, would eventually lead to *Crossroads, A True Story of Gina Dimant in War and Love* (K&O Harbour, 2014), a biography by Medvedeva-Nathoo.

The origins of the Korczak Association can be traced back to Warsaw-born Alexander Dimant whose family was stranded in the Warsaw Ghetto. After he was able to escape to the Aryan part of the city, it's possible the rest of his family witnessed Dr. Korczak's famous walk with 192 orphans to the *Umschlagplatz* to board the cattle train to Treblinka.

In 1996, Alexander Dimant spearheaded an event to honour and popularize in Canada Janusz Korczak's life and work, during preparations for an exhibition commemorating the Warsaw Ghetto Uprising. This event was organized by the Vancouver Holocaust Education Centre and the Consulate General of the Republic of Poland. After his untimely death in 1998, his wife Gina sought to continue his educational efforts. In November 1999 she organized a screening of Andrzej Wajda's film *Korczak* at the Vancouver Jewish Community Centre. The popularity of this event was the springboard for the formal creation of a Korczak Association to mount further events and to publish its own newsletter edited by Olga Medvedeva-Nathoo.

Gina Dimant returned to Szczecin, Poland, in 1946, as Hinda Wejgsman.

Gina Dimant was born as Hinda Wejgsman on January 11, 1926, in Warsaw. (A younger sister, Lina Wejgsman, born in 1937, worked many years as a radio announcer in Szczecin, Poland, before moving to Canada where she died in

Vancouver in 2016.)

Fleeing the Nazis, the Wejgsman family wisely left their home in Pelcowizna, a suburb of Warsaw in September of 1939 and travelled by train and by foot, staying for a time in Biesankovicy, Belarus, before reaching the Soviet border where guards registered Hinda's name as Gina.

In December of 1939, the family began a six-week journey to Leninogorsk (now Ridder, in Kazakhstan) where Gina worked at the brick factory, at a timber mill and eventually at the local cinema.

As Tamara Szymanska has noted in her book review: "*Crossroads* follows the Wejgsmans family, their extraordinary journey in a cattle car from the eastern border of Nazi-occupied Poland to the Union of Soviet Socialist Republics, and of their fight for survival there. The cold in the car was intolerable, and the Wejgsmans slept on straw, bodies side by side, trying to keep warm. They travelled for more than a month. They were sent to Leninogorsk in northeastern Kazakhstan, near the Altai Mountains, where temperatures dropped to minus 41°C in winter.

"After their arrival, Gina did not go to school because local authorities considered her an adult at age fourteen and gave her a construction job carrying bricks, four at a time. Gina reflects: "… my main memory from Leninogorsk is not what we ate there, but how terribly hungry we always were. With the feeling of hunger, you couldn't even fall asleep and, if you fell asleep, then it was with night dreams of food until you woke up with the same daydreams. In winter evenings when the frost was absolutely intolerable and it was inconceivable even to attempt lying in bed, so as not to freeze to death, we would pace the room in circles, single file."

At war's end, Gina married a Polish Jewish hairdresser, in January of 1946. Crossing the Polish border to return to live in Szczecin, Gina's name was changed to Longina because the name Gina did not appear in the official Polish list of first names. Gina's son, Saul, also known as Salek, was born on February 1, 1947. Gina and Jan divorced in 1948.

Gina met her second husband, Alexander Dimant, at the Jewish

Centre in Szczecin. Born on September 17, 1922, his birth name was Szaja Dymant, and he died in Vancouver on March 9, 1998.

The Dimant family had lived on Mila Street in Warsaw's Jewish Quarter. They married in 1952. Alexander graduated with a Master of Economics from the Polytechnic in Szczecin and Gina worked in health care. In 1968, her son Salek was arrested after attending an anti-government meeting at Szczecin University.

The Dimant family left Poland in September of 1969 after their citizenship was revoked.

Supported by the American Jewish Joint Distribution Committee, the Dimants lived in Vienna and Rome before Gina and Alexander immigrated to Vancouver in August of 1970. He opened an accounting firm; she found work with the Finance Department at UBC in 1973 and stayed there until her retirement.

Salek followed his parents to Vancouver in 1971 and married Rosalie Neuwirth in 1974, giving rise to grandchildren Henry "Dov" Dimant and Sally Dimant.

In 1993, Alexander Dimant travelled to Poland to participate in the fiftieth anniversary of the Warsaw Ghetto uprising. In 1996, he was involved in preparations for *The Warsaw Ghetto: A Pictorial Remembrance* exhibition at the VHEC (1996).

On May 3, 2013, Gina Dimant was awarded the Order of Merit of the Republic of Poland for her efforts in strengthening cordial relationships between Poles and Jews.

Dr. Olga Medvedeva-Nathoo has written and edited three books about Janusz Korczak, including the first extensive English bibliography about Korczak, himself a prodigious author.

As a joint project of the Janusz Korczak Association of Canada and the Adam Mickiewicz University (Poland), her *May their lives be easier . . . Of Janusz Korczak and his pupil* concerns the World War II relationship between the famous Holocaust orphanage manager in Warsaw and his ward Leon Gluzman, who had been living in Canada since 1930.

MERMELSTEIN, Robert

A CHILD SURVIVOR who came to Canada in July 1951, Robert Mermelstein earned a Ph.D in chemistry from the University of Alberta and worked 28 years for the Xerox Corporation in Rochester, NY, before becoming a Vancouverite. In *My Life: A Journey from Mukacevo to Vancouver: Prevailing Over Adversity and Challenges* (Vancouver, 2018), he mentions he has made it a practice to search once a year for any new mentions of his little-known birthplace, variously known as Munkacs or Mukachevo, at Hungary's eastern border, where deportations to the concentration camps from Hungary began. The Jewish population of Mukachevo, now situated in western Ukraine, hovers at around one hundred. When it was called Munkacs and he was born there on April 20, 1936, there were about 12,000 Jews comprising about 40 percent of the population. The Munich Agreement enabled Adolf Hitler to wrest political control of the Carpathian region from the former Czechoslovakia. The final deportation train left on May 23, 1944, carrying 3,080 victims.

In a preface, Mermelstein writes, "This chronicle of our family's history and of my professional life is addressed primarily to my five grand-nieces... I want to highlight some lessons I learned in life. I want to emphasize the importance of perseverance and of taking preventative action."

Robert Mermelstein has also recalled:

"Two days after the end of Pesach in 1944, my father Salamon (a leader in the town's Jewish community), was arrested, while my mother Blanka, my brother Paul and I were marched with a group of Jews to the local brickyard. There we met my mother's sister Janka, her physician husband and their two children.

"About a week after being imprisoned in the brickyard, Paul and I were separately smuggled, inside empty soup pots, into the ghetto by Rose Goldberger, one of the women escorts of food supplied to the ghetto. Rose, known to us as Rozsi, was the senior saleswoman in my parents' glass and china store, located on the main street in Munkacs. She also escorted our mother from the brickyard into the ghetto, where my parents were briefly reunited, and my father urged my mother to, 'Go and save the children!'

"That was the last time I saw my father.

"My mother and I hid in a room in the ghetto for about a week; I was told that my new Hungarian-sounding family name was Meszaros, and warned never to undress in the presence of strangers. I was also told not to ask questions, to memorize some basic Christian prayers, and to follow the instructions of family members.

"My brother Paul was in hiding with our Aunt Ilonka at another location in the ghetto and given identical instructions.

"One evening at dusk, my mother and I left our room and passed through a gate to where a taxi, with a Christian electrician sitting in the front passenger seat, waited. The taxi took us to a railroad crossing close to the train station and the three of us walked between the tracks for about 200 meters and boarded a waiting train from the back. Our overnight ride was uneventful; fortunately, at that early stage of Jewish persecution, there were no document checks at the station in Budapest.

"My Uncle Emil, stationed with a labour battalion in a Budapest suburb, was able to rent us a room for a month. Paul and Ilonka, who had made the same journey with the electrician a few days earlier, were in that room waiting for us. We had forged Christian identity papers which were obtained by my father and were able to avoid any situation in which they might be closely inspected.

"Between June and early December 1944, our mother and aunt arranged for Paul and I to live in a Franciscan monastery's orphanage near Budapest's Elisabeth Hospital. It provided refuge to a number of hidden Jewish children. There I learned the Lord's prayer, Psalm 23 and how to make the sign of the cross, along with basic arithmetic, reading and writing. I got along well with the other boys and played games with them during recess.

"By mid-December we heard the sound of Russian heavy weapons and saw bright flashes in the sky at night. Ilonka appeared and ordered us to pack our small suitcases. She insisted to the guards at the monastery gate that these two small boys had to join their relatives for the upcoming Christmas holidays.

"She took us to the nearby apartment of a Communist couple, named Rakosi, who were hiding several Jews, including our mother. We spent nearly two weeks in their apartment, until the sound of approaching artillery shells chased us to the basement of the building.

"On the third or fourth of January 1945, the first Russian forces entered our shelter, which was crowded with frightened women and children.

"We returned to Munkacs in March 1945 to establish which of our relatives had survived and what property or assets, if any, could be recovered. All of the returnees were anxious to locate surviving family members. Most survivors left to restart their lives elsewhere in Europe, the British-mandate Palestine, or North America.

"It soon became apparent that our father, grandparents, aunts (save for one), uncles and cousins had all been murdered. Several of our former neighbours told us that our father and closest relatives were on the last train transport from Munkacs, which arrived in Auschwitz two days before Shavuot, 1944.

"Our looted home, with most of its furnishings and contents stolen, became a temporary haven for several friends and acquaintances. Conversations primarily revolved around the severe conditions in concentration camps and how most inmates' fates depended on the duration of their confinement—although determination, perseverance and luck also played a role.

"I listened intently to the returning adults talk about the past several months of their lives, but most of the names they mentioned were unfamiliar to me. Our neighbour's son, Amos Rubin, who had hid with a local Righteous Gentile family, was the only Jewish adolescent I encountered during our brief return to Munkacs.

It became apparent to me that Amos, Paul and I were the only survivors younger than sixteen out of an estimated 3,000 Jewish youth who lived in the Munkacs region in April 1944.

[After Mermelstein's book was published, he discovered two other Jewish boys, Zoltan Matyash and Michael Pinto-Duschinsky, had also survived.]

"In mid-July 1945, about six weeks prior to the scheduled closing of the Russian-Hungarian border, we returned to Budapest with nothing but a change of clothing. I was nine years old and had very little understanding of what had occurred in the world between April 1944 and our liberation from hiding.

"We resumed our lives using our real name, Mermelstein, and also resumed our education. While there was a strong effort by the Jewish community to involve its youth in social, cultural and recreational activities, neither Paul nor I met anyone from Munkacs in these Jewish youth groups.

"My Bar Mitzvah celebration was a very modest event, held in school due to our dire financial situation.

"Our family of four (mother, aunt and two boys) left Budapest for Vienna, Austria in 1949, with the intention of moving to Israel.

"We eventually decided to immigrate to Canada. The foundation of my Jewish identity was formed during these turbulent five to seven years, between the end of the Shoah and our first couple of years in Canada.

"We arrived in Halifax on July 4, 1951, and travelled to Montreal. The next fifteen years can best be described as a typical immigrant experience: two adults struggling with a difficult financial situation due to limited employment skills, while Paul and I concentrated on our education.

"My science teacher, Mrs. Gottesman, awakened in me an interest in science which ultimately led to a Ph.D in chemistry and two years of post-doctoral training in life sciences.

"At the age of thirty, I joined the Xerox Corporation as a research scientist."

Michael Mielnicki (left), reunited with his brother after fifty years

MIELNICKI, Michel

IN 1989, MICHEL MIELNICKI learned from a Simon Wiesenthal newsletter that an Auschwitz-Birkenau camp selection SS officer named Heinrich-Johannes Kuehnemann had been identified singing opera in Essen, Germany, by Auschwitz escapee Rudolf Vrba.

In 1991, Michel flew to Germany with his wife, June Frischer Mielnicki, also a Holocaust survivor, in order to corroborate evidence against Kuehnemann at a trial in Duisberg, Germany. Initially, he had worried that he might be murdered by "some old Nazi or some new neo-Nazi skinhead" if he testified in public.

Kuehnemann, known for his brutality, was identified by Mielnicki and other witnesses for his role in selecting inmates for the gas chambers and he was convicted. The defendant had argued unsuccessfully that he was unaware of any systematic process for murdering inmates at Auschwitz.

Appreciative, the German prosecutor asked Mielnicki if there was any favour to be done in return. Mielnicki told this prosecutor that he remained troubled by never learning the fate of his brother. About a year later, the German prosecutor called Mielnicki and told him he'd come across the contact information for a Ukrainian named Aleksei Mielnicki who had visited Auschwitz seeking documentation of his imprisonment there.

Perhaps this was a relative of some sort? The prosecutor gave Mielnicki the contact info. He was unaware of other branches of his family beyond Poland and Aleksei is not a Polish name but as soon as Mielnicki made the phone call he knew he had found his brother. Aleksei Mielnicki had simply adopted a different first name. Michel Mielnicki and his wife flew to Poland where he was re-united with his brother after a fifty-year separation.

BORN IN WASILKOW, a few kilometers from Bialystok in northeastern Poland, in 1927, Mielnicki was one of 1,500 Jews in a town of 5,000 people. Following the conquest of his area of Poland by Germany in 1941, he lived in the Bialystok Ghetto, then was sent onto the Pruzany Ghetto for fourteen months, before he was deported, at age sixteen, with his brother Aaron, his parents Esther and Chaim, and his sister Lenka, in a cattle car to Auschwitz-Birkenau. His mother died on the train and his father was beaten to death shortly after arriving at Auschwitz. He witnessed both deaths.

At the concentration camp, Mielnicki's sister was sent off with the other women. Aaron became ill and was sent to the so-called hospital. The siblings promised they would try to return to Bialystok if they were separated. While in Birkenau, it was memories of his mother's cooking that gave Mielnicki "the saliva necessary to chew bread that was at least twenty-five percent sawdust."

Michel survived a death march, worked in the slave labour camp at Buna, then at Mittelbau-Dora in Germany and was finally liberated by the British Army from Bergen-Belsen in 1945. Mielnicki returned

Hitler used repressive police tactics to suppress other political parties to declare victory in the 1933 German election with only 43.9 percent of the vote.

to Bialystok to wait in vain for his brother. Arriving at his hometown in the middle of the night, he found the train station was rubble. It had been destroyed by a German air raid six years before. A switchman kindly pointed to a wooden bench, seeing he was obviously Jewish and entirely alone. "I wouldn't wander the streets at night if I were you," he said. "At best you'll be beaten and robbed. At worst you'll be murdered."

The racist reality of Mielnicki's homeland became increasingly clear. In the two years following the end of the war, more than 100,000 of Poland's remaining Jews fled the country of their birth in fear for their lives. The Red Cross had no answers regarding his missing brother, so Mielnicki eventually immigrated to Canada where, from his home base in Montreal, he became known as "Mr. Michel," one of Canada's premier fur fashion designers.

The emotional cost of survival is made clear in his memoir *Bialystok to Birkenau: The Holocaust Journey of Michel Mielnicki* (Ronsdale 2000) in which he provides harrowing, first-hand accounts of Birkenau, Buna, Mittelbau-Dora and Bergen-Belsen. He recounts the gallows humour that prevailed when prisoners were forced to stand en masse and witness yet another execution ("Want to split his bread portion tonight?") and he references Hannah Arendt's famous phrase about the banality of evil. He has recalled:

> The Nazis had created a subterranean world at Auschwitz that was inhabited by scurrying, craven, little people like myself, and ruled by diabolic, troll-like creatures beyond the imagination of even a Tolkien.
>
> As Himmler's slaves, we lived our lives at a level so primitive that the reader's imagination is undoubtedly strained in trying to come to grips with such a reality. For example, when the physical event called sunshine did occur at Birkenau or Buna, I jumped at any chance to stand or sit in it. If I could find a place away from the ever-prying eyes of killer guards and murderous Kapos, that is.
>
> . . . You cleaned your teeth with your dirty fingernails or

> slivers of wood... and you rubbed your gums with your fingers in hopes that this might prevent pyorrhea. Among the last things you wanted on earth, this side of being gassed or burned, was to lose your teeth.
>
> And because the Grim Reaper was our constant companion in the death camps, we prisoners tended to run each waking hour on pure adrenaline. Which is more than most human bodies or psyches can endure.
>
> Studies show that most of those who did survive, like many combat war veterans, continue to suffer from post-traumatic stress disorder as a result. But unlike sailors, soldiers or airmen, we had no guns with which to fight. Consequently, survivors have few tales of personnel daring-do to share. Just those of unremitting horror. And terror.

Mielnicki's story ends with a blistering indictment of the callousness of the British liberators, and his discovery on returning to Poland that no Jew was safe there. John A. Munro, who co-wrote Mielnicki's memoir, has recalled Mielnicki's profound depression. "I can only guess how ghastly this must have been for him. For me, his Holocaust experiences filled my dreams to the point where constant nightmares interrupted my sleep, which caused me to begin to worry about my own sanity."

Michel Mielnicki increasingly volunteered to speak to high school students about the Holocaust. His daughter Vivian Claman recalled in 2018: "It was cathartic for him to tell his story, and he believed that passing it over to students was of utmost importance. I cannot deny that he is a complicated man, whose identity was forged by the trauma and loss he endured during and after the war. He was emotionally volatile and haunted by memories of what he went through.

"He spoke endlessly about the Holocaust to anyone who would listen, sometimes to the detriment of his mental health. But in spite of his experience and his need to talk of these heinous crimes, he always advocated for tolerance, education and love as the antidote to hatred, racism and genocide."

MINES, Rachel

ONE OF THE IMPACTS of the Holocaust is that it hastened the decline of the Yiddish language. Approximately, 85 percent of the Jews who died in the Holocaust could speak the Yiddish language. The monolingual stance of the Zionist movement further generated the modern dominance of Hebrew over Yiddish as the official, most common tongue of Israel. There were perhaps fewer than two million speakers of Yiddish remaining in 2020, whereas there were approximately eleven-to-thirteen million Yiddish speakers worldwide prior to World War II.

The rich history of Yiddish literature is therefore in jeopardy, soon to be overlooked and ultimately forgotten, unless retrieval and revival actions are taken. One attempt to revive Yiddish has led to the creation of the loosely-knit Vancouver School of Yiddish translators that includes Rachel Mines, Seymour Levitan, Helen Mintz and Faith Jones. As a translator of Yiddish into English, Rachel Mines has concentrated on disseminating, into English, the stories of Jonah Rosenfeld, a major literary figure and frequent contributor to the Yiddish-language newspaper *Forverts* in the United States from the 1920s to the mid-1930s.

Mines' translation from the Yiddish of nineteen stories by Rosenfeld, *The Rivals and Other Stories* (Syracuse University Press 2020), showcases Rosenfeld's dark, Chekhovian style which foregrounds loneliness, social anxiety and people's frustrated longing for meaningful relationships. "Today, Rosenfeld is almost entirely unknown," says Mines, "since he wrote only in Yiddish." Only a handful of his short stories, and none of his plays or longer works, were previously translated into English.

Both of Rachel Mines' parents were Holocaust survivors who spoke Yiddish at home. Her father Sender Mines was born in Skuodas, Lithuania, in 1909, the youngest of nine children. Her mother Jennie Lifschitz was born in Montreal in 1924 as the third of three children. When Jennie's parents split up in Montreal, she and two

FONCIE PULICE PHOTO

Rachel Mines with her mother, on the 700-block Granville Street, Vancouver, 1959, where nearby the family operated the Ideal Lunch restaurant.

siblings were taken reluctantly to Latvia by their mother. The cover of this book shows Jennie Lifschitz as a schoolgirl in Liepaja, Latvia, prior to the Holocaust.

Mass murders and dreadful privations ensued during the Holocaust in Liepaja, where the family lived. Jennie was incarcerated first in the Liepaja Ghetto, then interned at Kaiserwald (in Riga, Latvia) and at Stutthof (near Gdansk, Poland).

After the war, Rachel's mother-to-be, as Jennie Lifschitz, returned to Canada as a natural-born Canadian, rather than as a refugee, in March of 1946. After her arrival in Montreal, a newspaper article about her return to Canada on the *Aquitania* appeared in the *Montreal Gazette*. Legally, it became possible for a limited category of Jews to immigrate two months later, but, in reality, large-scale immigration of Jewish refugees did not occur until 1948.

Rachel Mines has written an account for *Canadian Jewish Studies* of how her mother survived and returned, via Halifax, as quite likely the only Canadian-born, Holocaust prison camp survivor.

The story of how Jennie Lifschitz married Sender Mines in Montreal is more complicated than it is romantic; and it certainly qualifies as unusual.

Daughter Returns to Father Here After 20 Years and Nazi Terror

Rachel Mines' mother Jennie Lifschitz returned to Montreal in 1946, before any other Jews were allowed into Canada in the aftermath of the Holocaust. As Jennie Lifschitz, she was likely the only Canadian-born Jew to survive the death camps as a Canadian citizen. She married twice and became Jennie Mines and Jennie Phillips.

In Lithuania, Sender was required to leave school at age eight to work on a neighbour's small farm; later he worked in his uncle's shoe factory. After his father died in 1931, he moved with his mother to Kaunas, the capital of Lithuania, in 1936. In 1937, he married his cousin Chaja, daughter of Yosef Mines, the shoe factory owner. She already had a daughter born in 1932. Their first son, Emanuel, was born in 1938.

Kaunas fell to the Nazis on June 25, 1941. All Jews were forced into a ghetto of 30,000 people in the Slobodka area of the city. During the winter of 1941–42, Sender was deported for forced labour in Riga, Latvia. His wife and son were among the non-labourers in the ghetto who were rounded up on March 27 and 28 by the Gestapo and sent to either nearby Ninth Fort where they were shot or sent to Auschwitz where they would presumably be gassed. Meanwhile, when the Riga Ghetto was liquidated in 1943, Sender was sent to the nearby Kaiserwald concentration camp in November where he first saw Jennie—although there is no memory of them speaking to one another at the time.

On August 6, 1944, Kaiserwald was evacuated. Both Sender and Jennie were transferred by boat to the Stutthof concentration camp in Poland where Sender became Prisoner #56524. In the spring of 1945, with Russian troops approaching, Sender and Jennie were among the 5,000 viable workers who were loaded onto barges in April for delivery to Germany. Without food and water, during ten days at sea, approximately half of the prisoners died.

The hellish voyage ended on May 3, tragically for most. Abandoned by the SS guards and accompanying tugs, the barges drifted onto a beach at Neustadt in Holstein. Many survivors were shot and killed by German soldiers, if the survivors had the strength to wade to shore, and others died a few hours later when an Allied aerial attack on the Neustadt harbour erroneously sunk some ships in the harbour loaded with concentration camp survivors. At 4 p.m., British troops liberated the surviving prisoners who included Sender and Jennie. Both were hospitalized.

Jennie was able to return to Canada the following year. After Sender immigrated to Canada on December 28, 1951, he went to Montreal in January, reconnected with her and soon found a job in a shoe factory. The couple planned to marry until they learned that Sender's first wife, Chaja, had survived the war and remarried. Both Sender and Chaja had assumed the other was dead. Coincidentally, Chaja had also immigrated to Montreal. Were the storylines not so bleak, this situation had the makings of a Shakespearean comedy.

Arrangements were made for Sender and Chaja to be granted a legal divorce in June of 1952 enabling Sender and Jennie to marry in March of 1953. In 1954, they came to Vancouver, bought a house, opened a restaurant and raised their three children (Michael, Paula, Rachel). Sender Mines died in August of 1982.

Jennie Mines remarried to B.C. labour movement organizer, Jack Phillips, who wrote for the *Tribune*, a Communist newspaper. The couple lived for a time in Prague during which time they visited the remains of the Nazi transit camp of Theresienstadt on Remembrance Day, November 11, 1983.

Mainly used as a holding compound for Czech Jews, Theresienstadt served as a "show camp" to disguise the murderous mandate of the Holocaust. When Red Cross representatives were allowed to inspect the premises in July of 1944, fake stores, a cafe, a kindergarten and flower gardens were added; inmates painted fake house fronts along the inspection route and were given additional food. Conditions were nonetheless sufficiently deplorable that many elder inmates died there while awaiting transport.

During their visit to Theresienstadt, Jack Phillips took a photo of Jennie and labelled it "Return to Stutthof" because clearly Theresienstadt was a ghost-ridden representative of her incarceration in Stutthof (since renamed Sztutowa) in Poland, 36 kilometres east of Gdansk (formerly Danzig).

Stutthof is significant as both the first concentration camp to be erected beyond German borders, in September of 1939, as well as the last camp liberated by the Allies, on May 9, 1945. Executions/murders began at Stutthof in January of 1940. A crematorium and a gas chamber were added in 1943. Poland held four trials in Gdansk to prosecute former guards, kapos and administrators accused of crimes against humanity. There were 99 convictions, including eleven death sentences.

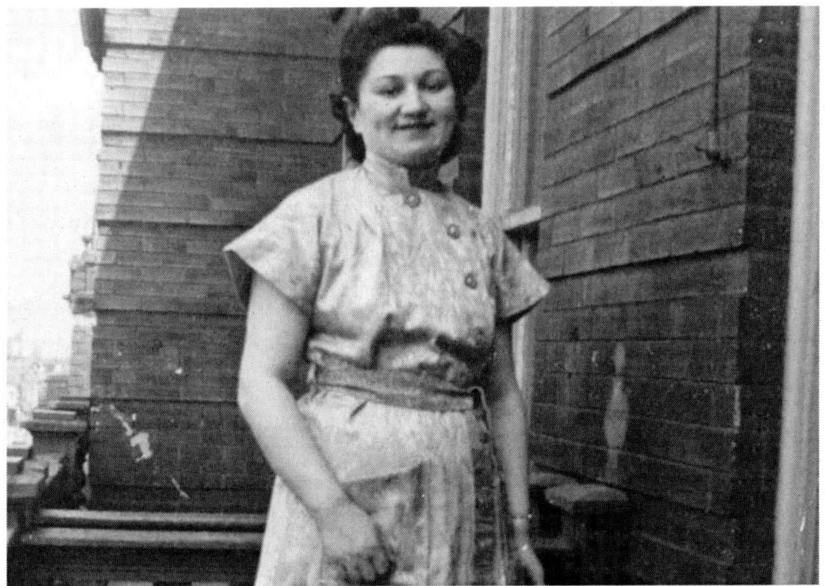

Rachel Mines' mother on a porch in Montreal as Jennie Lifschitz in 1946, before other Jews were allowed into Canada in the aftermath of the Holocaust.

Jennie and Jack Phillips did visit Stutthof in July of 1984 but there are no known photos of the visit. Subsequently, they were able to arrange for a copy of her official registration as a Jewish prisoner of the camp named Jennie Lifschitz in 1944.

"IN 2007, I VISITED Latvia where I met my mother's cousin, who had survived the Holocaust with my mother in some of the same camps," says Rachel Mines. "Meeting Bella inspired me to start studying Yiddish, and it was my Yiddish studies that led me to translation and Rosenfeld's stories and to Holocaust memorialization in general."

Simultaneously, Rachel Mines has been involved in Holocaust education and outreach in Skuodas, Lithuania, where her father was born and raised. Between 30 percent and 50 percent of the town's population were Jewish prior to the Nazi occupation of the town in June of 1941. Most of Skuodas's Jews were murdered during the Holocaust. The once-thriving Jewish community has one cemetery memorial and three Holocaust memorials dedicated to the murdered Jews of Shkud (the town's Yiddish name). Mines has created a website about the prewar Jewish community of Skuodas.

While an instructor at Langara College, Mines also created, coordinated and taught the "Writing Lives: The Holocaust Survivor Memoir Project," with the assistance of Gene Homel, Ph.D., teaching the history portions. This was a second-year, two-semester course that teamed Langara students with local Holocaust survivors to help them create written memoirs of their wartime experiences. The program has since been extended to First Nations survivors of residential schools.

One of the Writing Lives participants, Serge Haber, a Holocaust survivor, told the *Jewish Independent*, "It is very crucial to me, because, for the last thirty-five years, I have been thinking of writing my experience in this life. I never had a chance, the time or the person to listen to me. I hated the machines that record, so [a] personal touch was very important to me. And here it was, presented by Langara. I worked with two students, and I think we created a relationship, a personal understanding of what I went through.

"It is important to know that the Holocaust happened not only in camps but also in many cities around Europe, where thousands upon thousands of Jewish people, young and old alike, perished for nothing, only because they were Jewish. I profoundly remember three words that [I was told] while I was watching what was happening on the streets below, where thousands of people had been killed—my father said to me, 'Look, listen and remember.' And I remember."

Born and raised in Vancouver, Rachel Mines received her Ph.D. in English from King's College, University of London, in 2000 as a specialist in Old English language and poetry but has since realized "the world is not crying out for specialists in Old English poetic metre." She became a Yiddish Book Center Translation Fellow in 2016.

Her fellow Yiddish translator Helen Mintz has revived Abraham Karpinowitz's stories memorializing the pre-war Jewish community of Vilnius, Lithuania, for *Vilna, My Vilna* (Syracuse University Press

2016). Faith Jones has translated *The Acrobat: Selected Poems of Celia Dropkin* (New World Translation Series, Tebot Bach 2014).

Seymour Levitan received the 1988 Robert Payne Award of the Translation Center at Columbia University for his translation of *Paper Roses*, a posthumous poetry collection by Rachel Korn, one of Canada's most important Yiddish writers. He has also translated Yiddish author Rokhl Auerbach's autobiographical *A Soup Kitchen in the Warsaw Ghetto*. Levitan was born in Philadelphia in 1936 and educated at the University of Pennsylvania before coming to B.C. in 1965 to teach at UBC. His work is included in *The Penguin Book of Yiddish Verse, A Treasury of Yiddish Stories, The I. L. Peretz Reader, The Second First Art* and *Beautiful as the Moon, Radiant as the Stars.* He has edited and translated a volume of Rukhl Fishman's poems, *I Want To Fall Like This* and contributed articles to the revised *Encyclopedia Judaica.*

MOORE, Gudrun

IN 1965, HAVING LIVED in Canada for one year, Gudrun Moore read in *Time* magazine that her father was one of those accused of killing 33,771 Jews in the Babi Yar Gorge outside Kiev in present-day Ukraine. Babi Yar was one of the largest-scale, murder-by-bullets massacres during the Holocaust.

In two days in September 1941, following Nazi Germany's invasion of the Soviet Union in June, Nazi forces captured Kiev, capital of the-then Soviet Ukraine, now capital of Ukraine, whereupon SS and German police units and their local auxiliaries, along with members of Einsatzgruppe C, gunned down some 34,000 Jews in the Babi Yar ravine outside Kiev. Soon after Babi Yar, there were again minimal objections from European powers and the U.S. when 50,000 more Jews were murdered in Odessa.

The overlooked atrocities that had occurred during the murderous terrorism of Kristallnacht, followed by the Babi Yar and Odessa massacres, in effect proved to Hitler he could get away with murder.

The historical supposition that Hitler was emboldened by impunity was supported by Rabbi Meir Lau in Kiev when he participated in a 2006 commemoration of the Babi Yar massacre. "Maybe, say, this Babi Yar was also a test for Hitler," he said. "If, on September 29th and 30th in 1941, Babi Yar happened and the world did not react seriously, dramatically, abnormally, maybe this was a good test for him. So later in January of 1942, near Berlin in Wannsee, a convention can be held with a decision, a final solution to the Jewish problem. Maybe if the reaction [of the western powers] had been a serious one, a dramatic one, in September 1941, the Wannsee Conference would have come to a different result."

GUDRUN MOORE had known for years that her father had long been expecting some sort of arrest, but she had no idea why. She also knew about Babi Yar because she had read the poem about it by Russian poet Yevgeny Yevtushenko [a charismatic figure who gave a packed reading at the Vancouver Art Gallery in 1974 and died in Tulsa, Oklahoma, age 83].

The great Russian composer Shostakovich based part of his thirteenth symphony on Yevtushenko's poem and D.M. Thomas portrayed the horrors of Babi Yar in a climactic scene for his novel *The White Hotel* in 1981. Soviet writer Anatoly Kuznetsov had first published a censored version of his own novel *Babi Yar: A Document in the Form of a Novel* in 1966.

"I did not understand how my father, who I knew to be intelligent, honest and kind, could be involved in this," Moore has written, "When I learned about the Third Reich and its part in German history my soul became mired in outrage and confusion, then pain and shame. I could not understand."

Her mother confirmed her father's arrest with a letter. The trial process against August Haefner lasted more than one year. He was sentenced to nine years imprisonment. Thirty years later, in 1996, Gudrun Moore asked him to tell her the story of his life. It was the beginning of a long process to get members of her family to record their lives and experiences.

Gudrun dug up diaries, journals, letters and nagged her family endlessly for more stories.

"I wanted to find out why they all had so enthusiastically joined the Nazi Party and been part of everything that happened thereafter. I learned that men and women who became Nazis were ordinary people who wanted a future for themselves and their fatherland after all the misery of the Depression. I also learned that men who joined the SS were often idealistic young men or just regular men who needed a job. Today, I thank my family for their honesty."

Gudrun Moore's subsequent book about two German families and personal responsibility recounts "how three generations were sucked up in the maelstrom of history: first they lived through WWI, the war to end all wars with sixteen million lives lost, then they slid into a terrible world-wide depression for which, in Germany, Hitler promised a way out with hope and honour, which sadly resulted in WWII, a scourge that cost another sixty million lives."

After WW I, the intellectual Ernst family and the "burger" Haefner family both struggled through extreme poverty and desolation before falling prey to the rhetoric of Adolf Hitler promising work for all. All members of these two families became involved in the dream of National Socialism and the actual reality of 1939-1945.

Moore called her book *A Duty of Remembrance* (Trafford 2010) because she believed liberal democratic societies, such as Canada today, are not dissimilar to societies of the 1920s and 1930s, because "the liberal democratic parties, the press, the universities, the unions, the arts and churches are reluctant to come together to assert their moderating positions in a corporate state." This reluctance, she believes, enables the disenfranchised, educated or not, and the poor and the unemployed, to turn towards charismatic demagogues or fascist-like movements.

Trumpism and Nazism can be seeded by liberal complacency.

"I wanted to show that war brings nothing but destruction, suffering and death. There is no glory. War is a waste of material and human resources, and it marks everything that is touched by it forever. We still have wars. We still have the disenfranchised, the unemployed and the poor, the very groups Hitler roped in so easily. Have we not learned the lessons of history? Could it not all happen again?"

Born at the outset of World War II, Gudrun Moore was evacuated from Berlin during the Allied bombing. As a child, she was later forced to flee from a house at Lac Constance by French troops in 1945. Her mother, pushing a pram with her sister in it, with Gudrun at her side, spent months on the road. They eventually gained sanctuary at Gudrun's grandparents in southern Germany.

An education in the Helene Lange Boarding School in Markgroeningen opened Gudrun's mind to music and literature, as well as "the power of feminism and the possibility of civil disobedience, a new concept after the mental stultification of the Third Reich."

Gudrun studied literature and then medicine in Heidelberg and Munich.

Halfway through her medical training program, Gudrun met and married Englishman Jim Moore. They immigrated to Canada in 1964; their son Jamie was born in 1965; then both husband and wife taught school at a small Métis colony and later on for twenty years in the village of Hines Creek in northern Alberta. This led them to a life of farming in the Peace River country on their 4,000-acre property, mainly raising Maine Anjou cattle.

Gudrun Moore very happily became a Canadian citizen in 1970. After selling their farm in 1990, they adopted two children. A year of backpacking through Asia and Europe with their pair of pre-teens, and two dogs, resulted in her first memoir, *Borobudur by Chance* (Outskirts 2009), describing their shared adventures as vagabonds.

They retired from teaching jobs in 1996 to live in Malta, then France. The Moore family eventually came to the south Okanagan Valley where they built a house on five acres at Oliver, and started a Bed & Breakfast.

MOSZKIEWIEZ, Helene

AT 19, HELENE MOSZKIEWIEZ was a superb liar and an excellent tease. For six harrowing years she survived by her wits, infiltrating the Brussels Gestapo headquarters where she posed as a secretary (she could not write a letter in German), collecting information for the Belgian Resistance.

While residing in West Vancouver under a different name, having married her second husband and moved to Canada after the war, Moszkiewiez co-wrote her memoirs, *Inside the Gestapo: A Jewish Woman's Secret War* (Macmillan, 1985), with former *Province* editor turned Book Page editor Geoffrey Molyneux, uncredited.

Whereas the 2006 feature film *Zwartboek* [aka *Black Book*] directed by Paul Verhoeven can only be loosely described as a Dutch variant of her story, the earlier TV movie in 1991, *A Woman at War*, starring Martha Plimpton, is intended to directly portray the real characters in Belgium.

THE STORY OF HOW Helene Moszkiewiez maintained three identities (Jewish, Belgian and German) while working with Franz Boehler, a brave mastermind, reads like a thriller. She was married to her first husband (both named Albert) for just one week before he was detained and later murdered at Auschwitz. Her parents were sent to the concentration camps in 1943. Helen used her multilingual charms for revenge.

The Germans took control of Belgium when she was nineteen. Two years earlier, she had met a handsome young Belgian soldier named Francois in a Brussels library. When she met Francois again, he was operating as Franz while wearing a German uniform. After two successful, life-saving missions, Franz asked her to help him daringly infiltrate the Gestapo with falsified identity papers, posing as Olga Richer. He suggested she could gradually get to know two Gestapos chiefs, Mueller and Schwenke, who met regularly at the Cafe

Louise. Over weeks or months, Helene/Olga was expected to somehow inveigle a job for Franz, her supposed fiancé, inside Gestapo headquarters. She accomplished this on her first visit to Cafe Louise.

"They were so stupid," she told Geoffrey Molyneux in 1985. "They thought only in caricatures. You know, the Jewish man with a long black beard and a large hooked nose. Many of the Gestapo were the dregs. They were just there because they were cruel. The Abwehr intelligence men, now they were bright and you had to be careful when they were around."

Next, after Franz had secured a high-level intelligence position within the nondescript Gestapo headquarters at 453 Louise Avenue, she obtained her own security clearance to work for him, posing as his secretary, after first necessarily rejecting an offer to work for the top-ranked Mueller. All the arrogant and contemptible Gestapo chiefs hoped and expected to seduce her but she maintained the façade of her betrothal to Franz. For most of the war she lived under an assumed name at 46 Leon de Lantsheere Street.

Moszkiewiez's story recalls screams of SS victims, stealing information to rescue Jews scheduled for transport, helping a truckload of POWs escape by driving them to the Swiss border and killing a senior Gestapo officer in cold blood in a public park. She declined an invitation to work for British intelligence after the war and received a Certificate of Service, signed by Field Marshall Montgomery, in 1946, made out to Mademoiselle Helene Moszkiewiez.

Perhaps not surprisingly, since she excelled at being secretive, there is precious little information to be found about her on the internet where her name has been misspelled (as Moszkiewicz) by Amazon. Born on December 20, 1920, she died on June 18, 1998.

NEDERLANDSE OSCAR® INZENDING
CARICE
VAN HOUTEN
SEBASTIAN
KOCH
THOM
HOFFMAN
HALINA
REIJN
venezia 63
competition
OFFICIËLE SELECTIE
FILMFESTIVAL VENETIË 2006
'Een prachtrol van CARICE VAN HOUTEN...
als liefhebbers van VLIJMSCHERP GEREGISSEERDE FILMS
zijn we erg gelukkig dat Verhoeven er weer is'
Veronica Magazine
TORONTO
INTERNATIONAL
FILM FESTIVAL
OFFICIAL SELECTION
2006
van de regisseur van BASIC INSTINCT en SOLDAAT VAN ORANJE
PAUL VERHOEVEN
ZWARTBOEK
sms zwartboek naar 4443 en ontvang gratis mobiele downloads (eenmalig € 0,70)
WWW.ZWARTBOEKDEFILM.NL

"We heard about the camps from the BBC but so many Jews seemed to think it couldn't happen to them. You know, it could happen again. Jews have to be ready to fight."
— Helene Moszkiewiez

IN THE YEAR THAT her memoir was published, Moszkiewiez incurred the wrath of the Jewish community by expressing her feelings in a *Vancouver Sun* article, by Joanne Blaine, entitled How one Jew fought the Nazis (November 1, 1985). According to Blaine, Moszkiewiez commented upon "how meekly most of her fellow Jews went along with the German invaders . . . allowing themselves to be taken away to concentration camps without a fight . . . like sheep waiting to be slaughtered."

Bronia Sonnenschein issued a firm and important rebuttal in the *Jewish Western Bulletin*:

"Mrs. Moszkiewiez has tarnished the memory of every man, woman and child who was killed during the Holocaust and cannot defend himself against her accusations of being meek or acting like sheep. She has opened up the wounds of those who survived the Holocaust —by the grace of G-d—and feel the anguish of being criticized by someone who had the opportunity through a chance encounter with a young Belgian soldier to be actively involved in working for the Underground.

Helene Moszkiewiez, 1985

"As Mrs. Moszkiewiez says, she herself was a 'naïve' girl when she entered the Resistance. Once there, she would not have been able to leave, comparing the Resistance to a 'Mafia'. But even her heroic work does not give her the right to call those who were killed and tortured beyond belief meek or to compare them with sheep. Not all of us had guns or knives handy to attack the beast that tortured us.

"We were herded at gunpoint to the ghettos, the cattle-cars, the concentration camps. Would Mrs. Moszkiewiez regard Elie Wiesel as meek or a sheep? Does Simon Wiesenthal fit into this category? Would thousands upon thousands of courageous people deserve to be called meek for having worn the Star of David when all they had to fight back with were only their two hands? How does Moszkiewiez regard hostages? Are they also meek and behaving like sheep instead of fighting back against their captors with their bare hands?

"I am a survivor. I had to endure Nazi atrocities from March 1938, when Hitler marched into Vienna, 'til the day of our liberation on May 8, 1945 in Theresienstadt. I cannot take credit for having saved lives—does that make me a meek person, acting like a sheep? Or does it make me a victim who was robbed of the dignity to defend herself by having been stripped of every possible defence action?

"We can't all be heroes. Mrs. Moszkiewiez must be aware of this as even her own parents perished at the hands of the Nazis.

"To be courageous also means to have compassion for the less courageous ones, the 'meek' ones of this world. The world does not consist of heroes only."

NICHOLLS, William

"MANY JEWISH WRITERS have said, quite simply, that the Nazis chose the Jews as the target of their hate," William Nicholls has written, "because two thousand years of Christian teaching had accustomed the world to do so.

"Few Christian historians and theologians have been sufficiently open to the painful truth to accept this explanation without considerable qualification. Nevertheless, it is correct."

Christian scholar William Nicholls was one of the early founders of Vancouver's Annual Holocaust Symposium in 1976 as well as one of its first featured speakers. As a defender of Israel, he worked to free Jonathan Pollard, the U.S. intelligence analyst who was convicted in 1987 for providing top-secret, classified information to Israel. [Sentenced to life imprisonment, Pollard was finally released and welcomed as a hero in Israel in 2020].

Nicholls persistently fought against Holocaust denial as a minister in the Anglican Church and founder of the Department of Religious Studies at the University of British Columbia in 1964. "From the Holocaust experience there is a message of hope," he said, in 1984, "that it is possible to triumph only when we dare confront the worst." At the time, Nicholls was speaking at UBC in support of a new book by Irving Abella, author of *None is Too Many*, who observed, "Although most Canadians believe that Canada is a country with a long history of accepting refugees and contains little European bigotry, Canada's attitude towards the Jews during the Holocaust punctures a hole in that myth."

Later, Nicholls most significantly wrote *Christian Anti-Semitism: A History of Hate* (London: Jason Aronson Inc 1993), a 499-page, scholarly book dedicated "To the survivors of the Holocaust, and in particular to those who have undertaken the task of bearing witness to a new generation."

In the *Jerusalem Post* in 2011, David Turner wrote, "Dr. Nicholls' book is unrelentingly honest and powerful, a carefully constructed and well-written indictment of a religion that sees itself as embodying the high ideals of 'Love, Charity and Forgiveness.' Whatever else these ideals refer to, as Dr. Nicholls describes in this volume, clearly they do not apply to the Jews."

According to Turner, Nicholls describes Augustine's rationale providing for Jewish survival in Christendom as punishment for Jews' crimes: from the fifth through the 16th centuries Jews were the property of the church or princes and with few exceptions lived in poverty and despair. Their purpose in Christian society was to provide a warning against Judaizing or unbelief. But Nicholls reserves his harshest criticism for Martin Luther, a father of his own reformed church.

"In the early years of his conflict with the Church," Nicholls writes, "Luther assumed that, freed of the whip of Church anti-Judaism and the thousand-year-long persecution it inspired, the Jews would abandon Judaism and enthusiastically accept conversion to his reformist Christianity.

When the Jews failed to fulfill his expectations Luther's venom towards them was perhaps unmatched until four hundred years later when Hitler sought to fulfill Luther's instructions to the princes before his death. Nicholls writes, "At his trial in Nuremberg after the Second World War, Julius Streicher, the notorious Nazi propagandist, editor of the scurrilous anti-Semitic weekly, *Der Sturmer*, argued that if he should be standing there arraigned on such charges, so should Martin Luther."

William Nicholls came to UBC in 1961, retired in 1984 and died on November 10, 2014.

OBERLANDER, H. Peter

"In the summer of 1940, more than 3,000 refugees—including some 2,300 German and Austrian Jewish refugee males, many between the ages of sixteen and twenty years— were transported to Canada and interned in guarded camps in Ontario, Quebec and New Brunswick."

—Adara Goldberg, *Holocaust Survivors in Canada*

WHEN HITLER INVADED Austria in March of 1938, H. Peter Oberlander, at age fifteen, was away on a school ski trip. He and other Jewish boys were soon segregated and locked up for two days. They returned to Vienna in a separate rail car.

His father Dr. Fritz Oberlander (1889–1953) was soon arrested, taken to Gestapo headquarters, interrogated and severely beaten even though he had been wounded twice during World War I and decorated for his services in the Austrian Imperial Army, widely acknowledged as a human rights lawyer, accepted as a Master of Vienna's Masonic Lodge and a recipient of Austria's highest civilian honour, the Knight's Cross, in 1935, for his work on behalf of army widows and orphans.

Fritz Oberlander was not seen by his family for four months. His law office was ransacked; his Doctorate of Law was revoked; his Knight's Cross was abrogated; former colleagues and friends grilled him; his teeth were knocked out; and he was sent to Mauthausen to work as a labourer to build the camp. Only the intervention of Vienna's Deputy Minister of Justice, Peter Sippl, gained a reprieve. Sippl was then removed from his position.

Upon his release, Oberlander was forced to forfeit all his assets to the Nazis and given 48 hours to leave Austria. This is why his son H. Peter Oberlander arrived in London with his family in September of 1938, only to be later arrested himself as an enemy alien.

Oberlander's younger brother George was allowed to accompany his parents, Fritz and Margaret, when they immigrated to New York in 1940, but Peter was deported to Canada and held in various internment camps as a presumed "dangerous enemy alien."

Released in early 1942, Oberlander received a Bachelor of Architecture degree from McGill University in 1945. After he became the first Canadian to obtain a Master of Urban Planning degree, he became the first Canadian to gain a Ph.D in Urban and Regional Planning from Harvard.

Oberlander then founded the School of Community and Regional Planning at the University of B.C. in 1952 and the Centre for Human Settlements in 1975. He worked around the world spreading his integral message: "The city is humanity's greatest achievement."

Oberlander was also integral to convening the first UN Conference on Human Settlements in Vancouver in 1976 and the third session in 2006.

His daughter Judy Oberlander later founded the SFU City Program on Urban Issues. Peter Oberlander and his wife Cornelia Oberlander, a landscape architect, both became Order of Canada recipients.

In 2009, Peter Oberlander was posthumously accorded the United Nations Human Settlements Programme's 2009 Scroll of Honour Award, the most significant human settlements award in the world, "for a lifetime of promoting the urban agenda around the world." Born in November 29, 1922, he died on December 27, 2008 at age eighty-six.

Ken Cameron's book, *Showing the Way: Peter Oberlander and the Imperative of Global Citizenship* (Tellwell 2018) pays tribute to Oberlander's influence as a planner and author, but it was left to his daughter, Wendy, to discern and retrieve the impact of the Holocaust on her father's life.

In a *Zachor* article in 2013, Wendy Oberlander described her own investigations into her father's reticence to discuss wartime experiences and their personal repercussions. She describes her visit to the remains of Camp B in Ripples, New Brunswick, where her father was held for the winter of 1940–1941.

"For a myriad of reasons," she writes, "my father Peter Oberlander did not talk about his wartime experiences when I was young. Stray references to 'camp' (always spoken without an article) alluded to some kind of deprivation here in Canada; much later, in 1991, he briefly spoke about one night spent on Ile Saint-Helene in 1941."

Her investigations and questions led her to make a 1996 video, *Nothing to be written here*. The title arose from Prisoner of War stationery internees were forced to use.

After her father died, Oberlander found the draft of a letter he wrote to his parents the night he was released from Camp 'I' in November of 1941, free at last in Montreal: "So strange, so queer, I can hardly put it in words. My vocabulary fails me. All seems like a dream, so unnatural, nearly impossible. Often I had to pinch myself, to know whether it was reality or just one of those mad nightmares.... I at first had a deep breath of freedom and then went to bed. Imagine, in a bed for myself with white linens, and I could sleep as long as I liked, and I could turn the light off when I liked."

PRINGLE, Heather

THE MASTER PLAN: *Himmler's Scholars and the Holocaust* (Viking 2006) by journalist Heather Pringle unravels the little-known story of the ridiculous but lethal Nazi think-tank, Ahnenerbe, that used bogus science to corroborate racism and justify the murder of six million Jews, intellectuals, gypsies (Roma) and homosexuals.

As depicted in the *Raiders of the Lost Ark* movie, Adolf Hitler's SS (Security Squad) was not only infamous for running the concentration camps and gas chambers, and for serving as the Fuhrer's bodyguards, the world's most notorious terror force also played a key role in unearthing antiquities to ostensibly prove links to ancestral greatness for their unfounded belief in a so-called Aryan race.

In 1935, Hitler sanctioned an obscure but powerful research arm of the SS, the Ahnenerbe—meaning "something inherited from the forefathers"—to uncover ancestral treasures, to reconnect with past glories and to present the Third Reich as a model for fairness and middle-class decency. This "Nazi think-tank" recruited scholars to invent crackpot theories and to undertake archaeological digs around the world in order to authenticate Hitler's view of Aryans as a master race (tall, blonde, blue-eyed men and women).

The dreamer and mover behind the Ahnenerbe was SS director Heinrich Himmler, a thin, pale man who never exercised. His head appeared to be too big for his body but he was nonetheless obsessed with Aryan perfection. It was Himmler who decided his SS men ought to look elegant in newly designed black uniforms from Hugo Boss, complemented nicely by a silver death's-head on their hats. This look, according to Himmler, would engender fear in men and "success with the girls." An avid reader and self-designated intellect, Himmler maintained a list of favourite books to recommend to others.

Himmler originally wanted Ahnenerbe-sponsored research to stimulate his SS men to learn more about Germanic folklore, religion and farming techniques, encouraging them to promote the values of the Aryan race. In the 1930s, Ahnenerbe resurrected the debunked

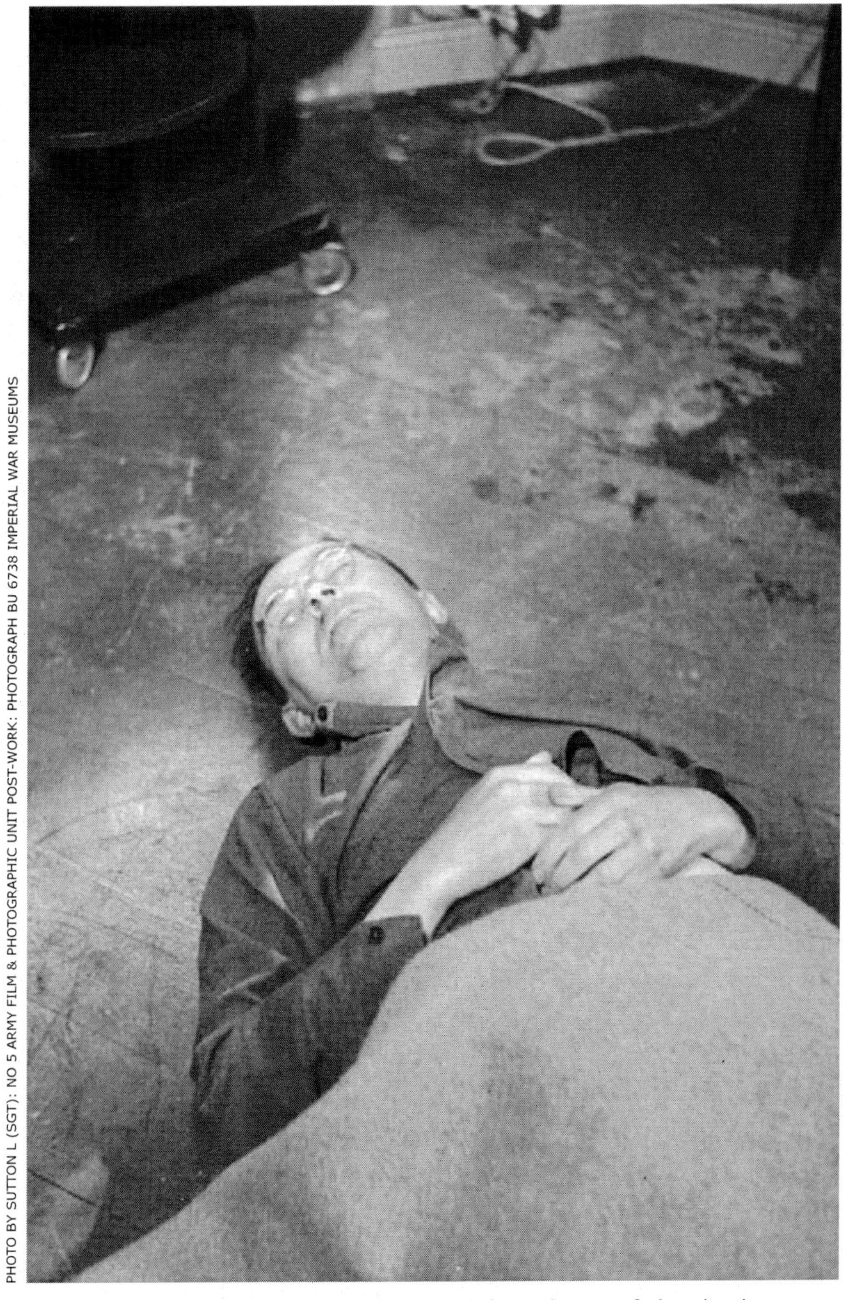

PHOTO BY SUTTON L (SGT): NO 5 ARMY FILM & PHOTOGRAPHIC UNIT POST-WORK: PHOTOGRAPH BU 6738 IMPERIAL WAR MUSEUMS

The body of Heinrich Himmler (1900-1945), architect of the death camps, lying on the floor of British 2nd Army HQ after his suicide on May 23, 1945.

notion that measuring cranial features could indicate intelligence and superiority. Nazi scholars hoped to discover racial data that might be useful in justifying the removal of all "mixed-races" from the Reich.

In order to channel ancient knowledge, one of Himmler's scholars, Karl-Maria Wiligut, would go into trances. Wiligut, a violent alcoholic and ex-mental patient, changed his name to Wisethor. Equally bogus, the prehistorian Herman Wirth claimed to have unearthed an ancient holy script that would help Germany resurrect its former greatness. Other notables were the classical scholar Franz Altheim and his lover, the rock art researcher Erika Trautmann, who had turned down a proposal of marriage from Hermann Goring.

To explain the origins of the universe, Himmler and Hitler were particularly excited about the Ahnenerbe-sponsored "World Ice Theory." Its chief proponent, Hans Horbiger, prided himself on never performing calculations and thought mathematics was "deceptive."

The Ahnenerbe's researchers plundered foreign museums, art galleries, churches and private homes carting off valuable relics and masterworks of art. But with the onset of World War II, the activities of the Ahnenerbe became far more sinister. The Ahnenerbe began using prisoners as guinea pigs to measure the effects of mustard gas and typhus. When some SS members complained about the stress of shooting large numbers of women, children and babies in the Crimea, as they did elsewhere, Himmler's henchmen in the Ahnenerbe ranks introduced mobile gassing wagons that could kill 80 people at once. With three mobile wagons in the Crimea, the SS was able to kill nearly 40,000 people, mainly Jews.

Human endurance at extremely high altitudes was tested using concentration camp prisoners in a vacuum chamber, resulting in extreme suffering and many deaths. Painful sterilization experiments were also conducted on humans. Himmler's "scientists" were keen to know how long parachuting aviators could survive in freezing waters and still be revived. Male prisoners were placed in ice-cold tanks for hours and then laid on beds where naked female prisoners were instructed to warm them up and engage in sex.

Originally reliant on grants from a scientific and agricultural agency, Ahnenerbe also received financial help from corporate donors that included BMW. One of the organization's key sources of loot was Adolf Hitler's chauffeur. In 1936, when Nazi party member Anton Loibl wasn't driving the Fuhrer to and from work, he was moonlighting as an inventor. One of his inventions was the shiny piece of glass now commonly mounted on bicycles to make them more visible at night. When Himmler learned of Loibl's "bicycle reflector" innovation, he inked a deal to produce the new product. As head of the German police, Himmler was able to ensure the passing of a new traffic law that required all new German bicycles to have a reflector.

In 1945, before Hitler and Eva Braun committed suicide in their bunker in Berlin, Himmler, a sycophant whom Hitler never liked, fled using the stolen police identification of a Sergeant Heinrich Hitzinger. After only a few weeks on the run, Himmler swallowed a lethal cyanide capsule during a medical examination and strip search at the headquarters of the Second British Army at Luneburg in Lower Saxony.

Some of the Ahnenerbe scholars were arrested, tried, disgraced, executed or killed themselves, but others enjoyed highly-respected careers. In the last chapter, Heather Pringle tracks down ninety-year-old Ahnenerbe member Bruno Berger in a quiet German town. Berger, a so-called expert in racial studies, only displayed emotion when discussing the war crime trial he had endured, muttering about "how the law is biased." During several hours of conversation, he was unrepentant, believing that Jews should be regarded as a mongrel race.

As a science journalist based in B.C., Heather Pringle has been a long-time correspondent and editor for *Equinox* magazine and has contributed to publications such as *Omni, National Geographic, New Scientist*, *Discover*, *Science*, *Geo* and *Saturday Night*. Her study of the Ahnenerbe movement is a restrained work of reportage, without proselytizing from its author, but Pringle takes care, on page 316, to cite a 1971 survey that revealed 50 percent of the German population believed "National Socialism [Nazism] was fundamentally a good idea which was merely badly carried out."

PROPP, Dan

JEWS HAVE BEEN in Bolivia since the 16th century. A wave of Jewish immigration to Bolivia from 1938 to 1940 was largely facilitated by the German-born Jewish businessman Maurice Hochschild. The "Bolivian Schindler" was an avid mountain climber who first came to Bolivia in 1921. As one of Bolivia's three foremost tin barons in the early part of the 20th century, he convinced President Germán Busch Becerra to provide visas for an estimated 10,000 Jews—about five times more than Schindler saved as a member of the Nazi party. Like Schindler, Hochschild used business as a rationale for saving Jews. He successfully argued that Jewish immigrants could undertake farm work in the coca-growing region of Yungas, east of La Paz.

The Bolivian Schindler, Maurice Hochschild

Consequently, Dan Propp of Steveston, B.C. was born in Sucre, Bolivia, on October 16, 1944. His parents, Arthur and Elsa Propp, had fled the Nazis to South America. His mother had first taken a ship to Brazil. Imprisoned by the Nazis after Kristallnacht, his father, who had been born in Konigsberg (later Kaliningrad) in 1890, managed to escape from Berlin by air with the assistance of a woman from the British underground. From England, he sailed in 1940 from Liverpool to Hamilton, the capital of Bermuda, en route to Chile. The Propps eventually settled as a couple in Bolivia because it was one of the few countries willing to accept Jewish immigrants.

The Propps came to B.C. in 1950. After a few months in Vancouver, they settled in Gibsons Landing on the Sunshine Coast where Arthur Propp, in his sixties, started the Sucre Lumber Co. Dan Propp of Steveston studied photography in Los Angeles during the 1960s, worked for the *Richmond Review* and the *Surrey Leader*, then taught in the Surrey school system for twenty-three years. After his father died in 1965, Dan Propp wrote to Elie Wiesel about his parents' experiences and Wiesel provided numerous notes of encouragement to Propp until April of 2013.

Propp has produced four self-published books and arranged for the publication of his father's memoirs, written in German, as *Von Koenigsberg nach Kanada* (2017), translated into English as *Where the Straight Path Leads* (2017), both available via Amazon. Dedicated to the children of the Holocaust, Dan Propp's own collection called *3 Stories* opens with a story about a child of the Holocaust who searches for a sense of belonging in Los Angeles and Vancouver. Another story, "A Nobody From Powell River," describes a son's upbringing in an isolated Jewish family and his attempts to untangle his parents' post-Holocaust trauma.

Dan Propp offered these words of remembrance at the outset of his poem called "Kiddush in Bolivia":

I remember Kiddush in Bolivia
A handful of children we were
The rabbi's, the lawyer's, the beggar's
The grocery store owner's, and me

Gestapo, German, Yiddish
Eyes that reflected the tide
Schiller, Goethe, Talmud
A difficult mixture to hide

ROGOW, Sally

AS A COMPILATION of true stories of rescue during World War II, Sally Rogow's *They Must Not Be Forgotten: Heroic Catholic Priests and Nuns Who Saved People From The Holocaust* (Holy Fire Publishing 2005), has been recognized and honoured by both Yad Vashem and the Catholic church. Having developed and directed a graduate program for B.C. teachers working with students who are blind, visually impaired and/or have multiple disabilities, Rogow was also motivated by the courage of those children to create an inspirational collection of twelve stories about teenagers in Europe who resisted the Nazis during World War II, *Faces of Courage: Young Heroes of World War II* (Granville Island Publishing 2003).

Among the heroes and heroines profiled by Rogow are Jacques, a blind French teen who organized a student resistance group; Yojo, a Gypsy who guided downed British pilots over the Pyrenees Mountains; Kirsten, a Danish girl who helped Jewish children defy the Nazis; and the 'Eidelweiss Pirates', a group of German teenagers who opposed the Hitler Youth.

Three stories are based on actual teenagers, most notably Jacques Lusseyran, the blind resistance leader who later wrote a book called *And There Was Light*. Born in Paris in 1924, he was physically blinded by a collision at school at age eight.

At age sixteen, during the German occupation, Lusseyran headed a resistance movement of 600 French youth. Betrayal led to his arrest and imprisonment at Buchenwald. He survived and wrote several books in which his own blindness is interpreted as a spiritual advantage. "Lusseyran," wrote Oliver Sacks, "sees the 'task' of blindness as reminding us of our other, deeper modes of perception and their mutuality."

In *Faces of Courage*, Rogow has reprinted the following quotation from Adolf Hitler about his Hitler Youth groups. "I want a brutal, domineering, fearless, cruel youth. Youth must be all that. It must bear pain. There must be nothing weak and gentle about it. The free, splendid beast of prey must once again flash from its eyes. That is how I will eradicate thousands of years of human domestication. That is how I will create the New Order."

In addition to Rogow's dramatizations based on historical events and circumstances, she has published an article, 'Hitler's Unwanted Children: The Story of Children with Disabilities in Nazi Germany' (1999). It appears in the *Journal of Holocaust Education*. According to the United States Holocaust Museum: "In the autumn of 1939, Adolf

Hitler secretly authorized a medically administered program of so-called mercy death, code-named Operation T4, in reference to the address of the program's Berlin headquarters at Tiergartenstrasse 4. Between 1940 and 1941 approximately 70,000 Austrian and German disabled people were killed under the T4 program, most via large-scale operations using poison gas. This methodology served as the precursor to the streamlined methods of the Holocaust. Although Hitler formally ordered a halt to the program in late August of 1941, the killings secretly continued until the war's end, resulting in the murder of an estimated 275,000 people with disabilities."

Born in Brooklyn, New York, on May 9, 1930 to May (nee Weinberger) and Gustave M. Levine, Vancouverite Sally Rogow came to Canada in 1966 to teach at Simon Fraser University.

Rogow was both a Canadian and U.S. citizen who obtained a B.A. from the University of Wisconsin, an M.A. in Anthropology from Columbia University, an M.A. in Special Education from Michigan State and a Ph.D in Education in 1971 from the University of British Columbia.

At UBC, having taught at the Michigan School for the Blind, she was hired to develop a school program for teachers of those with multiple handicaps or visual impairment, directing the program she created from 1971 until 1995.

After her retirement from UBC, Rogow became project director of "The Person Within," a program to prevent abuse and neglect of children and young people with disabilities.

Sally Rogow's uncle was the first Jewish man to be a Lieutenant Colonel in the Canadian Army. Her charitable works were recognized by Jewish Women International and the American Printing House for the Blind inducted her into its Hall of Fame for Leaders and Legends of the Blindness Field in 2011.

Her final years were lived at the Weinberg Residence, a Vancouver facility for Jewish seniors, until her death on December 21, 2012.

SALCUDEAN, Martha

BORN INTO A JEWISH FAMILY in Cluj-Napoca, Romania, on February 26, 1934, Martha Eva Salcudean (nee Abel) was the daughter of two physicians. Martha's mother Eta overcame anti-Semitism and gender discrimination to graduate from medical school in 1925. Her courtship with Martha's father Odon Abel began after she treated him for wounds from an attack by a rabid dog. They established a joint medical practice in his village.

As a Vancouverite, Salcudean recalled what happened to her family in 1944 when she was a ten-year-old in the village of Chiocis, Romania, in Northern Transylvania, now part of Hungary. Imprisoned in ghettos by the invading Nazis, she experienced cruelty and hatred that robbed her of her childhood. When her family was taken to the train station and lined up in front of a cattle car bound for Auschwitz, Martha's father made a split-second decision that enabled them to be transported instead to Bergen-Belsen.

Having been incarcerated in Bergen-Belsen as a child, Martha Salcudean became the first female head of an engineering department at a Canadian university.

Martha's life was spared due to the efforts of Rudolf Kasztner, the Hungarian Zionist, journalist and lawyer who undertook negotiations with the Nazis. As part of the "Blood for Goods" bartering that occurred to save a relatively few privileged Jews, the Salcudeans were allowed to leave Bergen-Belsen and reach Switzerland as promised. This reprieve would carry a heavy psychological price. The U.S. Holocaust Museum has provided a succinct, uncritical overview:

"Beginning in April 1944, Kasztner and Joel Brand entered into negotiations with Dieter Wisliceny and Adolf Eichmann of the SS in the hope of suspending deportations of Jews from Hungary. In late April 1944, Adolf Eichmann proposed "selling" 10,000 Jews in exchange for trucks delivered to the Nazis. Brand travelled to Turkey to present the proposal to the Allies and representatives of the *Yishuv* (the Jewish community in Palestine). After Brand failed to return from Istanbul, Kasztner took over negotiations with Eichmann and Kurt Becher, even as the mass deportation of Hungarian Jews began in May 1944.

"In June 1944, Kasztner convinced Eichmann to allow nearly 1,700 Hungarian Jews to escape Hungary and the deportations to Auschwitz. A small committee headed by Otto Komoly, chairman of the Relief and Rescue Committee, Kasztner, and other Hungarian Jewish leaders selected the passengers for the rescue transport.

"The list of nearly 1,700 Jews slated for release included wealthy Jews, Zionist leaders, prominent rabbis (including the Satmar Rebbe, Joel Teitelbaum), and perhaps most controversially, Kasztner's own friends and family members. Kasztner would later argue that he had insisted on the inclusion of his own family to convince others of the safety of the convoy. There were 338 Jews from Kasztner's home city of Cluj. Other passengers on the 'Kasztner train' represented a cross-section of Hungarian Jewry: journalists, teachers, artists, nurses, housewives with small children, peasant farmers, and small businessmen.

"On June 30, 1944, the 'Kasztner train' left Budapest, carrying 1,686 individuals in exchange for an unclear sum of money—some reports indicate perhaps $1,000 per person paid in currency, gold, jewels, and shares of stock collected by the Jewish committee. Despite a promise from Adolf Eichmann that the train would travel directly to Switzerland, the transport reached Bergen-Belsen on July 8, 1944. The passengers were held in the camp for several months in the

Ungarnlager (Hungarian camp).

"In late August 1944, 318 Jews from the Kasztner train were released from Bergen-Belsen and transported to Switzerland. On December 7, 1944, the remaining 1,368 Jews from the transport reached Switzerland. Kasztner travelled to Switzerland in late November 1944.

"After the war, Kasztner intervened on behalf of Kurt Becher, Dieter Wisliceny, and Herman Krumey with whom he had negotiated in Hungary. He declared to the International Military Tribunal in Nuremberg that Becher in particular was one of the few SS leaders who had the courage to resist the Nazi plan for annihilation of the Jews and that he had, in fact, attempted to rescue Jews. Thanks in part to Kasztner's statement, Becher was not prosecuted as a war criminal.

"Kasztner moved to Israel after the war and continued his active role in Labor Zionist politics, becoming a spokesman for the Ministry of Trade and Industry in 1952.

"Kasztner's controversial role in negotiating with the SS became prominent news in 1953 when Malkiel Gruenwald published a leaflet accusing Kasztner of having collaborated with the Nazis. Gruenwald was a Hungarian Jew who had lost dozens of relatives in the Holocaust. He charged that through the negotiations with Eichmann and Becher, Kasztner had participated in the destruction of Hungarian Jewry. He also charged that Kasztner had personally benefitted from his negotiations with the SS while failing to warn Hungarian Jews of the impending deportations, even though he was among the first to receive a copy of the Auschwitz Protocols—the Vrba-Wetzler report—from Slovakian Jewish leaders in late April 1944.

"Gruenwald sought to expose what he saw as Kasztner's crimes. A member of Ha-Mizrahi (the religious Zionist party), Gruenwald also hoped to denounce Mapai (the Labor

Martha Salcudean, circa 1941, after her family moved to Szamosujvar, Hungary (previously Gherla, Romania).

Zionist governing party) and force the government to appoint a commission that would investigate the events leading to the destruction of Hungarian Jewry.

"Kasztner subsequently sued Gruenwald for libel. Because of his position as a government official, Kasztner was represented at trial by Haim Cohen, Israel's attorney general. The trial of Gruenwald for libel would become known as the "Kasztner Trial." Gruenwald's defence attorney, Shmuel Tamir, succeeded in turning what was supposed to be a libel trial against Gruenwald into an indictment of Kasztner and the ruling Mapai Party.

"Four key charges against Kasztner were outlined in Gruenwald's pamphlet:

—Collaboration with the Nazis

—'Paving the way for the murder' of Hungarian Jewry

—Partnership with a Nazi war criminal [Kurt Becher] in acts of thievery

—Saving a war criminal from punishment after the war [Kurt Becher]

"In his judgment on June 22, 1955, Judge Halevi accepted most of Gruenwald's accusations against Kasztner. He ruled that by saving the Jews on the Kasztner train while failing to warn others that their resettlement was in fact deportation to the gas chambers, Kasztner had sacrificed the majority of Hungarian Jewry for a chosen few. It also had become clear during the trial that Kasztner had indeed submitted testimony on behalf of Becher after the war, a fact he had earlier denied. The verdict triggered the fall of the Israeli Cabinet after the government sought to appeal on Kasztner's behalf.

"The Supreme Court of Israel overturned most of the judgment in January 1958, stating that the lower court had "erred seriously" in its decision. Before the highest court returned this verdict, however, Kasztner was assassinated near his home in Tel Aviv on the night of March 4, 1957, by three

> veterans of the right-wing pre-state militia group Lehi, once a splinter group of the Irgun. He died of his injuries twelve days later."

Returning home at war's end, Martha found her life under the new Communist regime was another descent into cruelties and fear. During her studies, Martha met and married George Salcudean whose family members, though not Jewish, suffered torture under Communism. Their only child, Tim, was born in 1957.

The Salcudean family, including Martha's mother, immigrated to Canada in 1976. As an internationally-recognized researcher in fluid mechanics and heat transfer, she was able to teach at the University of Ottawa before moving to B.C nine years later where she became head of mechanical engineering at UBC.

Salcudean was later Associate Vice-President of Research, working extensively with the forest industry. She then became chair of Weyerhauser Industrial Research. In 1991, the Science Council of British Columbia awarded her the Science and Engineering Gold Medal. Also a fellow of the Royal Society of Canada and the Canadian Academy of Engineering, Martha Salcudean received the Order of British Columbia in 1998 and became an Officer of the Order of Canada in 2004. After she became one of the most effective voices for Holocaust education in British Columbia, speaking to hundreds of school children, she died on July 17, 2019, just three months after her memoir was published.

With an introduction by Zoltan Tibori-Szabo, Salcudean's 184-page memoir, *In Search of Light* (Second Story 2019), contains illustrations, portraits and maps. Canadian publisher Anna Porter previously wrote *Kasztner's Train: The True Story of Rezso Kasztner, Unknown Hero of the Holocaust*, issued by the B.C.-based imprint Douglas & McIntyre in 2007. It largely exonerates Kasztner, contending that some poor Jews were accorded transit for nothing.

"If you're in hell," Porter writes, "who do you negotiate with but the Devil?"

SCHALLIE, Charlotte

BY OCTOBER OF 1944, when the Nazis were making raids on Jewish homes in Hungary, the Danube was strewn with Jewish corpses.

As Vice-Consul at the Swiss embassy, Carl Lutz negotiated with the Nazis, including Adolf Eichmann, to enable him to issue "protective letters" for Jews to emigrate. About 3,000 Jews received temporary sanctuary in a former glass factory, dubbed the Glass House, living in extremely crowded and unsanitary conditions, hoping to be processed. One of the Jews who was saved by the interventions of Carl Lutz was Andras Spiegel who changed his name to Andrew Simon and became the producer for the long-running CBC Radio program *Cross Country Check-up*. "I thank him for my own life and my parents' lives," said Simon in 2018.

Several other diplomats in Hungary were taking similar measures to safeguard Jews. These included the Spanish Charge d'Affaires, Angel Sanz Briz, who saved the lives of Sephardic Jews and became the subject of a dramatic, 2011 film by Luis Oliveros, *Angel of Budapest*.

Lutz has been credited with saving the lives of between 40,000 and 60,000 Jews overall but he remains far less known as a saviour than Swedish diplomat Raoul Wallenberg, German businessman Oskar Schindler and Chiune Sugihara, the Japanese vice-consul in Lithuania.

Charlotte Schallie's *Under Swiss Protection: Jewish Eyewitness Accounts from Wartime Budapest* (Columbia University Press 2017), co-authored with Agnes Hirschi, has recounted Carl Lutz's Holocaust rescue operations, as verified by Jewish eyewitnesses in Canada, Hungary, Israel, Switzerland, the U.K. and the United States.

As the head of the foreign interests division in the Swiss legation in Budapest, it is estimated that Lutz—with the help of his wife, Gertrud Lutz-Fankhauser, Moshe Krausz, the director of the Palestine Office in Budapest, fellow Swiss citizens Harald Feller, Ernst Vonrufs, Peter Zurcher, and the underground Zionist Youth Movement—issued more than 50,000 lifesaving letters of protection (Schutzbriefe)

MIKE MORASH PHOTO / UNIVERSITY OF VICTORIA

Charlotte Schallie (left), Holocaust survivor David Schaffer and graphic artist Miriam Libicki at Schaffer's home in Vancouver on Jan. 3, 2020. A documentary film about their collaboration for a graphic novel has been posted as *If We Had Followed the Rules, I Wouldn't Be Here.*

and placed persecuted Jews in 76 safe houses as annexes of the Swiss Legation during World War II, between March 1944 and February 1945.

Born in London near the outset of World War II, Charlotte Schallie's co-author for *Under Swiss Protection*, Agnes Hirschi was raised in Budapest and spent two months in a bomb shelter with the Lutz family. Her mother Magda married Carl Lutz in 1949 and so he became Agnes' father in Switzerland. Yad Vashem accorded Carl Lutz "Righteous Among The Nations" status in 1965.

Charlotte Schallie has also co-edited *After the Holocaust: Human Rights and Genocide Education in the Approaching Post-Witness Era* (University of Regina Press 2020). Along with "new" Holocaust survivor stories, now ostensibly among some of the last in living memory to be collected, this composite volume combines Jewish scholarship, activism and poetry with perspectives on Canadian anti-Semitism, the legacy of human rights abuses of Indigenous Peoples in Canada as well as the internment of Japanese Canadians in World War II.

As an Associate Professor and Department Chair in the department of Germanic and Slavic Studies at the University of Victoria, Charlotte Schallie is an expert in contemporary German, Austrian and Swiss culture and literature; as well as diasporic, transnational and postcolonial literature. Her research interests include post-1945 diasporic and transcultural writing/filmmaking, memory studies, Jewish identity in contemporary cultural discourse, as well as teaching and learning about the Holocaust.

At the outset of 2020, Schallie developed a new program to foster collaborations and intercultural exchanges entitled Narrative Art and Visual Storytelling in Holocaust and Human Rights Education. It expands upon a literary form that was first explored in B.C. by David Lester with his graphic novel, *The Listener*, in 2011. Specifically, Schallie has instigated collaborations for new, Holocaust-themed graphic novels.

"If you read a graphic novel," she told CBC's *All Points West*, "it is as if you're watching and reading a movie at the same time. Visual storytelling in graphic narratives is especially effective for life stories and memories of survivors who were children during the Holocaust, as images often tend to be so deeply imprinted in a child survivor's memory."

Under Schallie's direction, graphic novelists have been paired with four survivors: Emmie Arbel of Kiryat Tiv'on in Israel; Nicole and Rolf Kamp in Amsterdam, Holland; and David Schaffer of Vancouver. After his family was deported to Transnistria, Schaffer survived the Holocaust as a boy in Romania. Miriam Libicki, a graphic novelist based in Vancouver, is paired with him. Her own grandfather, also a survivor, died three years prior to the project and she regrets not having learned his Holocaust story.

"We have fewer and fewer survivors left," Miriam Libicki told *All Points West*, "and I think it's really important to have the stories first and to not only have them as documents, but to know what the survivors themselves think is important about their stories, what they care about, what are the lessons or the facts they want future generations to take from this story."

SCHOCHET, Simon

BORN IN POLAND of Jewish parents in 1926, Simon Schochet was a prisoner in Dachau, where all his family perished, before he was sent to Feldafing, in Bavaria, the first all-Jewish, DP [Displaced Persons] camp in the U.S.-controlled portion of post-war Germany.

For those who seek to appreciate the pain and resilience required to survive the Holocaust, the clarity and intelligence of Simon Schochet's writing makes his only book, *Feldafing* (November House 1983), a hidden gem. Here he recalls a young woman who arrived at Feldafing in 1945, when she was heavily pregnant:

> Despite her condition and ragged clothing, she was immediately noticed, for she had long brown, thickly-plaited hair and an unusually luminous and spirited face. She lived in a room with a few elderly women, and shortly after giving birth, when her body resumed its normal proportions, she took off and left Feldafing for Munich. Since then, she is often spoken about by the men who have seen her in Munich, mostly with the Americans, riding about in their cars and dressed in American clothes, high heels and heavily made-up. They call her *kurva* (whore) and then praise her beauty, and with a mixture of anger, jealousy and pity, condemn her for not having found a husband amongst us instead of running about with the American soldiers.
>
> Only today I heard the story of this young woman from one of the men who was in hiding with her in a little Ukrainian village during the war. A group of well-to-do Jews were

> hidden by a Ukrainian in an abandoned barn. Among them was this young beauty with her fiance. The war dragged on, and the money used to buy their safety drained away. At last, when there was little left, the Ukrainian farmer demanded a new sort of payment in exchange for his protection. It was the young woman. She was to be placed at his disposal, to save the others. She consented.
>
> They were liberated by the Russians and followed the troops westward in order to leave that swinish place. After a few days of the pilgrimage towards greener and freer pastures, the girl's fiance disappeared. Shortly thereafter, she left the group and was lost in the chaos despite a desperate search by the others who had shared in her grief and were alive because of her. Her fellow captive had tried to communicate with her when he had met her in Munich, but she had refused to recognize him. "And so," said the man who was telling the story, "don't call her a *kurva*. The world is a *kurva*."

Opened by the U.S. Army, near the town of Tutzing, in May of 1945, Feldafing was created as an emergency measure to accommodate Hungarian Jews from liberated cattle cars near the Tutzing railway station. Some of the Nazi personnel who had deliberately delayed the embarkation of the train with its doomed prisoners (from the Mittergars, Muldorf Wald Lager / Ampfing / and Muhldorf-Mettenheim concentration camps) were accorded lenient treatment.

In *Feldafing*, using the voice of an anonymous narrator, Schochet recalled his experiences serving as a teacher of English and History for his fellow concentration camp survivors, all of whom were attempting to adapt to post-war life.

"I received a comb today," he writes. "What a luxurious and civilized feeling it is, to be able to use one again."

A progressive educational mandate for Feldafing was encouraged by the Army's Civil Affairs commander, First Lieutenant Irving J. Smith, a Jewish soldier and peacetime attorney. Feldafing benefited from separate visits in 1945 by General Dwight D. Eisenhower in

Simon Schochet, upper left, with his fellow teachers at Feldafing in 1948.

September and David Ben-Gurion in October. In 1946, Feldafing boasted several newspapers, its own magazines, theatre troupes, an orchestra and its own camp court system for 4,000 Jews. By the time control of the facilities was shifted from the U.S. military to the German government in 1951, the population of Feldafing had dwindled to 1,500 Jews.

Schochet immigrated to the U.S. where he taught history, married, had two children and worked as a commodities broker. He remained obsessed with trying to unravel the truth about a massacre that occurred in April of 1940 in Katyn, Poland. Specifically, he wanted to uncover the extent to which Jews had been victimized in the mass murder by Soviet troops. Eventually, in his paper entitled 'An attempt to identify the Polish-Jewish officers who were prisoners at Katyn,' Schochet identified approximately 800 Polish Jewish officers who were murdered. He used a list of names compiled by the historian Adam Moszynski and another compiled by German investigators in April of 1943.

Cover art of *Feldafing* by J. E. Sherwood

The tragic story of the Katyn massacres is only now emerging. The government of Nazi Germany announced the discovery of mass graves in April of 1943 but Stalin's administration denied all responsibility. Until 1990, the USSR insisted the Nazis had killed the victims. This is known as the Katyn Lie.

The religion of the soldiers was not noted on either the Officers' Almanacs or the list compiled by the Germans, but Schochet painstakingly estimated there were at least 700, and perhaps as many as 800, Jewish officers in the three internment camps of Kozielsk, Starobielsk and Ostaszkov whose internees were killed. He was able to identify 262 names of Jewish officers from the Kozielsk internment camp alone, about five percent of the officer population. The lone reference to Jewish faith was the name of Major Baruch Steinberg, Chief Rabbi of the Polish Armed Forces, who was originally imprisoned at Starobielsk. He was among the first to be massacred, on April 9, 1940. But not all Polish military prisoners and intelligentsia were killed by the Soviets. The Polish historian Zibigniew Siemaszko calculated that between 20–25 percent of all Poles deported by the Soviets from Eastern Poland to the camps and settlements in Siberia were Polish Jews.

On October 14, 1992, Rudolf Pikhoya, chairman of Russia's Archives Commission and a personal envoy of Boris Yeltsin, delivered to the Polish President Lech Walesa, a rare parcel containing forty-two, previously secret documents about the Katyn massacres of April and May, 1940, when approximately 22,000 to 26,000 Polish officers and intelligentsia were killed by Soviet Security Services, specifically NKVD. This Soviet verification of responsibility for a hitherto denied mass extinction under Stalin would have come as no surprise to the sophisticated researcher Simon Schochet who contributed his research materials to the United States Holocaust Memorial Museum before he died in 2011.

SCHOCHET'S VERY READABLE yet little-known memoir was one of the final books published by Cherie Smith, who had started November House in 1969, as a thirty-six-year-old mother of two. Her publishing company was named November House after the month in which she was born.

As one of the five founding members of the Association of Book Publishers of B.C., Smith released twenty-one titles before closing up shop in 1983. In 1984, she founded (and became the namesake for) the Jewish Book Festival in Vancouver, and she later turned her hand to writing her own family memoir, *Mendel's Children* (University of Calgary Press, 1997), a history that charts the course of the Russian-Jewish immigration to the Canadian prairies over 100 years.

Cherie Smith's grandfather Solomon Steiman was sent to Viatka in the Urals, 450 miles north-east of Moscow, in 1914, as a political exile. His wife and family later joined him there. Born in Latvia in 1898, Cherie's father Iser Steiman was sent to Canada in 1912 when he was fourteen. His experiences as a teacher in northern Manitoba, starving and freezing, are recounted in *Mendel's Children.* As a physician he started King Edward Hospital in Kamsack, Saskatchewan, where he married Laura Shatsky. Their daughter, Cherie, was born November 13, 1933. She died of cancer on July 13, 1999.

Cherie Smith, founder and namesake for the annual Jewish Book Festival in Vancouver, was also the publisher for *Feldafing*.

SCHOEN, Walter

IN HER LITTLE-KNOWN Masters thesis for History at Malaspina College in 2002, *Three Times Betrayed: The Sudeten Germans of Tomslake, B.C.*, Margaret Melanie Drysdale writes:

> Few people equate the hamlet of Tupper (now Tomslake), a small community in the Peace River district of northeastern British Columbia, with international events that plunged the twentieth century headlong into a second devastating world war. Betrayed by the international community and abandoned by the Czechoslovakian government, a small group of German Social Democrats escaped pre-war Europe only to be confined to a northern wilderness.
>
> Despite their ignoble beginnings and limited assistance from the Canadian government, and being trapped by bureaucrats to endure miserable conditions, the new inhabitants of Tupper worked hard to build a viable community. While the emergence of Tomslake was the direct result of events that transpired on the world stage, the community survived due solely to the hard work and persistence of its residents.

The subject of the Sudeten settlement in B.C. is germane to Holocaust studies because it forces one to consider the volume of immigration of German-speaking immigrants to Canada during World War II (versus the volume of Jewish immigrants allowed entrance during the same period).

Walter Schoen was born on March 2, 1931, in the Sudeten area of what was then Czechoslovakia. Sudetenland was a German-speaking area that had been affirmed to be part of Czechoslovakia in the aftermath of World War I. Schoen's parents sympathized with the Social Democrats, a minority group that was opposed to the ambitions of Hitler's Nazi party to annex the territory to Germany, partly to salve the wounded pride of Germany after its devastating defeat in The

Great War. Eventually Britain's Prime Minister Neville Chamberlain infamously agreed to have Sudetenland ceded to Germany in 1938 as the price to pay for "Peace in our Time."

This turning-point-truce with Hitler was a compromise that signalled to him that the West would not have the courage to halt Nazi aggressions. It was called the Munich Agreement. It was made when Hitler hosted Chamberlain in his luxury Munich apartment that he shared with his mistress Eva Braun. The luxury apartment was paid for by a German newspaper publisher who provided vital support for the Third Reich. [During this time a daring, neophyte news photographer, Tim Gidal, took possibly the only unsanctioned photo of Hitler ever published without his permission during his rule. It shows the newspaper publisher with Hitler in an outdoor café in Munich, not far from Hitler's apartment. The photograph is now owned by Yosef Wosk of Vancouver. It has been reprinted in two books that Wosk has produced about Gidal, credited as being one of the world's first photo-journalists. This unique photograph was an act of defiance, taken surreptitiously, by a Jewish photographer who refused to be intimidated.]

Walter Schoen and his parents were among a group of 518 people from the affected Sudetenland region who feared incarceration or death due to their political beliefs. Even though they were mostly office or factory workers with no experience in agriculture, they chose to accept an offer of asylum in Canada if they were willing to become farmers. Therefore, in 1938, Walter Schoen accompanied his parents, via Denmark, as part of a contingent of 518 refugees that were brought to the remote settlement of Tupper in the Peace River district of northeastern B.C. These constituted more than half of the 1,024 Sudeten German refugees accepted by Canada.

This venture was supervised by the Canadian Colonization Association, a subsidiary of the Canadian Pacific Railway, as much to benefit Canada as it was to save the refugees on humanitarian grounds. Workers were needed to tame wilderness for the expansion of transportation and industries.

Walter Schoen completed Grade 8 in a rural school, then attended high school in Dawson Creek. Schoen obtained his MEd at UBC and taught in secondary schools from 1955 to 1988. He married and lived in Dawson Creek, B.C. In retirement, he became active in the Kiwanis Club, his local history society and he played tenor sax in the community band. His self-published memoir is *The Tupper Boys, a History of the Sudeten Settlement at Tomslake, B.C.* (Trafford 2004). We learn that about forty men among the Sudeten immigrants in the area enlisted to fight against the Nazis in the Canadian army. Also relevant is Bruce Ramsey's *A History of the German-Canadians in British Columbia* (Winnipeg: National Publishers Ltd. 1958).

During World War II, the Canadian High Commissioner in London, Vincent Massey, the scion of the wealthy Massey family, was decidedly anti-Jewish, influenced by the prominent and largely pro-German and anti-Semitic Cliveden set centred around Lord and Lady Astor. Meanwhile, the Canadian Committee for Jewish Refugees was formed in December of 1938, under Canadian Jewish Congress president Samuel Bronfman, and a second Jewish refugee committee was formed in March of 1939 under Montreal lawyer Saul Hayes. The racist views of the Anglophile aristocracy prevailed.

On June 7, 1939, Canada denied entry to 907 Jewish refugees aboard the MS *St. Louis* that was forced to return to four European ports, and thereafter 254 of its passengers lost their lives due to the Holocaust. Out of the 2,300 Jews transferred from British to Canadian internment camps in 1940, only 972 were permitted to become Canadian citizens.

By 2016, according to the Canadian Census, 3,322,405 Canadians (nearly 10 percent of the population) reported German origins, and 404,745 people in the country reported German as their mother tongue. In 2010, according to the *Canadian Encyclopedia*, German Canadian Congress president Tony Bergmeier "sparked controversy as he objected to the prominence to be given to the Holocaust exhibit in the Canadian Museum for Human Rights, slated to be opened in 2013. Other ethnic group representatives, such as the Ukrainian

Canadian Congress, voiced similar opinions. The GCC press release argued that the museum should "recognize that human suffering is equal to all people. No suffering by one group of people can be more important than the suffering of others."

Bernie Farber, then president of the Canadian Jewish Congress, stated he was surprised and saddened by the GCC objections. Wendy Lampert, writing for the *National Post* on December, 28, 2016, pointed out that "to suggest the Holocaust was just like any other genocide, undeserving of special recognition, is to ignore the reality of its impact on 20th-century society."

SHANDLER, Rhodea

RHODEA SHANDLER'S *A Long Labour: A Dutch Mother's Holocaust Memoir* (Ronsdale 2004) not only recounts a story its author felt unable to tell her family for most of her life, it also accommodates Dr. Lillian Kremer's fierce indictment of Dutch collaboration in the persecution of their Jewish neighbours.

Born Henriette Dwinger in Leeuwarden, Netherlands, on August 26, 1918, Rhodea Shandler became a nurse and married Ernst Bollegraaf before she became a fugitive in the Dutch countryside during the five-year German occupation of Holland. When the Nazis began rounding up Jews, Rhodea, her husband and their youngest daughter went into hiding with sympathetic Christian families, assisted by the underground Resistance movement. They travelled to rural Holland where anti-Nazi sentiment was strongest, and Nazi patrols less frequent. Over the ensuing war years, they moved frequently, as one hiding place after another proved untenable. Found and paid for by the underground, their main home was a former pigsty, whereas a wealthier Jewish couple who could afford to pay more was accommodated in the house with the host family. Their protector's attitude, kind at first, changed overnight to hostility when Rhodea discovered she was pregnant.

Rhodea nevertheless felt gratitude to the family. She was fully aware of the risks taken on their behalf. Their hosts would have been shot instantly for harbouring Jews. She also understood their mutual risks were greatly increased by the presence of a baby on the premises. In spite of severe privations, Shandler remained on friendly terms with her hosts and visited them after the war. Her baby was delivered in the unheated pigsty on a frigid December day, with unsterilized equipment, and with help from her husband and a fellow fugitive who had some nursing training. Once the child was born, the Resistance movement arranged for her to be placed with a Gentile family. Rhodea and her husband were dispatched to separate hiding places, not far from each other. When convoys of German soldiers searched the area, Rhodea hid in a shallow dug-out, like a grave, in the ground. The first member of the underground who helped them was captured and shot.

After the war, when Shandler returned home to Amersfoort, she discovered that her parents, brother, and many members of her extended family who had been transported to Poland, supposedly for relocation, had been killed in the concentration camps. She also found that the neighbours to whom she and her husband had entrusted their money and possessions for safe-keeping were unwilling to return them. Her story ends as the couple and their children start a new life in Canada.

Shandler immigrated with her family in 1951. In spite of the gruesome circumstances, Rhodea's tone is surprisingly benign and tolerant, not so much because of the mellowing effect of old age as the result of an enviably optimistic outlook that helped her during her ordeal. She speaks sadly but rarely in anger. Any incipient bitterness is either suppressed quickly or tempered with understanding. Rhodea manages to sympathize with the young German soldiers she saw in the last years of the war. She saw that they were little more than children, drafted unwillingly into the depleted army.

When she visited a German town after the war, she was greatly moved by the plight of German mothers who had lost their sons. Like many survivors, Rhodea remained tormented by guilt over her own choices—for her abandonment of the mental patients it was her job to care for before she became a fugitive, for leaving her older daughter to the protection of others when she fled, and for failing to convince her parents to go into hiding, rather than making the fatal journey to Poland.

In her introduction, Dr. Lillian Kremer, professor emerita of Kansas State University, states the percentage of Dutch Jews who perished in the Holocaust was slightly higher than the number in some other western European countries; that Dutch civil servants often cooperated in the disenfranchisement of Jewish citizens; and that the Dutch police sometimes actively participated in the deportations.

After the war, Jewish survivors found little support from their Dutch compatriots, who were interested mainly in re-establishing their own lives. It is alleged they had little sympathy for the greater losses and the atrocities suffered by the Jews. Starting in the 1960s and 1970s, the Dutch population that had lived through the war years, like that of other European countries, came in for severe criticism by a younger generation. The myth of a widespread heroic response to Nazism was exposed as a lie; numerous publications indicted the wartime generation for the abandonment and betrayal of Dutch Jewry.

Rhodea Shandler died on February 17, 2006, at the age of eighty-seven, soon after completing her book.

SICHERMAN, Claire

CLAIRE SICHERMAN of Salt Spring Island grew up reading Anne Frank's diary and watching *Schindler's List* with almost no knowledge of the Holocaust's impact on her own specific family. Though most of Sicherman's ancestors were murdered in the Holocaust, her grandparents didn't talk about their trauma and her mother grew up in Communist Czechoslovakia completely unaware she was even Jewish.

Now a mother herself, Sicherman uses vignettes, an epistolary

Claire Sicherman on Salt Spring Island

style, and other unconventional forms in *Imprint: A Memoir of Trauma in the Third Generation* (Caitlin 2018) to explore the ramifications of the inter-generational transmission of trauma. In essence, we learn the theory that genes can carry memories that are passed down as a genetic imprinting.

We learn the word holocaust is derived from the Greek word *holos* or "whole" and the word *kaustos*, to burn, and that Claire Sicherman is named after her great-grandmother, Klara, who lived in Prague but was killed by the Nazis in August 1942 in Belarus. Whereas family lore suggested that Klara had been shot in the back of the neck, Sicherman scoured the internet to discover Klara was more likely killed in a van outfitted with poison gas. There is no known marker or gravesite.

Sicherman's son, Ben, was named after her husband's favourite uncle, Ben Zion, who survived the Holocaust. Through a series of journal entries and letters to her son, we learn how she wrestled within herself, trying to discern the best way to pass along the ancestral legacy of grief, and ultimately breaking the silence surrounding her family's stories.

In his review of this book for *The Ormsby Review*, Mark Dwor, a member of the Vancouver Holocaust Education Centre, writes: "In the Book of Exodus, Jews are required to tell their children every year about how God freed them from slavery and the going out from Egypt. One of the questions that comes up in this annual re-telling is, 'what does it mean to be freed from slavery?' Is this simply the opportunity to choose to be freed from something? Or is it, more purposefully, the gift of allowing someone to do something with this freedom? Claire Sicherman has faced this conundrum head on and has chosen the opportunity to analyze, to prevail, and to know that she's not an unhealed victim of history."

SIGAL, Ruth Kron

ON THE ANNIVERSARY of Hitler's birthday on April 20th, 2002, swastikas were found painted on almost all of the gravestones of Jews in the Kristijonas Donelaitis cemetery in Siauliai [also known as Shavl] in Lithuania.

The following year, in January, neo-Nazis disrupted the town's Hanukkah celebrations, pulling down a menorah. Supporters of the country's main neo-Nazi party staged a rally with anti-Semitic signs and slogans.

News reports of these events motivated Ruth Kron Sigal to tell her family's story in *Ruta's Closet* (Shavl Publishing 2008, Unicorn 2013), co-written with *Vancouver Sun* journalist Keith Morgan and touted by Sir Martin Gilbert as "one of the finest Holocaust memoirs."

Published more than a half-century after Ruth Kron Sigal left Lithuania, *Ruta's Closet* is the survival story of the Kron family and their neighbours during the Nazi occupation of Lithuania, beginning in 1941. The story concerns the murder of an estimated 190,000 to 195,000 Lithuanian Jews during the Holocaust, roughly 90 percent of the Jews in the country.

"My story was locked away in a mental closet of my own making for many years," she writes.

Her father Meyer Kron was a chemical engineer. Her mother Gita had a law degree. Ruta (or Ruth) was born on July 28, 1936. About half of the townspeople were Jews. When the Nazis invaded Lithuania in 1941, the Kron family hid in the fields. Ruta's grandmother was the first to die, hit by a stray bullet in her backyard. The family returned to their home and found it occupied by two German officers. The well-educated Krons managed to befriend the officers who temporarily protected them so they were not rounded up for the camps.

On August 24, 1941, Ruta Kron and her family, including her sister, Tamara, born in 1939, were forced into the burgeoning ghetto of approximately 5,000 Jews at Siauliai. Inside the ghetto, her father's essential work in the leather industry prevented them all from being selected for culling and being sent by trainloads to Auschwitz. The local Jewish Council submitted to Nazi dictates that no more Jewish babies could be born.

The Krons succeeded in smuggling food into the ghetto. Ruth Kron Sigal later recalled: "My parents' determination to survive grew as members of our family and good friends died or suffered at the hands of the Nazis or the Lithuanian fascist collaborators. They became more inventive and daring in their bid to keep our family together. No matter what our tormentors did we were not going to allow them to beat us into submission."

Eventually, Ruta, too, was apprehended and placed on the last truck, with her sister, during a round-up of Jewish children—referred to as a *Kinderaktion*—on November 3, 1943. Ruth later recalled how her uncle pleaded with one of the guards to spare the girls. She was reprieved because she appeared old enough to work. In his book, *Child Holocaust Survivors*, Robert Krell reported in 2007 that it was Dr. Wulf Peisachowitz, a first cousin, who pulled her off that truck. The other 823 children in the convoy, including Tamara, were sent to Auschwitz.

Thereafter, Ruta, as the precious child who was spared, was taken secretly to the farm of a Catholic family, giving rise to the title of her memoir. At age eight, she remained hidden in a closet for between three and four months. She had to remain in hiding for her own safety and the safety of the host family until she could speak Lithuanian fluently. With hair dyed blonde, she became known as cousin Erika. The transformation was more complete than hoped. She became a devout Catholic.

The ghetto was liquidated and all inhabitants were sent away on the trains with the rare exception of her resourceful parents, who had escaped into hiding just a week prior. Ruta was reunited with them when the Soviets liberated Lithuania in September of 1944. This reunion did not go smoothly. It took several months of parental visits before she would agree to leave her Catholic home. Strong-willed, Ruth negotiated the terms of their reunion. Her parents had to agree not to speak Yiddish at home and she must be allowed to continue to attend Catholic services.

Not long after this rapprochement, Ruta switched her belief system

Ruth Kron Sigal at a memorial stone for murdered Jews buried in trenches at Panevezys, Lithuania.

from Catholicism to Communism. Her father was arrested as a Zionist but he managed to evade prosecution and escape with his family to Poland where Ruth's brother was born. The Krons had planned to forge a new life in Israel but were instead granted immigration to Canada—where Ruta became Ruth.

The Kron family of four arrived in Halifax, Nova Scotia, on March 11, 1951, and continued to Montreal where her father Meyer spent three months in hospital with infectious hepatitis. Her mother Gita started a new career as a teacher by attending the Jewish Hebrew Teachers' Seminary. Meyer left Montreal in March of 1952 to operate a government-run tannery in Regina; he was joined by the rest of the family later in the year—but the factory burned down in May of 1953.

A client in Winnipeg offered Meyer work at the J. Leckie Company, in New Westminster, near Vancouver, where he stayed until 1964. Gita obtained a teaching post at the Beth Israel Religious School and Talmud Torah Day School, in Vancouver. Meyer died October 10, 1986 and Gita died on November 10, 1994.

As an expert on the stresses of being a hidden child, Robert Krell writes, "Ruth, a thoroughly indoctrinated Christian by the time she was returned to her parents, would probably have remained a Christian, had they [her parents] not survived. Slowly, she was brought back into the fold. Her personal recovery, while guided by her parents to a large degree, came from a renewed sense of community offered through school friends in Feldafing and Munich. It was there she received toys and candy, Baby Ruths and Butterfingers.

"She returned to school and studied Hebrew with teachers from Israel. It was her friends of these previous years of recovery and recuperation that she sought out at the First International Gathering of the Hidden Child in New York in 1991. She found one, and through her, others."

Ruth Kron married Dr. Cecil Sigal in 1957. In 1995, as Ruth Kron Sigal, during her visit to Lithuania and Latvia, revisiting her birthplace at Siauliai, she recorded a documentary about her family's experiences. The rise of anti-Semitism in the 21st century made her feel obliged to record her family's story for posterity.

According to Keith Morgan, "The late Meyer Kron left behind a substantive unpublished memoir entitled 'Through the Eye of the Needle' from which the basic story outline was drawn. Similarly, members of the Peisachowitz, Gotz-Ton, Luntz and Perlov families graciously provided unfettered access to unpublished memoirs and personal documents, enabling a better description of events and even the inclusion of near contemporaneously recorded conversations." A diary of ghetto life, kept by Eliezer Yerushalmi, a scribe for the ghetto's *Judenrat*, was also published by Yad Vashem in 1950, in Hebrew.

Ruth Kron Sigal graduated from UBC in Bacteriology. After doing research and social work for ten years, at age thirty-nine, she went back to UBC and received her second degree in Counselling Psychology. She was also a founding member of the Vancouver Crisis Centre and of SAFER (Shelter Aid for Elderly Renters). As a Registered Psychologist, she was the founder and Director of UBC's Women's Resources Centre for 25 years. Among the many honours she received were the YWCA Woman of Distinction Lifetime Achievement Award in 2001, the UBC AMS Great Trekker's Award and the UBC President's Award.

Ruth Kron Sigal was a co-founder of the Vancouver Child Survivors of the Holocaust group and was active in Holocaust education. Shortly before the publication of her memoir, she died at home of kidney cancer on December 16, 2008, whereupon the $500 Kron Sigal Award for Excellence in Holocaust Education, established in memory of her parents, Meyer and Gita, was renamed to include Ruth Kron Sigal. It is presented annually to an elementary or secondary teacher in any discipline who has shown a commitment to teaching students about the Holocaust and its lessons for humankind.

Ruth Kron Sigal told children when she gave talks in schools: "Our elders told us, 'You did not suffer. You were safe. You were hidden in the homes of rescuers.' We, 'the hidden children,' as we are known, were left feeling that our stories were not as important as those told by older people who had survived Hitler's concentration camps."

SLYOMOVICS, Susan

BORN IN 1926, in the village of Bushtyna, on the Tisa River, now part of western Ukraine, Vera Hollander survived the Auschwitz, Plaszow and Markkleeberg camps with her mother, Gizella Elefant Hollander.

Upon liberation, the pair disagreed about applying for the post-World War II Wiedergutmachung ("to make good again") reparations. Their varying attitudes to restitution gave rise to *How to Accept German Reparations* (University of Pennsylvania Press 2014) by Vera's daughter, Susan Slyomovics. Her two female subjects are so interesting that this is likely one of the most engaging academic books that one is likely to come across.

Gizella persisted in presenting herself as younger than she was. She would toss her head and say, "*Raboyne shel oylam* [Master of the Universe] knows my age and that's enough for me." She later claimed this approach saved her life when she passed through the selection process at Auschwitz, chosen for work detail with her daughter instead of being sent to the gas chambers.

Thereafter, Gizella bought cemetery plots wherever she lived. Each time she imagined her temporary residence would be permanent. First, there was the family plot in the hometown cemetery in Bishtine, former Czechoslovakia. Only once did Vera ever succeed in dissuading her mother Gizella from buying a place to be buried with her name on it—in Prague from 1945 to 1948. Afterwards she went on to purchase plots in Budapest, Havana, Montreal, Brooklyn and, finally, Netanya, Israel (where she now rests next to the second of her three husbands).

Such are the deviations from the subject of reparations in Slyomovics' study of her mother and grandmother. [Whereas there are some twenty monuments to the Holocaust in Montreal's Jewish cemeteries, it wasn't until 1987 that a major Holocaust memorial monument was erected in Vancouver's Orthodox Jewish cemetery, actually located in New Westminster. The cost of commemorating a murdered ancestor's name was only $200 in 1987.] "In my photograph taken during fam-

TWIGG PHOTO

New Westminster memorial provides the names of 1,200 murdered relatives.

ily visits to the dead," writes Susan Slyomovics, "my mother gestures to her father's name, Samuel Hollander.... My maternal grandfather's grave is nowhere on earth, yet his name is inscribed everywhere my mother resides."

Vera studied medicine at Charles University in Prague, Czechoslovakia, where she met her husband, Josef Slyomovics, a Czech furrier and veteran of the Czech Brigade that was attached to the British Army during World War II. After the Soviet takeover of Czechoslovakia in 1948, they fled to a DP camp in Salzburg, Austria, where their son Peter Slyomovics, was born. Canada granted the three of them immigration and they arrived to Montreal in October 1948.

Interviewed by Robert Krell in 1981 for VHCS archives, Vera Slyomovics described hiding in a church, then giving herself up to the Gestapo so she could join the Mateszalka ghetto to be with her family. She proceeded to describe her Auschwitz experiences, including the selection process and "showers."

Susan Slyomovics' mother, Vera, and her grandmother, Gizella (Prague, 1946), were among 10,000 Jews selected from Auschwitz to construct the German military barracks at the Plaszow Camp, site for the movie *Schindler's List*. Her mother said Plaszow was worse than Auschwitz, overseen by a brutal female commandant named Ilse (Else Lieschen Frida Ehrich) who shot people on the spot, wielding a gun from a holster like a cowboy.

Transferred to forced labour at the nearby Plaszow camp near Krakow, Vera received help adapting from other prisoners before being transferred back to Auschwitz. She further described the cruelty and abuse from female guards, conditions at the camp, and how she and her mother helped each other.

Later transported to Markkleeberg, seven kilometres south of Leipzig, Vera was one of approximately one thousand Jewish women and 250 female, French Resistance fighters who did forced labour in a factory. Collectively, they were subjected to a death march to Theresienstadt. During a bombing, some of her French companions helped her escape the deadly transport with her mother but they were returned to captivity.

In her interview with Krell, Vera recalled a chance meeting after she arrived in Australia with the Jewish kapo who had tattooed her identity number onto her arm. As a main tattooist at Auschwitz, Ludwig "Lale" Eisenberg, born to Jewish parents in Slovakia in 1916, reportedly remained silent about his role at Auschwitz for fifty years. Eisenberg had arrived in Auschwitz, at age twenty-six in April of 1942, where he became Prisoner #32407. After recovering from typhoid, he became the assistant of the camp's tattooist, a French academic named Pepan. Due to his ability with languages (Slovakian, German, Russian, French, Hungarian and a bit of Polish), Eisenberg was accorded the job when Pepan was removed.

The first series of prisoner numbers was implemented in May of 1940. The practise of tattooing was conceived in October of 1941 and was introduced the following month for Russian inmates. According to the United States Holocaust Museum, only prisoners at Auschwitz I (Main Camp), Auschwitz II (Auschwitz-Birkenau) and Auschwitz III (Monowitz and subcamps) were tattooed during the Holocaust

Eisenberg, the tattooist, soon fell in love with Gita Fuhrmannova, a Jew in the woman's portion of Birkenau, and protected her. Reunited with difficulty after the war, they married in October of 1945 in Soviet-controlled Czechoslovakia where they changed their last name to Sokolov. They escaped to Vienna, lived briefly in Paris and eventually sailed to Sydney, Australia. They lived mainly in Melbourne. Gita died in 2003. Prior to his death in 2006, Eisenberg spent three years recounting his story to Heather Morris who then produced a bestseller, *The Tattooist of Auschwitz*, in 2018. This novelized biography, panned by some critics, evolved from Morris' attempts to write a screenplay.

The Tattooist of Auschwitz was promoted as a revelation but Vera Hollander had spoken of her tattooist's existence in Vancouver in 1981. In her interview with Robert Krell, Vera also discussed her own number and tattoo; her identity as a survivor; why she did not feel survivor guilt or a need for revenge; her experiences watching Holocaust films and Holocaust-related television programmes; the shortcomings of such depictions; her Jewish identity; the importance of Israel; her horrific experiences with her children; and her motivations for rendering testimony.

Vera Hollander died on January, 25, 2014. Her daughter, Susan Slyomovics, received her Ph.D at the University of California Berkeley in 1985. As a professor of Anthropology and Near Eastern Languages and Cultures at UCLA, Susan Slyomovics has written and edited various books including *The Object of Memory: Arab and Jew Narrate the Palestinian Village* (University of Pennsylvania 1998) about the former Palestinian village called Ein Houd. The book received the 1999 Albert Hourani Book Award of the Middle East Studies Association and the 1999 Chicago Folklore Prize. In it she examines how and why two villages—Jewish Ein Hod and a renewed Arab Ein Houd—continue to exist in dynamic opposition.

In her *How to Accept German Reparations*, Slyomovics examines differences between German reparations and French restitution for Algerian Jewry, then raises the even thornier issues as to whether or not reciprocal reparation models ought to be made morally and financially applicable for victims of contemporary conflicts between Israel and Palestine.

"When human rights violations are presented primarily in material terms," she writes, "acknowledging an indemnity claim becomes one way for a victim to be recognized. At the same time, indemnifications provoke a number of difficult questions about how suffering and loss can be measured: How much is an individual life worth? How much or what kind of violence merits compensation? What is 'financial pain,' and what does it mean to monetize concentration camp survivor syndrome?"

After the Holocaust, Germany created the largest sustained redress program in history, amounting to more than $60 billion. Unlike her daughter, Gizella Elefant Hollander accepted German reparations money as soon as it was offered in the 1950s. She died in Netanya, Israel, in 1999, at age ninety-six, living for more than fifty years on her monthly stipend of approximately $600.

Vera Slyomovics' involvements with B'nai Brith led her to become the vice-president in 1957. As chair of public relations for the Canadian Jewish Congress, she worked with anti-racist and anti-hatred groups. She moved with her family to Vancouver in 1969. She co-founded the CJC's Holocaust Remembrance Committee and worked to teach youth the importance of respecting diversity. In 2002, Vera Slyomovics received the Governor General's Caring Canadian Award.

SONNENSCHEIN, Bronia

HAVING BEEN BORN into a Jewish family on July 12, 1915, in Zloczow, Poland (now Ukraine), Bronia Sonnenschein grew up in Vienna where her father worked in the family textile business. A sister was born in 1919. After Austria was annexed by Germany on March 13, 1938, their family was evicted from their home and they were forced to live in the Lodz Ghetto in Poland for five years.

With her German-language and office skills, Bronia worked as a secretary in the ghetto's Jewish administration. She was first married to Erich Strauss by Chaim Rumkowski, the head of the Council of Elders in the Lodz Ghetto. From 1940 to 1944, more than 180,000 Jews and 5,000 Roma and Sinti lived in the ghetto's cramped quarters, mostly forced to work in factories. Lodz was renamed Litzmannstadt.

Before the Lodz Ghetto was destroyed in August of 1944, Sonnenschein and her family were transported in cattle cars to Auschwitz where the family members were separated from her father.

After only six days in Auschwitz, they were sent onto the Stutthof concentration camp where she was reunited with her sister, Paula. Her father and her husband Erich died in Stutthof.

Along with her mother and sister, she was then forced to work in a munitions factory in Dresden where she was recognized from the Lodz Ghetto by director Hans Biebow and appointed to work in the factory office. All three women survived the infamous fire-bombing of the city by the Allies on February 13, 1945. In response to the advance of Russian troops, they were sent on a twelve-day death march in April to the Theresienstadt Ghetto in Terezin, Czechoslovakia (near Prague).

In order to persuade Jews that liveable conditions would be provided for their "resettlement," Theresienstadt was a Nazi "show camp" cynically described as a "spa town" in Nazi propaganda. In reality, nearly 90,000 people were transported from Theresienstadt to the murder camps, chiefly Auschwitz, Majdanek and Treblinka. Approximately 33,000 died in Theresienstadt itself, mostly from starvation or disease.

Bronia Sonnenschein often quoted Elie Wiesel's saying: "Not every German was a Nazi but every Jew was a victim."

In June of 1944, visiting dignitaries and representatives of the International Red Cross were permitted to visit Theresienstadt for an elaborate charade. After houses were painted and gardens planted, visitors were entertained by the ghetto's resident orchestra. Outstanding Jewish artists from Germany, Austria and Czechoslovakia

TWIGG PHOTO

Burial plaque for Bronia Sonnenschein in Burnaby, B.C.

were permitted to provide a facade of civility. In reality, the unintentional death rate in Theresienstadt was so high that Nazis had built a crematorium there in 1942 that could process 200 corpses per day.

The "camp-ghetto" collected approximately 15,000 children and approximately 90 percent of those did not survive. Children were nonetheless encouraged to undertake works of art at a Drawing Office and an Art Workshop, resulting in thousands of works of art that could demonstrate that detainees were housed in livable conditions. The ruse was successful; the delegation left impressed; and mass deportations resumed until October of 1944.

Theresienstadt maintained its bizarre character until Soviet troops cut off the main road and rail connections to the killing grounds of Auschwitz. Thereafter, Heinrich Himmler and Security Chief Ernst Kaltenbrunner agreed to release 1,200 detainees from Theresienstadt after Jewish organizations placed five million francs into an escrowed account in Switzerland. These German, Dutch, Austrian and Protectorate Jews arrived in Switzerland on February 5, 1945. The Swedish

Red Cross was permitted to take 423 Danish Jews out of Theresienstadt on trucks headed to Denmark on April 14-15.

Bronia Sonnenschein did not arrive at Theresienstadt until April 24th. The Red Cross officially took over administrative control of Theresienstadt from SS Commandant Karl Rahn on May 2, 1945. She recalled she never felt officially liberated until May 8, 1945. On that day a young Russian soldier on horseback greeted them saying, "You are free, you can go home again." Describing this scene ("but we had no home to go to") was an essential part of her talks to students and teachers from 1987 until 2008. From Theresienstadt, Bronia made her way to Prague where she worked for the Joint Distribution Committee and met her second husband, Kurt Sonnenschein.

After managing to leave Communist Czechoslovakia with very few belongings, the couple relocated to Israel briefly in 1949, where a son was born, but they immigrated to Canada in 1950.

Her second husband died in an automobile accident in 1952, leaving her with two infants to raise. With ongoing help from her mother and her married sister to help raise her children, Dan and Vivian (Herman), she became her family's chief breadwinner, working for the Alaska Pine Company.

Bronia Sonnenschein was known for her cheerful, upbeat attitude. As a Holocaust educator, she spoke to thousands of people and received the Queen's Golden Jubilee Medal for volunteer service.

First published in 1998, Bronia Sonnenschein's *Victory over Nazism: The Journey of a Holocaust Survivor* (Vancouver: Memory Press) was compiled and re-edited for a third edition by her son Dan Sonnenschein in 2013. He also recorded an audio interview about his mother after her death. An audio interview with Bronia Sonnenschein and her sister is available from the Jewish Museum and Archives of British Columbia, as well as a video interview. VHEC also has video interview material. Bronia Sonnenschein died in Vancouver on January 26, 2011.

SUEDFELD, Peter

AS THE SON OF assimilated Jewish parents, Peter Suedfeld was born in Hungary on August 30, 1935. His father worked as a musician and his mother, a secretary, was from a wealthy family. In 1944, his mother attempted to stop a Gestapo raid at the business where she worked and she was arrested. She would perish in a concentration camp, likely Auschwitz.

When his father was sent to Germany to work as a forced labourer, Peter lived temporarily with an aunt. He was lucky. With blond hair and blue eyes, he escaped incarceration with falsified Christian papers while hiding in a Red Cross orphanage.

Decades later, as a psychologist concerned with PTSD, Peter Suedfeld would write, "Recent research has shown that survivors of concentration camps and of hiding report such symptoms in roughly equal proportions (Yehuda et al. 1997), so that even children who were not interned were susceptible."

At nine years old, when the Soviet army liberated Budapest, Peter was reunited with his aunt and uncle. He subsequently lived with his father in Vienna as a displaced person until the American Joint Distribution Committee (a Jewish charity) facilitated their immigration to the U.S. where he attended school in Harlem. At Stuyvesant High School he won a scholarship to Queens College of the City University, but dropped out and served in the U.S. Army for three years. With a B.A. from Queens College, he eventually earned his M.A. and Ph.D in experimental psychology from Princeton University.

Peter Suedfeld was admitted to the Order of Canada in 2019 for his 55 years of research into how people respond to extreme environments.

Suedfeld taught at the University of Illinois and at Rutgers University prior to joining the University of British Columbia in 1972 where he became head of the Department of Psychology and later Dean of the Faculty of Graduate Studies. As a professor emeritus in UBC's psychology department, Peter Suedfeld told *Ubyssey* reporter Sabine Villorakin, in an interview, that people, including psychologists, tend to underestimate or overlook human adaptability, resilience, human strength and psychological stability.

"They tend to think we are more vulnerable and weak than we really are," he explained. "I did research with survivors of genocide . . . many of them put together normal lives and live happily."

More specifically, among his seven books, Suedfeld edited *Light from the Ashes: Social Science Careers of Young Holocaust Refugees and Survivors* (Ann Arbor: University of Michigan Press 2001), a project that originated from a session at the 1996 meeting of the International Society of Political Psychology. *Light from the Ashes* examines the effects of Holocaust trauma on child and adolescent survivors of the Holocaust such as himself. He contends that "very many child survivors and refugees are psychologically well-adjusted, socially integrated, emotionally warm and healthy, professionally successful and, in general, productive and valuable citizens."

Seventeen other social scientists, all of whom were profoundly affected by the Holocaust as children, contributed autobiographical essays and examined how their values, personalities and careers were influenced by being targets of Nazi persecution. Four of the seventeen contributors are women.

Suedfeld asserts that arguments as to who should merit true survivor status are "unproductive and demeaning." Each chapter explores the perceived connections between early years of survival and their subsequent adult attitudes, political orientations, ethics, family lives and religion. One contributor suggests that "risk taking," a craving for "curiosity" and humour as a defence mechanism are key personality characteristics of members of this group culture.

It is notable that all seventeen contributors had already attained a degree of professional success that enabled them to validate Suedfeld's hypothesis, one that could be crudely encapsulated by the aphorism, "when the going gets tough, the tough get going."

In a review of the book, Shirley Cohn summarized Suedfeld's main psychological findings about the effects of the Holocaust: Child survivors demonstrate a desire to make the most of every moment. Jews in Europe had been told they were worthless. Work is a way of disproving that; there is a heightened awareness of death, leading to the desire to leave traces of one's existence; and the indignities of the Holocaust can generate a search for status.

In a separate research paper, "Homo Invictus: The Indomitable Species" (*Canadian Psychology* #38, 1998) Peter Suedfeld examined human toughness and the ability to benefit from stressful experiences.

Suedfeld is a Fellow of the Royal Society of Canada, the Canadian Psychological Association, the American Psychological Association, and the Academy of Behavioral Medicine Research. He is a full member of the International Academy of Astronautics, a Fellow of the Explorers Club and the only psychologist elected as an Honorary Fellow of the Royal Canadian Geographical Society. He was also awarded the Lawrence J. Burpee Gold Medal by the Royal Canadian Geographical Society. He has received the Canadian Psychological Society's Donald O. Hebb Award, its highest award for distinguished scientific contributions, as well as the Society's Gold Medal for distinguished and enduring lifetime contributions to Canadian psychology and its Award for Distinguished Contributions to the International Advancement of Psychology.

Suedfeld's other awards include the Canadian Polar Medal, Queen Elizabeth II's Diamond Jubilee Medal, the highest award for scientific contributions from the International Society of Political Psychology, the Antarctica Service Medal of the U.S. National Science Foundation and the Zachor Award for contributions by Holocaust survivors to Canadian society. Among his many articles is "Life after the Ashes: The postwar pain, and resilience, of young Holocaust survivors" published by the *United States Holocaust Memorial Museum: Center for Advanced Studies* (pp. 1-24) in 2002.

TREGEBOV, Rhea

IN RHEA TREGEBOV'S *Rue des Rosiers* (Coteau 2019), a young woman accepts an opportunity to stay in Paris, hoping to find new direction and purpose after being fired from a job in Toronto. Searching for her own identity in 1982, she comes face-to-face with the terror of an age-old enemy when she reads the writing on the wall above her local metro subway station: *Death to the Jews*. Soon shadows from her childhood emerge once more. This novel received the Nancy Richler Memorial Prize for Fiction (Western Canada Jewish Book Awards) in 2020.

In Tregebov's previous novel, *The Knife Sharpener's Bell* (Wolsak & Wynn, 2009), a girl leaves Winnipeg at age ten with her parents to escape from the faltering of the North American capitalist economy in the 1930s. They return "home" to Stalinist Odessa, then must flee to Moscow to avoid the approaching Nazi forces in World War II. In the post-war years their family is threatened by anti-Semitism and the

"Jews are not wanted here." This was a typical sign erected by Nazis at parks, movie theatres and restaurants in Germany and conquered territories.

repressive totalitarianism of Stalin. This novel received the J.I. Segal Award for creative works on Jewish themes in 2010.

Born in Saskatoon in 1953 and raised in Winnipeg, Rhea Tregebov moved from Toronto to Vancouver in September of 2004 to commence teaching as an Assistant Professor of Creative Writing at the University of British Columbia in January of 2005. She retired in 2017. Now professor emerita, Tregebov has published five children's picture books and edited nine anthologies of essays, poetry and fiction.

An extensive overview of Rhea Tregebov's poetry output concerning her Jewish legacy and the Holocaust has been provided by Donna Hollenberg in *Canadian Jewish Studies* Vol 11 (2003), starting with *Remembering History* (Guernica 1982), her first collection of poetry that received the Pat Lowther Award in 1983. Poems in subsequent volumes such as "Vienna, November 1983" (*No One We Know*) and "Kristallnacht, 1988" and "DPs" (*Mapping the Chaos*) also reflect Holocaust themes.

WATTS, Irene N.

WITH HER FATHER gone into hiding, eleven-year-old Marianne Kohn keeps hoping her situation will improve in Irene Watts' autobiographical novel for children, *Good-bye Marianne*, but it's cold in Berlin and a sign on a shoe repair shop reads ARYANS ONLY.

Another sign tells her AS OF TODAY, NOVEMBER 15, 1938, JEWISH STUDENTS ARE PROHIBITED FROM ATTENDING GERMAN SCHOOLS.

A billboard warns AS OF DECEMBER 10, 1938, JEWS ARE PROHIBITED FROM LIVING IN THIS BUILDING. PLEASE VACATE APARTMENT TWO BY DECEMBER 9TH AT TWO O'CLOCK. HEIL HITLER.

A notice on a boarded-up clothing store is more succinct in its hatred: KEEP OUR STREETS JEW FREE. Subject to cruel taunts, hate propaganda and her mother's warnings not to be noticed, Marianne must eventually travel without her mother, via Holland, to arrive at Parkstone Quay, Harwich, England aboard *De Praag*, in December of 1938.

Illustration by Kathryn E. Shoemaker, from the 2008 graphic novel *Good-Bye Marianne: A Story of Growing Up in Nazi Germany*

Like her heroine, Watts once lived at Richard Wagnerstrasse 3, Charlottenburg, Berlin until she went to England—at age seven-and-one-half—on the Kindertransport trains that evacuated approximately 10,000 Jewish children (none of them accompanied by parents) from continental Europe prior to the outbreak of war in September of 1939.

Born in Berlin, Germany in 1931, Irene Watts emigrated from England to Alberta in 1968. Since coming to B.C. in 1977, she has published an impressive array of books and often gives workshops as a storyteller in schools. She is also a co-founder of the Vancouver International Children's Festival.

Good-bye Marianne won the Geoffrey Bilson Award for Historical Fiction and Isaac Frischwasser Memorial Award for Young Adult Fiction. It was re-issued and co-authored with illustrator Kathryn E. Shoemaker for *Good-Bye Marianne: The Graphic Novel.* To mark the 75th anniversary of the Kindertransport exodus, Watts re-released her three volumes of juvenile fiction on the subject, made available for an omnibus edition entitled *Escape from Berlin*, (Tundra 2013) including *Goodbye Marianne, Remember Me* and *Finding Sophie.*

Worth $10,000 each, the national Vine Awards for Jewish Literature in Canada are presented by the Koffler Centre for the Arts in four categories. The 2017 winners for Children's/Young Adult were Watts and Shoemaker (illustrations) for *Seeking Refuge* (Tradewind 2016) another graphic novel arising from the Kindertransport. The story depicts the protagonist's estrangement in England as a refugee, missing her family and needing to learn English.

"I came to London, England, in December 1938," says Watts, "as a seven-year-old refugee. When war broke out, I was evacuated with three million British children to the safety of the countryside, to Lanelly, South Wales, where I was educated. I did not come to Canada with my husband and four children until 1968. *Seeking Refuge* is not my personal story, it is based on the kinds of experiences many of the refugee children went through."

Watts's children's book *Touched by Fire* (Tundra 2013) recalls the terrible Triangle Shirtwaist Factory fire in New York City in 1911, during which 146 garment workers lost their lives due to fire, smoke inhalation or jumping from the building in which the doors had been locked by the employers. Watts follows one family's flight from the pogroms of Russia, to Berlin, onto steerage passage to Ellis Island, then onto New York's Lower East Side, through the eyes of teenager Miriam who gratefully lands a job as a cuff setter at the factory.

When the Bough Breaks and *Flower* are both books about "Home Children" who were sent from Britain to Canada as either orphans or as children whose parents could not fully provide for them. Watts' *A Telling Time* (Tundra 2004) recalls the Biblical story of Purim from the Book of Esther. Her anthology *Tapestry of Hope* (Tundra 2003), co-edited by Lillian Boraks-Nemetz, includes content from Jewish Canadian writers such as Ellen Schwartz, Karen Levine, Kathy Kacer, Mordecai Richler and Leonard Cohen. It won the Ca-

Illustration by Kathryn E. Shoemaker, from *Good-Bye Marianne: A Story of Growing Up in Nazi Germany*

nadian Jewish Book Award and a Yad Vashem award for Holocaust Studies.

In 2001, Watts was honored with a Playwrights' Union of Canada lifetime membership for her outstanding contribution to Canadian drama and theatre. She has won three Canadian Jewish Book Awards and lives in White Rock, B.C.

WILKES, Helen

WITH A PH.D. IN French literature, Helen Waldstein Wilkes of Vancouver, born in 1936, has examined her Jewish/Czechoslovakian background in *Letters from the Lost: A Memoir of Discovery* (Athabasca University Press 2009). Much of this material is derived from a treasure trove of letters received by Wilkes' parents in Canada from family members in Europe from 1939 to 1948. Wilkes rescued this cache from an Eaton's Christmas box after her father died in 1959.

As Nazis closed in on war-torn Czechoslovakia, her father had managed to escape from Prague with his young family in 1939. In her foreword, Elizabeth Jameson writes: "Both the United States and Canada refused entry to most Jews in the immediate pre-war years. Both had admitted Jews through the early twentieth century. Canada, unlike the United States, had permitted Jewish agricultural colonies on the prairies. But neither welcomed Jewish immigrants during the 1930s. The United States severely restricted European immigration in 1924, and during the 1930s resisted appeals on behalf of European Jews. Canada separated Jews as a class from others who shared the same citizenship and then quietly restricted Jewish immigration.

"Canadian immigration policy was more generous after the War, and thus most Canadian Holocaust memoirs have been written by survivors who emigrated after years in hiding or in concentration camps. *Letters from the Lost* differs from most narratives of the search for lost relatives because Helen Waldstein Wilkes was one of very few children to escape with her parents, and one of even fewer to enter

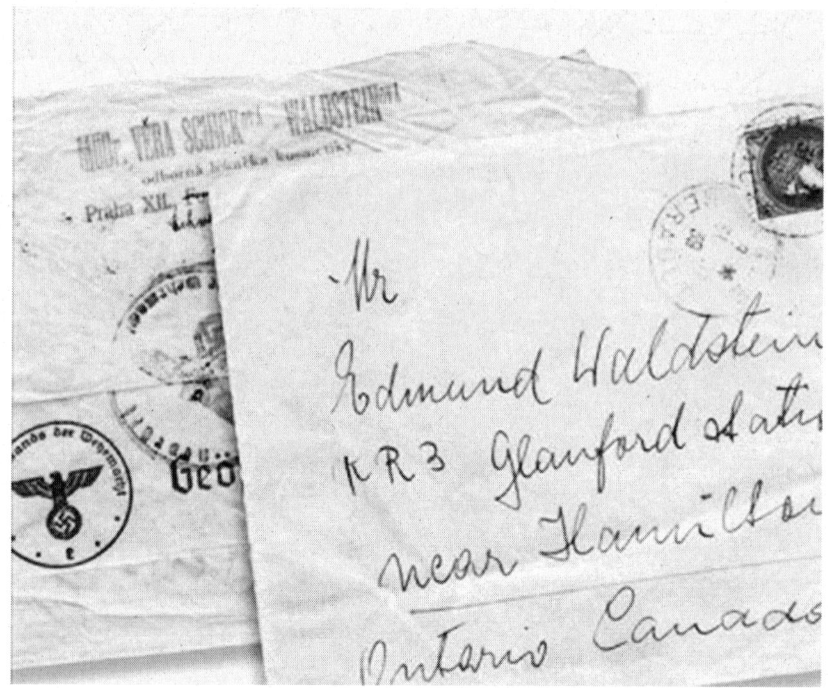

"My parents had done a lot of forgetting. It was their way of coping. The details of their trauma had always been a shadowy presence in my life. As I celebrated my 60th birthday, I knew it was time to unravel the mysteries in order to be present in my own life." — Helen Waldstein Wilkes

Canada before the formal onset of the War."

In 2011, *Letters From the Lost* won both the Alberta Readers Choice Award for best book published in Alberta (fiction or non-fiction) and the Edna Staebler Award for Creative Non-Fiction.

"I think involuntarily of Hilderl," Wilkes writes, "a relative on my mother's side. Hilderl was a beautiful child known to me only through my photo album. In the photo she is perhaps five years old. Poor little Hilderl. Neither her name nor the details ever varied as my mother told the story: 'Poor little Hilderl was a delightful child, sweet, bright, charming. One day as she was walking home with her mother, a Nazi tank deliberately drove onto the sidewalk and killed Hilderl. I don't know how her mother survived. We all thought she would go crazy.'"

ZELDOWICZ, Lola

BETTY KELLER OF SECHELT, B.C., founder of that town's annual Festival of the Written Arts, received the province's George Woodcock Lifetime Achievement Award in 2021 for twenty books she has written as well as her role as a freelance editor for dozens of others. Of those, possibly the least-known but most important book she has guided into print is *In the Warsaw Ghetto 1940–1943, An Account of a Witness: The Memoirs of Stanislaw Adler* (Jerusalem: Daf-Hen Press / Yad Vashem 1982).

This incomparable record of Warsaw Ghetto life by the ghetto's brilliant but depressed one-time Director of Housing, Stanislaw (or Stanislav) Adler, is one of several hidden gems uncovered in the process of compiling *Out of Hiding*, although it's more demanding than Simon Schochet's *Feldafing* and Mary Gallant's *Coming of Age in the Holocaust: The Last Survivors Remember.*

Having escaped from the Warsaw Ghetto with its author Stanislaw Adler, and then having remained with him in hiding from the Nazis for a year while he wrote the manuscript, Vancouver's Ludmila "Lola" Fiszhaut-Zeldowicz, a UBC neurology professor, eventually arranged for Adler's sophisticated memoir to be published in 1977, in a Polish edition for which she contributed a foreword. After the manuscript had been translated in English from Polish by Sara Chmielewska Philip, Lola Zeldowicz approached Cherie Smith of November House, hoping to have the book published from B.C. Smith sought the services of Betty Keller in order to fashion a readable English version.

Lola Zeldowicz

"Unfortunately, Philip's English was imperfect, to say the least," Keller recalls, "and she had great difficulty with English sentence structures and idioms, and that's where I came into the picture. I would edit the easier sections, then Lola and I would do battle over the obscure sections together, she with the Polish version, a dictionary and her memory of the events in hand. It was a great experience—which is not always true of the substantive editing process as you know—and we became good friends. And by the time the edit was finished, she had found the necessary funding to have the book published by Yad Vashem."

Other ghetto memoirists have attempted to report on the social structures of the Warsaw Ghetto—such as Ringelblum, Katznelson, Kaplan, Levin and Brisker—but according to the Yad Vashem Editorial Board, "There is no one like Adler—an intelligent man with a broad education and sensitive to the needs of the public—to explain the motives and conflicts that arose between the Jewish police and the Jewish public in the ghetto."

Here is how Adler's book eventually entered the world via British Columbia.

AFTER THE NAZIS sent 300,000 Jews to the nearby Treblinka death camp in the summer of 1942, a Polish resistance group in Warsaw called ZOB, or Zydowska Organizacja Bojowa (Jewish Fighting Organization) issued a proclamation urging Jews to resist any transport by railroad cars.

This idealism sparked the first armed resistance in the Warsaw Ghetto, from January 18 to January 21, whereupon the Nazis massacred 1,000 Jews in the main square in January. Deportations were temporarily suspended and this partial success instigated by the boldness of the youthful ZOB, led by 23-year-old Mordecai Anielewicz, would later give rise to the extended Warsaw Uprising in April.

In January of 1943, during that spate of ZOB resistance, the beautiful, married physician Dr. Lola Zeldowicz had entered the Warsaw Ghetto on a special permit to tend to a very sick child. Trapped inside the ghetto due to an unforeseen blockade, she was forced to climb over dead Jewish bodies on a staircase and hide for days in a cellar bunker.

Inside the bunker with the young doctor were three others: Dr. Julian Lewinson, a physician for the Jewish Police, his elderly mother and Adler, a former lawyer. Forbidden to practice law as a Jew, Adler had resigned in disgust from the "Jewish Police" (Jewish Order Service).

Calls from outside, in Polish, saying, "Jews come out, it would be better for you," were met with complete silence in the bunker. After four days, once the explosions outside finally ceased, Dr. Levinson, dared to leave the bunker first. Streets were strewn with corpses. Houses were smouldering or in flames. But grisly evidence of the first Jewish armed resistance to the Nazis filled their hearts with joy.

By January of 1943, Adler, born in 1901, had already made known his intentions to escape to his superior, Marek Lichtenbaum, a philanthropist and a surviving member of the *Judenrat*. Lichtenbaum had given his consent by saying, "The captains are the last to leave the sinking ship. However, our ship has already sunk." By then, at the height of a typhus epidemic, the mortality rate in the Warsaw Ghetto reportedly exceeded 5,000 deaths per month.

In early February, Adler devised a hasty plan to escape by hiding among the dead bodies that were routinely hauled away on a hearse, drawn by horses. He later wrote:

> In the street every few hundred paces, one could see a human corpse covered with newspaper. Somehow, in the passage of time, people got used to this sight and only the most sensitive crossed to the opposite side of the street and turned their heads away. But even the most courageous or insensitive lost their nerve when, in the darkness of the night, they happened to accidently step on some soft object that turned out to be a cadaver. On those occasions, invariably, hysterical screams rang out.
>
> The number of burials rapidly increased. They used the

> old-fashioned type of horse-drawn hearse that carried eight corpses simultaneously. Six inside the hearse while two were placed on the roof. From beneath the sheets that covered them, it was quite common to see a brownish, emaciated leg sticking out.

A courageous driver bade Adler to don a gravedigger's cap instead of hiding among the corpses. Alongside him, Dr. Zeldowicz, with her medical pass, wore her doctor's coat. At midday, in the vicinity of the Schultz factory, when they were about to be inspected by gendarmes with machine guns at the ready, the hearse driver said, in garbled German, "*Alle Tote, alles Kaput!*" (all are dead corpses) and whipped the horses, speeding through, leaving the gendarmes bewildered.

To avoid inspection at another checkpoint, surrounded by throngs of German factory police and a "rat-faced gendarme" that Adler recognized, their daring driver gave the password to indicate he was carrying contraband, thereby gaining swift passage to the safety of Aryan streets. On Bonifraterska Street, they rushed into the waiting room of their devoted friend, Dr. Wladyslaw Jakimowicz; then went to the apartment of Polish underground members Henryik and Dr. Halina Kotlicki; then they found refuge in the apartment of the Polish writer Zenon Skiersky and his elderly mother in Saska Kepa.

Stanislav Adler

Finally, in April, Adler began his third attempt to preserve his memoirs in *A Chronicle of the Events Which Led to the Extermination of the Jewish Population in Warsaw, Poland.* "My memoirs from the first months of the war," he wrote, "were thrown into a stove by the border police. My reconstruction of those notes was lost when I moved into the Jewish Quarter of Warsaw in 1941."

When the Gestapo arrived to arrest them, they saved their lives with bribery and escaped from Saska Kepa to a villa in Anin owned by some of Lola's former patients, the Jaskiewicz family. They frequently had to hide in the attic until the approach of the Russian army in the autumn of 1944. Eventually, this final house of refuge was taken over by Nazis who failed to find their concealed hideaway.

Inside the walls, Lola and Adler had to take turns sleeping—this way they could prevent one another from any loud and protracted snoring. They used their minimal water supply as sparingly as possible to prevent the need for urination. They were in the darkness for so long they completely lost track of whether it was day or night. Finally, they were thrilled to hear exploding bombs. They joyously welcomed the opportunity to avoid starvation in the dark. They were either going to die or be liberated. When they assumed the house must be empty, they crept into the light only to discover a Nazi asleep nearby. They were forced back into hiding until finally the Nazis in Warsaw were defeated.

There is no clarity afforded in the manuscript as to whether Adler and Lola were ever romantically entwined. In his narrative, he introduces her as "a physician employed by Schultz and Co… who had been called to attend a sick child in the area of the brushmakers shop."

Editor Betty Keller has confirmed that Lola and Adler were lovers:

> In the course of long lunches and even longer editing sessions together, Lola told me many stories of those terrible war years in Poland. As more than forty years have elapsed since the telling, I cannot guarantee I have all the details correct. However, Lola Zeldowicz and Stanislaw Adler were most definitely lovers.
>
> That story actually began in 1939 when Hitler invaded Poland. At that time, she was a young neurologist, and Henry Zeldowicz, her husband, was a psychiatrist in Warsaw, but

> he was also required by law to belong to the Polish reserve army, and when the invasion began, he was on maneuvers in the countryside. His unit fled from the Germans and for the next five years Lola heard nothing whatsoever from him and believed him dead.
>
> Thus, she considered herself a widow when she entered the Warsaw Ghetto. However, at war's end the Red Cross erected bulletin boards all over Europe where people could put up notices about missing persons, and that's where one of Lola's friends found a note from someone who had seen Henry Zeldowicz in Palestine with the British Army. He, by the way, also believed her to be dead.

Born in 1905, Lola was the daughter of Jakub Fiszhaut and Salomea Czapek. At war's end, Adler opted to stay in Poland whereas Lola left to meet up with her husband, Dr. Henry Zeldowicz, who had managed to join the Allied forces. Married in 1932, the reunited couple planned to immigrate to Canada. Lola told Keller that, in fact, the couple had been planning to include Adler in their immigration plans, leaving Europe as a trio.

"However, at the last minute," according to Keller, "Adler was asked to take a role in the new Polish government, and he decided to accept the challenge; he would join them later."

When Lola was leaving from Warsaw for Prague on May 4, 1946, Adler handed her his unpublished manuscript. "My heart was heavy," she recalled. "All the letters and cables I sent to Adler during the months that followed, failed to lift his spirit. His own courage and the initiative for swift action that had supported him during the war now failed him. Anti-Semitism was still rife in Poland and when the news reached him of a pogrom against the Jewish survivors in Kielce, he was shattered."

Lola later elaborated for Keller; she said Adler had become deeply disturbed by the news that an orphanage for Jewish children that had been established in a small town outside of Warsaw had been attacked by local Poles who burned it to the ground, killing most of

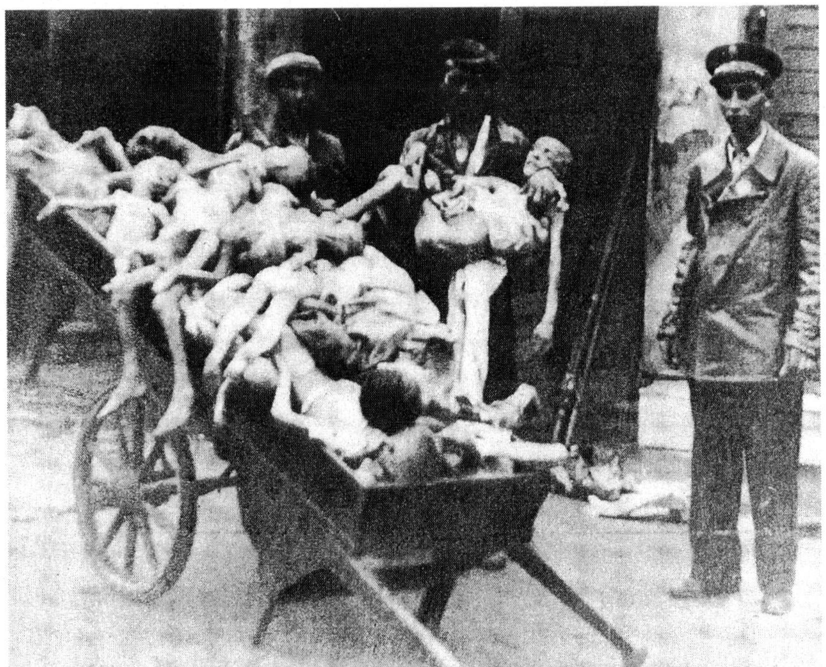

Emaciated corpses were gathered in the Warsaw Ghetto where typhus, starvation and bullets killed countless thousands.

the children. Whether it was this tragedy, or the end of his love affair with Lola, or the combination of both, Stanislaw Adler shot himself, at home, out of despair, on July 11, 1946.

There is one more explanation: guilt. Adler could not countenance any degree of complicity by the Jewish ghetto police in the earliest roundups for the labour camps. "It stopped at moaning and swearing at the fate that brought one to such detestable service. Evidently, it was preferable to catch than be caught.... Like the others, I did not take immediate measures to quit at once."

The degree of detail in Adler's 300-plus-page memoir makes it valuable to historians. Here, for instance, are some paragraphs about the complex nature of the Jewish Quarter:

> "For many scores of thousands of Jews, transfer to the ghetto meant complete material ruin. There were relatively few who could exchange their apartments with Aryans who had been

living in the area that was to be the Jewish Quarter. These exchanges, due to a greater demand for homes in the Quarter, were conducted with a much greater burden on the Jewish contracting parties. Usually, the Jew had to pay the Aryan a year in advance for the difference in rent when it was higher in the apartment he was receiving. He had to leave the Aryan his coal supply, part of his furniture, and so forth. A strange sort of wandering had begun. Two hundred thousand people were exchanging living quarters. The Aryans [Poles] carried out their moving operations with furniture trucks and lorries; the Jews pushed handcarts. It was a rare case when the modest chattels of a Jew were moved by lorry.

"The area of the Jewish Quarter was not accurately defined until the last moment. Originally, for instance, it had looked as if the boundary in the south and south-east would run along Chmielna and Marszalkowska Streets, and in the south-west along Wronia Street, but later it was decided that the dividing line should run along Zlota and Zielna. At the last minute, due to the impossibility of building an eleven-kilometer-long wall down the center of the street in a few months' time, the invaders adopted provisional measures. They erected fences, usually across streets, which closed them in such a way that, as a rule, the Quarter's boundaries ran along the external walls of apartment houses. The population did not realize that these arrangements were only temporary, and tens of thousands of them were faced with continuous wandering as a result of the endless population resettlement as the ghetto's boundaries changed.

"The outline of the boundary ran in fantastic zig-zags. Wherever a German industrial enterprise or any important German institution happened to be located on the periphery of the Jewish Quarter, it was sufficient reason for a whole complex of ghetto housing to be cut off and included in the Aryan sector. In such a way, an enclave was formed of Grzybowska, Walicow, and Ceglana Streets for the companies of Haberbusch, Schiele, and Ulrich; this was connected to the Aryan Quarter by a narrow neck only. Along both sides of Biala Streets, fences were erected to provide a passage to the courthouse, which had been excluded from the Jewish Quarter. Only a portion of that building remained, until the "resettlement action" that began on July 22, 1942, as a special place of meeting where Jews and Aryans could mingle more or less freely.

"The basic necessities, both economic and religious, of the Jewish population were not considered in the least; this population was not a subject for regulation but an object for destruction, all the more pleasing to the invader's eyes when it was accompanied by pain and suffering. The wooded areas, therefore, were purposely and maliciously excluded from the Quarter and the Morowska bazaars and adjoining streets, an area inhabited exclusively by Jews before the war, were cut out of the middle of the ghetto. The intention was clear: to prevent Jewish access to the largest market place.

"An additional result of this arbitrary boundary was the division of the Jewish Quarter into two parts. The smaller part, known as the 'small ghetto', was the seat of the more important pre-war Jewish institutions, including the Community Council, and had a population of nearly one hundred thousand. It was connected to the other part of the Quarter, or the 'large ghetto', where more than three hundred thousand people lived, by a single communication artery composed of Ciepla, Grzybowska, and Zelazna Streets. Where Zelazna intersected with Chlodna Street, the Jewish Quarter joined Aryan territory for a length of forty meters. . . . The extent of the traffic and masses of people who used this artery cannot be described and these crowded conditions contributed greatly to the spread of the typhus epidemic which decimated the Quarter."

Dr. Ludmila (Lola) Zeldowicz worked as a Clinical Assistant Professor of Neurology at UBC where her husband, Dr. Henry Zeldowicz, a psychiatrist, was a Clinical Assistant Professor of Psychiatry. She first met Robert Krell in 1976, at the Oakridge Auditorium, when they were guest speakers for the launch of the First Holocaust Symposium for High School Students. That evening she spoke about the Warsaw Ghetto. It wasn't until the early 1980s that she handed Krell a copy of Adler's memoir. Robert Krell recalls. "In her strong Polish accent, she said, 'Robert, this is my story, also.'"

After Dr. Lola Zeldowicz died of complications arising from Alzheimer's disease in 1991, Dr. Irene Bettinger of UBC donated funds from her parents' estate to establish the Ludmila and Henry Zeldowicz Award presented annually to support a resident physician to undertake studies and/or research in neurology. Bettinger's parents, Edwina (concert pianist) and Paul Heller, (B.C. lumber mill owner) were members of the Vancouver Jewish community that had fled Europe, shortly after the Nazi invasion of Warsaw, and befriended Henry and Lola.

IN COLLECTING THESE excerpts from B.C.-related sources, it is easy to include biographical details and moments of heroism and bravery to stress the dignity of the Jews. To do so exclusively, however, runs the risk of under-estimating and under-representing the extent and magnitude of cruelty and horrific behaviour perpetrated by German soldiers, SS personnel and collaborators on Jews and other victims.

A few historians, such as Martin Gilbert, have taken it upon themselves to divulge the evil degradations that evidently occurred routinely. Gilbert, for example, does not hesitate to quote sections of a 29-page notebook that was uncovered in 1952 near one of the crematoria at Birkenau. At the outset of 1943, a member of the *Sonderkommando* recorded how SS Staff Sargeant Forst "stood at the gate of the undressing room in the case of many transports and felt the sexual organ of each young woman that was passing naked to the gas chamber. There were also cases of German SS men of all ranks who put fingers into the sexual organs of pretty young girls."

The German soldiers often took pleasure, according to this Nazi diarist, in "torturing people and mastering their minds." For instance, when "shrivelled and emaciated" Jews arrived at Birkenau from another camp, "they undressed in the open and singly went to be shot. They were horribly hungry and they begged to be given a piece of bread at the last moment while they were still alive. Plenty of bread was brought; the eyes of those men, sunken and dimmed due to protracted starvation, now flashed with a wild fire of staggering joy, they snatched big chunks of bread with both hands and voraciously swallowed, at the same time descending the steps straight on to be shot."

Stanislaw Adler's memoir is unusual because he not only records his personal predicaments and emotions, as well as the nature of German and Jewish organizations within Warsaw. He also describes how, in January of 1943, naked and barefoot gypsies were loaded into wagons, and brigands from Treblinka set up tents at the *Umschlagplatz* in Warsaw in order to strip the doomed Jews of their money and jewelry, accepting bribes to forestall dreaded deportations to the death camp, only to be loaded onto the trains the following day.

Adler takes care to record how some of the SS men ostensibly befriended some of the German Jews and workers who were brought to the gathering grounds at the *Umschlagplatz*. When they went for drinks together, one of the SS officers asked if they had any wishes, whereupon one of the Jews had the courage to say his greatest wish was to not be sent to Treblinka. "Go back and don't worry," was the reply, "We shall see to it that you are not deported." Elated, the Jews mounted the stairs of a nearby house, whereupon, according to Adler's reportage, "they received from their saviours a volley of revolver shots that killed almost all of them on the spot. Thus, the SS men kept their promise literally."

Adler chooses to devote much of his final few pages to the story of Meir Alter, who had been a very successful cantor prior to the war. Alter had accumulated considerable wealth due to his foreign singing engagements as far afield as South America. After nearly four months without a single deportation, the Germans commenced their second major round of expulsions to Treblinka on January 18, 1943. On that Monday, 5,000 Jews were sent to their deaths, including 50 doctors—and the cantor Meir Alter. Adler writes:

> Alter was the first resident of our house whom the Nazis took away. . . .
>
> With him they dragged out his father and his brother Mieczyslaw. On the way to the *Umschlagplatz*, [Meir] Alter supported his father, who was moving with difficulty. When asked by the SS escort why the old man did not walk by himself, Alter explained that his father was blind. The Nazi fired a shot, killing the blind man instantly, and then ordered Alter to run. Alter pretended not to hear the order, but he understood that the executioner's intention was to shoot him if he started running, so he continued to trail along.
>
> Thanks to generously distributed bribes, Alter then spent twenty-four hours in the *Umschlagplatz*. Sometimes, in return for a substantial bribe, one could avoid deportation on the appointed day, and receive, in addition, a lavish supper, but one was pushed onto the train the following day. . . .
>
> Alter was placed in a freight car loaded, as always, with at least one hundred people. The cars were fastened with wire but the train did not start up. The prisoners began to suffocate—the Germans had released gas. Owing to his formidable strength, Alter was able to reach the little window, and help his brother Mieczslaw get some fresh air. Meanwhile, in the cars, people groaned and howled, tearing their clothes; completely naked and suffocating, they fell on top of one another. The train started to move and was shunted onto more distant tracks, probably to prevent the cries of the sufferers from reaching the town.
>
> The train was surrounded by soldiers in uniforms like

the ones worn by the Ukrainians during the "resettlement action." Alter, who could speak neither Russian nor Ukrainian, started begging the sentry for a bit of snow. Finally, they reached an understanding, and for the price of 100 zlotys Alter received a bit of snow, handed to him on the tip of a bayonet. Seven such portions quenched Alter's thirst, and enabled him, in the moments when the Ukrainian turned away, to renew his efforts to tear the barbed wire from the window. Some time later, when he had finally succeeded, he felt somebody energetically shoving him away and shouting to the supposed Ukrainian, "Listen, Karl, don't you remember me?" A minute later they were into a lively conversation in German. Karl, the masquerading Ukrainian, expressed—in excellent German—his willingness not to impede the prisoners' escape in exchange for 10,000 zlotys.

The stranger took out 3,000 and turned to his co-prisoners, asking for the rest. The remaining 7,000 was finally given by Alter, because none of the others had cash; the total amount was tossed over to the soldier. The "Ukrainian" counted the money, put it away, and gave the signal to jump and the first to get out of the car was the soldier's acquaintance. Before he could reach the ground, he was shot by the Ukrainian and fell dead on the spot.

Shortly afterwards, the train started. The majority of the Jews in the freight car were already dying. Alter held on to the window desperately, standing on a pile of corpses. His brother Mieczyslaw was losing his remaining strength. To place him at the window for a breath of fresh air, Alter had to enlarge the macabre pyramid. For this purpose, he began pulling a corpse by the leg when he heard a moan; he bent over and recognized the novelist, Jarecka. A moment later, she breathed her last breath. Then, in terrible torment, his brother Mieczylaw died, too.

Even before the train gained speed, people began to jump

out of the freight car. However, in the vicinity of Warsaw, the tracks were closely guarded by gendarmes and Ukrainians, who finished off these bold ones on the spot. The gendarmes rode in the last car which was equipped with lights that illuminated the tracks, so that in the fading light they could see and shoot anyone who jumped from the train. Even so, attempts to escape were repeated from time to time.

Only past Wyszkow, when the train accelerated, did Alter pluck up the courage to jump out; he chose to jump as the train rounded a curve, reckoning to fall as near as possible to the track. That way the escorting gendarmes, even when they noticed him, did not have time to aim carefully. They shot three times but missed, and soon the train disappeared from sight.

Alter got up, and dragging his legs, swollen because of the gas, he reached the highway. Here he noticed another three refugees; he joined them, and in the darkness they consulted.

Suddenly, Alter caught sight of another figure approaching them. He thought he could discern the glitter of a helmet, and jumped into a nearby thicket. A moment later, he heard four revolver shots, and then nothing.

His return to the ghetto took two days.... Now he had come to take his wife and children out of the ghetto. I look at Alter's hands wounded by the wire of the freight car window; I see his legs swollen like pumpkins in reaction to the mysterious gas, and I wonder if and when those guilty of the bestiality and tragedy into which Europe has now sunk will ever pay the penalty for their villainous deeds.

ZUEHLKE, Mark

"What is done cannot be undone,
but one can prevent it from happening again."
—Anne Frank, May, 1944

NEVER MIND SIDNEY CROSBY'S GOLDEN OVERTIME GOAL. The greatest Canadian victory was the liberation of Holland. It has been estimated this campaign cost more than four billion dollars. More than 7,600 Canadians died in the campaign. The Dutch remain grateful.

Canada's liberation of western Holland and the crucial Scheldt Estuary was its bloodiest campaign in World War II. The blow-by-blow progress of Canadian forces was under-appreciated until Mark Zuehlke's *Terrible Victory: First Canadian Army and the Scheldt Estuary Campaign* (D&M 2007) extensively documented the 55-day, mud-soaked struggle of the First Canadian Army to open the Antwerp coast for Allied shipping in 1944.

In a companion volume, *On to Victory* (D&M 2010), Zuehlke further described the fiercely-fought and bittersweet military triumph in Holland. These books are part of his Canadian Battle Series about Canada's military operations in Europe. According to the Victoria-based historian, more than 17,000 Jewish men and women served in the Canadian forces during World War II.

In 2021, when this manuscript was completed, Reuben "Rube" Sinclair of Richmond, B.C. was almost certainly Canada's oldest World War II veteran at age 109. He was born on his family's farm in Lipton, Saskatchewan, near Fort Qu'appelle, 70 miles northeast of Regina, on December 5, 1911, according to a birth certificate, but family history contends he was born even earlier. According to a profile in the *Jewish Independent*, Lipton was one of many "colonies" created by Baron Maurice de Hirsch in Canada, Argentina and Palestine to resettle oppressed Jews from Europe.

Sinclair's father, Yitzok Sinclair (born Sandler), travelled from Ukraine, via Liverpool and arrived at Ellis Island January 4, 1905, on the S.S. *Ivernia*, before he went to Saskatchewan. According to the *Richmond News*, in WW II, Reuben Sinclair served in the Royal Canadian Air Force as a wireless electronics mechanic. He installed navigational equipment which allowed aircraft to take off and land in total darkness before the widespread usage of radar. When radar came, Sinclair helped retrofit the planes. He did not serve overseas.

Shortly after the war, he moved his family to the Lower Mainland to run a service station, called Sinclair Bros. Garage and Auto Wrecking in east Richmond, with one of his younger brothers, Joe. Due to migraine headaches, he moved with his wife Ida to the drier climate of California in 1964. When he became successful in the furniture business in Los Angeles, he and Ida raised more than a million dollars for City of Hope, a cancer hospital and research facility. Both were active members of Schara Tzedeck Synagogue. Ida died in 1996, two years after they moved back to Richmond. At age 104, Reuben was still managing for himself in their apartment in Richmond.

CANADA'S TROOPS were involved in the liberation of three camps: Westerbork Transit Camp and Hertogenbosch Concentration Camp (known also as Vught) in the Netherlands and Bergen-Belsen in Germany. The widely-acknowledged Canadian involvement in the latter consisted of medical teams rushed to the camp to provide urgent care.

In *On to Victory*, Mark Zuehlke details the lesser-known Canadian liberation of Westerbork. On April 12, 1945, the armoured cars of 2nd Infantry Division's reconnaissance regiment—the 14th Canadian Hussars—were operating in northeastern Holland when they rolled up to the gates of Westerbork Transit Camp. Established by the Dutch in 1939 to intern Jewish refugees mainly from Germany, it was kept in service after the German invasion in May 1940. The camp served as a collection point through which almost 100,000 of the 120,000 Dutch Jews sent to the death camps in German-occupied Poland passed.

MARK ZUEHLKE PHOTO

Forced aboard a cattle car at Westerbork in the Netherlands on September 3, 1944, Anne Frank was transported to Auschwitz-Birkenau and later died at Bergen-Belsen. "What is done cannot be undone, but one can prevent it from happening again." — Anne Frank, May, 1944.

When the Canadian troops arrived at Westerbork, the camp population stood at 876. The guards had fled and the Jews were "delirious with joy" at being liberated. By evening, divisional medical teams and Provost police were on the scene to provide humanitarian relief. The following Sunday, the army's Senior Jewish Chaplain Sam Cass conducted a service. Writing his wife, Cass described the service as "the final evidence of their liberation" and that it "may be one of the most dramatic memories I shall bring back from the experiences of this war."

As of 2020, Mark Zuehlke had written 21 books about World War II. As a historian with Liberation Tours, a company that brings groups of Canadians to Westerbork as part of pilgrimages through the World War I and II battlefields, memorials, and cemeteries, he revisits the

Canada's oldest World War II veteran, Ruben "Rube" Sinclair in Richmond, at age 109, in 2021.

MARK ZUEHLKE PHOTO

At Westerbork, steel rails (at right) have been bent upward to symbolize that no train can ever again follow the route that led to the death camps.

camp almost every year. "The experience of introducing people to the story of the camp is always a grim highlight of each tour," he says. "Westerbork is a place that instills dramatic memories for most who visit it. Today, it survives as a museum and memorial to the memory of those who were held there until being loaded on railway cars for a final journey to their deaths."

One of the transits from Westerbork to the murder camp at Sobibor in Poland consisted of 1,400 children, age four to eight, sent alone to die without their parents. In 2021, after ten years of archeological excavations at Sobibor, Yoram Haimi from the Israel Antiquities Authority, assisted by Polish and Dutch associates, was part of a team that uncovered personal identity tags for four Jewish children from Amsterdam. These name tags were almost certainly prepared by their parents who were hoping their children could survive and possibly be re-connected with relatives.

"As far as we know," said Haimi, "identity tags with children's names have only been found at Sobibor." The name tags identified six-year-old Lea Judith De La Penha of Amsterdam, born on May 11,

1937, as well as Deddie Zak, Annie Kapper and David Juda Van der Velde. Archaeologists at Sobibor contacted staff at the Herinneringscentrum Kamp Westerbork visitors' site who responded almost immediately by email. "We received photos of smiling young children." said Haimi. "I looked at the photos and asked myself, how could anyone have been so cruel."

Of the 120,000 Jews from the Netherlands sent to Poland, according to Zuehlke, only 16,000 survived. In addition to the Jews, about 7,000 Sinti and Roma peoples were arrested in Holland and shipped to their deaths through Westerbork. "Near the centre of the camp where the prisoners assembled for roll calls, a large, tightly-arrayed collection of small red clay stones stand—one for each person who passed through the camp's gates. Nearby, a section of railway ends with the steel rails torn up and bent into a near circle to symbolize that no train can ever again follow the route that led to the death camps."

Inside the visitor centre/museum there is also a simple black-and-white photo of someone easily recognizable. It is a haunting image of Anne Frank, seeming so full of life and potential. She and her family had gone into hiding inside a secret annex at her father's business premises on July 6, 1942. They remained hidden until being arrested in a police raid on August 4, 1944. Taken to Westerbork, the Frank family were among 1,000 Jews loaded into cattle cars on September 3, 1944, and transported to Auschwitz-Birkenau.

"Anne and her sister, Margot, were subsequently transferred to Bergen-Belsen where they both contracted typhus and died as a result in February or March of 1945," says Zuehlke.

"The train that carried them from Westerbork was the last to rumble out of the camp's gates. Allied bombing soon after destroyed most of the rail system connecting Holland to Germany, leaving the Germans with no means for further deportations. Not that it mattered, hardly any more Jews remained. Looking, though, at her photo in the visitor centre—as I have done on numerous visits to the camp and will do so again—it's hard not to feel an ache in the heart.

"Had Anne missed that train, she would have undoubtedly survived the war. What would her life have been?

"Every time I look at that photo, I think of this and realize the same question should be asked for every person who went through the camp to a grim death.

"Indeed, it is a question that needs to be asked for all of those who perished in the Holocaust and even in a World War that took millions of lives."

ALAN TWIGG PHOTO

Anne Frank plaque on memorial wall at Jewish cemetery in Frankfurt, where she was born.

With essential support from Canadian donors, New York-raised Rabbi Marvin Hier from Vancouver was able to establish the essential Simon Wiesenthal Center's Museum of Tolerance in Los Angeles that opened its doors in 1993. The Vancouver Holocaust Education Center, spearheaded by Robert Krell, opened its doors in 1994, after its foundational society was formed in 1983.

PART THREE

Also Singing

BIDDISCOMBE, Perry

UVic historian Perry Biddiscombe has examined the vengeful Nazi terrorist movement that flourished from 1944 to 1946 in *Werwolf!* (University of Toronto Press, 1988). It was a corps of mostly drafted German young and elderly would-be resistance fighters in the last months of the war. Biddiscombe also published *The Last Nazis* (Tempus Club 2000). Consult ABCBookWorld.

BOEHM, Heige

Heige Boehm's debut novel for young adults, *Secrets in the Shadows* (Ronsdale 2019), concerns two boys growing up in Nazi Germany who think life is an adventure until they have to fight on the frontlines and are confronted by the reality of Hitler's propaganda and anti-Semitism. Consult ABCBookWorld.

CAMPBELL, Olga

After listening to a radio program about second generation Holocaust survivors, Olga Campbell started to explore and confront feelings of loss and grief by creating a solo, multimedia exhibition in 2005 combining prose, art and poetry. All members of her mother's family had been murdered in the Shoah but no details had ever emerged. For an exhibition called *Whispers Across Time*, she began imagining her family's story as best she could as an alternative to knowing nothing. Her exploratory journey into the inner darkness of the Holocaust and her repressed sorrow resulted in her self-published book of the same name, *A Whisper Across Time* (Jubaji Press 2018). While evoking one family's experience of the Holocaust as an inadvertent legacy of trauma, *A Whisper Across Time* led to an exhibit and book launch in November of 2018 at the Gertrude and Sidney Zack Gallery in conjunction with the Jewish Book Festival at the Jewish Community Centre in Vancouver. As a multi-dimensional reflection of family losses and inter-generational trauma, it eventually received the Kahn Family Foundation Prize for Holocaust Literature at the Western Canada Jewish Book Awards in 2020. The work has been cited as a healing ritual, a shamanic soul retrieval and a celebration of life. While this is clearly a story of remembering and healing, it is also a cautionary tale asking the reader to look at what is happening in the world today. If it happened before, it could happen again.

EDUGYAN, Esi

Esi Edugyan's second novel, *Half-Blood Blues* (Serpent's Tail 2011) is about an inter-racial jazz band in Nazi Berlin in the late 1930s. There's a brilliant, black trumpet player, Hieronymus "Hiero" Falk, as well as two African American musicians, jazz drummer Chip Jones and Sidney "Sid" Griffiths, a journeyman bassist who can pass for white and uses a distinctive German-American slang as a narrator. In an era when the Nazis were concocting their fallacy of a master race, the marginal acceptability of being black is increasingly jeopardized by increasingly repressive Nazi ideology. Hiero is denigrated as a *mischlinge*. When they learn that Goering is proceeding to sterilize mixed-race children, all three escape to Paris in 1939, but after Paris falls in 1940, Hiero Falk, a German citizen at age twenty, is arrested and never heard from again, seemingly another victim of one of the concentration camps. Sid, in his eighties, returns to Berlin in 1992 and begins to learn more about his friend's fate. When he learns Hier might be alive in Poland, he and Chip go on a quest to find their long-lost band mate. The novel gained global interest when it was shortlisted for the Man Booker Prize in 2011 and also received the Scotiabank Giller Prize in Canada. Although it can be cited as a Holocaust novel, it contains little content regarding the persecution and mass-slaughter of Jews.

DIXON, Jack

Based on interviews, Jack Dixon's *The Barn* (Friesen Press 2015) describes the ordeals and bravery of the Mollens, a family of nine in Arnhem, Holland, after their country was overrun in 1940. They took refuge in an empty barn for the remaining eight months of the war, surviving on turnips, beets and acorns, emboldened by BBC news via a secret radio hooked up to a Gestapo power line. Consult ABC-BookWorld.com

DRZEWIECKI, Mary A.

Polish Catholics were also interned in Auschwitz and Dachau. In her illustrated, 347-page family memoir of war-torn Poland, *Born and Raised Under a Straw Roof: A True Legacy of the Human Spirit* (Hignell Printing 2001), Mary Anna Drzewiecki pays tribute to the lives of her parents Sylwester Drzewiecki and Janina Horoszkiewicz (1926–2020) who survived persecution in Germany prior to immigration to Vancouver Island in 1949, settling in Cedar, near Nanaimo. The mayor of Warsaw, Piotr Drzewiecki (1865–1943), was arrested by the Nazis and died in prison in Berlin.

GERBER, Jean Miriam

Born in 1940, Vancouver-based Jean Gerber is not a JBB—a Jew by birth. She is a JBC—a Jew by choice. She has been a mainstay of Jewish Canadian journalism, via *Canadian Jewish News*, ever since she read the transcripts of the Nuremberg trials for a professor at Penn State and realized she had never been taught about the Holocaust in all her years of schooling. For 27 years, she contributed more than 300 columns to the CJN. After earning a B.A. in History at Penn State in 1961, and an M.A. in English from SFU in 1969, she received an M.A. in history from UBC in 1989 based on experiences of nearly 400 survivors of the Holocaust who came to the city. It was released as *Immigration and integration in post-war Canada: a case study of Holocaust survivors in Vancouver, 1947–1970.*

HIER, Rabbi Marvin

As the only rabbi who is also a member of the Motion Pictures Arts and Sciences, ex-Vancouverite Rabbi Marvin Hier has rubbed shoulders with the likes of Tom Cruise, Marlon Brando, Michael Douglas, Billy Crystal and Frank Sinatra; friendships described in his memoir, *Meant to Be* (Toby Press 2016). Born in 1939 in New York City, Hier was told, at age twelve, by his rabbi, "Every bar mitzvah boy has an opportunity to make up for what the Nazis took from us." Buoyed by substantial financial support from Vancouver businessmen Samuel and William Belzberg, and Toronto businessman Joseph Tannenbaum, Rabbi Hier was empowered to leave Vancouver's Congregation Schara Tzedeck after fifteen years as its spiritual leader, doubling as Hillel director at UBC, and create the Simon Wiesenthal Center (opened in 1977) and the eight-storey Museum of Tolerance (opened in 1993), both in Los Angeles. Twice named the Most Influential Rabbi in America by *Newsweek*, he was photographed in the Oval Office with President Ronald Reagan and Simon Wiesenthal and Samuel Belzberg in 1984 and he became the first Orthodox rabbi to give a benediction at the inauguration of an American president when he accepted an invitation to bless the new presidency of Donald J. Trump in 2016. Rabbi Hier subsequently participated in fundraising activities for Trump's re-election campaign. Four times larger than Yad Vashem, Hier's 185,000 square-foot Museum of Tolerance in Jerusalem, complete with a Conference Center, remained in the planning stages for more than two decades, mired in court challenges. Hier also founded Moriah Films. As a co-producer, he received

Academy Awards for the documentaries *Genocide* in 1981, narrated by Elizabeth Taylor and Orson Welles, and *The Long Way Home* in 1997, narrated by Morgan Freeman. Hier is also credited with co-producing and writing a documentary on European Jewish life before the Holocaust, *Echoes That Remain* (1990), as well as *Liberation* (1994). Well-known in Hollywood circles, he is cited as a consultant for Stephen Spielberg's *Schindler's List* and the ABC mini-series *War and Remembrance* based on Herman Wouk's novel.

KAELLIS, Eugene

Among Eugene Kaellis' many self-published books is *Making Jews* (Lulu 2008), a novel in which a medical doctor, Aaron Velinsky, believes the future of world Jewry is in danger of extinction, largely due to assimilation and declining birth rates. Despite Rabbinic opposition, the doctor launches The Return Movement to convert non-Jews to Judaism. The Return Movement he starts appears largely successful but a shocking event leaves him disconsolate and convinced his efforts were mistaken. Davida, the young, dynamic leader of the Movement, challenges his despair and vows to continue the struggle. Consult ABCBookWorld.com

KAPLINSKI, Solly

Solly Kaplinski's parents spent several years with the Bielski partisans in the Naliboki forest in Western Belarus engaged in rescue, resistance and sabotage missions. In 1947, they immigrated to South Africa where Solly was raised. He was kept largely ignorant of how his father, a doctor, and his mother had survived the Shoah until 1965 when his father was called to give evidence at a trial in Germany. "Until then, we lived in denial," he has said. "My brother and I were largely unaware of what they were experiencing." Kaplinski's parents died within six months of each other, prompting his visit to Poland in 1988, as part of the March of the Living, to connect with his roots. He visited the forest in Belarus where his parents had survived for two years. A former Head of Vancouver Talmud Torah Day School,

Kaplinski has published two books related to the Holocaust: *A World of Pains: A Redemptive Parable?* and *Lost and Found: A Second Generation Response to the Holocaust*. The latter is a collection of poetry dedicated to his late parents. In 2000, Kaplinski and his wife emigrated from Vancouver to Jerusalem where he became Director of the International Relations English Desk at Yad Vashem, then Executive Director of Overseas Joint Ventures at the American Jewish Joint Distribution Committee. Consult ABCBookWorld.

KARSAI, Andrew

Born in Slovakia to Jewish parents in 1942, Andrew (Andrej) Karsai grew up in Czechoslovakia after he and his sister were rescued by a Christian family in 1944. He immigrated to Canada in 1968 to escape the Communist regime. With memories of Slovakia and the Holocaust, his 60 poems arise from immigrant experiences in *Random Convergences* (Self-published 2011). The accompanying illustrations are by Vancouver-born Janet Lee whose parents emigrated from Shanghai in 1948. The pair appeared at the Jewish Book Festival in 2011 with cellist Lei Hui Hua and guitarist David Yeung.

KEMENY, Robert L.

Self-published as a lavish coffee table book, *My Life* (2016) is noteworthy for its high-quality photo reproductions of Hungarian life and Nazi militarism from Getty Images. Kemeny wore a yellow star and was sheltered for three days in a Jewish orphanage. His parents bribed their way out of the camps near Budapest but no details are provided. They changed their surname from Krausz to Kemeny at the end of the war. Born in Hungary in 1935, Kemeny had an uncle who became involved in copper mining in Chile in the 1950s. While in his thirties, Kemeny, London-educated, gained power and prestige in the mining industry of Chile in the following decade. He became a Chilean citizen in 1965 but left Chile for Spain in 1970 in response to the socialism of Salvador Allende. He brought his family to Vancouver in 1974.

LAMMERS, John

John Lammers' self-published autobiography, *A Castle on the Frontier: An Immigrant's Life Journey from Holland to the Yukon, 1921–1987* (Gray Jay Publications 2004), recalls the Nazi invasion of Holland followed by 35 years in the Yukon. Consult ABCBookWorld.

MARTIN, Nikolaus

Nikolaus Claude Martin's self-published memoir *Prague Winter* (Trafford 2002) recalls the terror of the Nazi occupation of Prague and his captivity in the Small Fortress of Terezin (Theresienstadt), a political prison administered by the Prague Gestapo. Consult ABCBookWorld.

MATAS, Carol

Carol Matas' novel set in Seattle and Vancouver, *The Whirlwind* (Orca,2007), describes severe prejudice against German Jewish refugees and immigrants in North America during World War II. Published by Orca Books in Victoria, *The Whirlwind* follows the plight of fifteen-year-old Benjamin Friedman who has escaped from Nazi Germany in 1941. Among Matas' twelve books for young readers about the Holocaust, *Daniel's Story* concerns Kristallnacht and, in *Lisa's War,* a Jewish girl, age twelve, fights back after the Germans have invaded Denmark in 1940. Consult ABCBookWorld.com for extensive information.

MENKIS, Richard

To boycott or not to boycott? Richard Menkis' co-written *More than Just Games* (University of Toronto 2015) explores Canada's participation in the controversial, pre-Holocaust 1936 Olympics in Berlin. At a closed-door meeting, self-interested Canadian Olympic representatives decided Canadian athletes would attend. A noteworthy critic of participation in Hitler's showcase was Matthew Halton of the *Toronto Daily Star*. Meanwhile, Prime Minister Mackenzie King pronounced Hitler to be, "a man of deep sincerity and a genuine patriot." This is easily one of the most significant works of the pre-Holocaust period from a B.C. author. An associate professor of History and Religious Studies at UBC, Menkis has been a co-editor of the *Canadian Jewish Studies Reader* and an integral VHEC advisor. See ABCBookWorld.

MIDDELMANN, Robert

Robert Middelmann of Squamish presents himself as a middle man. In his self-published memoir, *Fearless: A Jewish Boy in Nazi Germany* (2019), he claims, as a half-Jew, that he was forced to live by his wits ever since Hitler came to power, surviving amid a maze of double standards and deceits. Nobody can prove it was so or not so. He says he can still remember the lyrics and melodies for the hate-filled songs he was forced to sing in the Hitler Youth movement. *When the Jewish blood runs off our swords / things are going twice as good.* Some skepticism will be automatic if someone who wore a Nazi uniform claims he was forced to do so in order to survive. But American academic Bryan Rigg has interviewed hundreds of Jews or alleged half-Jews who fought for the Nazis. "Thousands of men of Jewish descent and hundreds of what the Nazis called 'full Jews' served in the military with Hitler's knowledge," Rigg writes. Mixed-race Germans were often classified as *mischlinge*, a derogatory term implying mongrel or hybrid or "half-breed" status. Robert Middlemann was born in the Ruhr Valley, in Herne, Germany, on July 10, 1927. Consult ABC-BookWorld for a lengthy review.

MILMAN, Isa

In 2021, Isa Milman published a memoir about her investigation into the lives of Jewish twin sisters who grew up in interwar Poland, *Afterlight: In Search of Poetry, History, and Home* (Heritage House 2021). The two women are Milman's mother, Sabina, who survived the Holocaust, and her mother's twin, Basia—who did not. Milman describes her fears and fascination as she traversed modern-day Poland and Ukraine, the lands of her ancestors, looking for Basia's vanished poems that were published when Basia was aged fourteen. As Milman delves into the complexities of what cultures choose to remember and what they erase, she visits places where her relatives had been, including where her aunt Basia and her own paternal grandmother Yalena were killed in Polish-held Ukraine.

"The last of Kostopol's Jews were murdered in Kostopol forest on August 25, 1942. Five thousand Jews in all, from neighbouring farms as well, were brought to the forest where huge pits had been dug. After they'd been forced to undress, they were lined up in rows, facing the pit, mounting with bodies of their friends and family, and shot in the back of the head or neck. Among them were Basia Kramer Fishman and Yelena Bebczuik Kramer, and the entire extended Bebczuk and Kramer families. The earth trembled for three days after as those still alive slowly suffocated beneath the weight of their dead....

"My mother [Sabina] rarely told the particulars of this horror, but I've known it as long as I've had consciousness, in one form or another. How could she speak of this to her children—that human beings have the capacity to reduce other human beings to garbage, to torture and kill and feel nothing of the pain? From the moment of learning the truth, sorrow raged through my mother's bones and lived in her marrow for the rest of her long life."

The poet Don McKay has described *Afterlight* as "a telling reminder that atrocity thrives in the dark and must be unearthed, whatever the anguish, in order to be overcome."

Born a displaced person in Germany in 1949, Victoria-based Isa Milman grew up in the United States and came to Canada in 1975. She is a graduate of Tufts University and holds a Masters of Rehabilitation Science from McGill, where she taught for a decade. Her first three poetry books all won the Canadian Jewish Book Award for Poetry. *Prairie Kaddish* in 2008 was inspired by the Ashkenazi Jews who migrated to the Canadian prairies near the turn of the 20th century, fleeing persecution about fifty years before the Nazis came to power. To cite this far lesser-known genocide, when thousands of Jews were being murdered in Eastern Europe in the late 19th century, one her poems titled "A Few Restrictions Regarding the Jews of Romania, 1885-1900" lists restrictions forbidding Jews to be peddlers, forbidding Jews from attending elementary schools, barring them from professions such as practicing medicine, or from being a patient in a hospital, or from owning a business or property. This collection was inspired by an epiphany Milman had in the Lipton Hebrew Cemetery in Saskatchewan where she realized she belonged in "the great tapestry of Jewish suffering and regeneration."

PÁL, George L.

Within the first half of the 20th century, while growing up in Mukachevo in the Carpathian Rus, a city now in Ukraine, George L. Pál variously lived under the rule of Czechoslovakia, Hungary, Germany and Russia. As he noted wryly, "At the age of seventeen, I had already had in several different countries, without ever having left town!" George L. Pál's self-published memoir *Prisoners of Hope: Rising from the Ashes of the Holocaust: An Eyewitness Account of Life in the Auschwitz Extermination Camp and Two Slave Labour Camps (1944-1945)* describes his internment in two Nazi camps, including Kittlitztreben, and his arrival at Auschwitz, in May of 1944, as Prisoner #42821.

The cover of *Prisoners of Hope* shows a photo of seventeen-year-old George, standing among a group of newly-arrived Auschwitz prisoners (at the far right of the image), looking straight ahead. Eventually, he would be liberated by the Russian army. His father (Victor), his grandfather (Leopold Neuman), and his Uncle Moric died during the Holocaust but Pál was reunited with his mother and sister in Mukachevo before he moved to Budapest. He graduated with a Masters degree in Engineering from the Technical University of Budapest in 1955. As a married engineer with two children, Tom (1951-2006) and Judi (b. 1954), Pál took his family to Austria from where he eventually found asylum in Canada. Pál soon learned English; he was already conversant in Czech, German, Hungarian and Hebrew and he had a smattering of Russian. He became Dean of Engineering at Mohawk College in Hamilton, Ontario in 1962. In 2006, to be closer to

JUDI PAL-LAKE PHOTO

George L. Pal

his daughter, he moved to Victoria where for ten years he shared his stories with students in Holocaust studies courses taught by UVic's Helga Thorson. An earlier version of his memoir was entitled *From Whistle to Smoke.*

As Sam Margolis has reported, in 2019, Pál began working with Vancouver editor Lisa Ferdman, who has also edited Silvia Foti's *The Nazi's Granddaughter: How I Discovered My Grandfather Was a War Criminal.* In one of his later chapters, Pál states: "I have often been asked, 'Do you hate the Germans?' My emphatic answer is always, 'No! If I were to blame the entire German people for everything that happened to me, my family and all those who did not survive, I would be making the same mistake that the Nazis made in blaming the Jews for all of Germany's woes.' Such generalizing, or demonizing, is dangerous." Pál died in 2021 at age 94. "Having survived one of the most monstrous events in human history," Pál wrote, "I believe that it is my duty to testify. This is crucial especially because Nazi sympathizers and followers continue to exist throughout the world."

PENN, Ian

In 2011, the Vancouver Holocaust Education Centre hosted Ian Penn's first solo exhibition, *Projections: A Monument to Personal Memory* that resulted in a book/catalogue issued with the same title. Consult ABCBookWorld.

RAVVIN, Norman

Norman Ravvin's inter-generational novel *The Girl Who Stole Everything* (Linda Leith 2019) connects an abandoned Jewish cemetery near the Polish village of Radzanow with Vancouver's Downtown Eastside, contrasting pre-war Polish shetl life and Jewish lives today. In Poland, a house stands empty on a village square for seventy years after its owners were killed. An unsolved murder in Vancouver must also be unravelled. Consult ABCBookWorld.

ROTBERG, Howard

Howard Rotberg's novel *Second Generation Radical: The Struggle Against the Second Holocaust* (Mantua Books 2003) concerns a Canadian professor who writes a book about Israel during the suicide bombings of the Second Intifada. It is an outgrowth of Rotberg's conviction that Jews must be vigilant to ensure there is never another Holocaust, hence they must remain wary of Islamic terrorists and the possibility of an Iranian nuclear bomb. Self-described as the son of a survivor of Auschwitz "whose parents' and sister's mere Jewishness proved their crimes against the Third Reich and justified their death in the gas chambers," Howard Rotberg was born in 1951 in Brantford, Ontario, received degrees in History and Law from University of Toronto. He came to live in B.C. in 2005. See extensive information in ABCBookWorld.

SEROTA, Phyllis

Born into a Jewish family in Chicago in the year of Kristallnacht, in 1938, Phyllis Serota first learned about the Holocaust from a book at age thirteen. Her family had kept silent. It wasn't until 1997 that the Victoria-based painter began to overtly be influenced by the Holocaust in her artwork. Immersing herself in written and visual documentation of the Holocaust, she began to be inspired by photographic imagery to lend "a sense of truthfulness" to her artworks. The following year, her exhibit, *Order And Chaos: The Holocaust Paintings of Phyllis Serota*, was presented at the Jewish Community Centre in Vancouver. Serota later published *Painting My Life: A Memoir of Love, Art and Transformation* (Sono Nis 2011) with art about her Chicago childhood, family violence, police brutality and echoes of the Holocaust.

UPTON, Colin

Commissioned by the Vancouver Holocaust Education Centre, Colin Upton's limited edition, 24-page comic book *Kicking at the Darkness* (2016) depicts Canadian soldiers liberating the Bergen-Belsen concentration camp. "When I look at Donald Trump, and the conspiracy theories I see on the Internet," said Upton, "it's very depressing but necessary that we have to tell these stories again and try to convince people that these things actually did happen." Research and writing for the VHEC's accompanying exhibit, Canada Responds to the Holocaust, 1944–1945 exhibit, afforded first-person perspectives from soldiers, survivors, aid workers and chaplains. Under the direction of Richard Menkis and Ronnie Tessler, it was touted as "the first major project of its kind, examining the encounters between Canadians and survivors of the Holocaust and the evidence of Nazi crimes at the end of the Second World War and its immediate aftermath."

Kicking at the Darkness (Vancouver Holocaust Education Centre, 2016)

WINDLEY, Carol

As is made clear in Carol Windley's fourth novel, *Midnight Train to Prague* (HarperCollins 2020), one of the many unmeasured costs of the Holocaust is the pain of being separated from loved ones compounded by the anguish of not knowing if your loved one is alive or dead. Born in 1910 with an English mother and a German father, Natalia Faber travels with her mother from Berlin to Prague in 1927, only to be delayed in Switzerland where she learns family secrets. In Hungary, she meets her future husband, a journalist named Count Miklos Andorjan, who will be accused of being a Communist. When World War II begins, Natalia loses contact with Miklos and hopes to reunite with him in Nazi-occupied Prague where she sets up shop as a fortune teller. But who can really foretell the future in such times? She is accused of spying and sent to "a camp for women, not far from Berlin" where she is classified as a political prisoner and wears a red triangle on her sleeve. At war's end she is reunited with her Jewish friend, Anna, who had expected to be sent to Theresienstadt but instead was one of countless Czech girls who were sent to be a domestic servant for German families. Slav girls "had what the Nazis called Aryan racial characteristics to behave and think like true Germans."

WILSON, Robert

As recorded in a *New York Times* article in 1983, Robert Wilson, a self-described former jewel thief and safe-cracker from Vancouver, at age fifty, went to Bolivia to steal gems in 1971 and became acquainted with Bolivian government ministers and the Nazi war criminal Klaus Barbie, the notorious Butcher of Lyon. Robert George Wilson claimed he subsequently based *The Confessions of Klaus Barbie* (Pulp Press 1984) on his taped interviews with Barbie as well as his access to Barbie's personal scrapbook and correspondence. Wilson reported that Barbie had thrived in Bolivia for thirty years due to CIA protection. Born in the village of Bad Godesberg in 1913, Barbie joined the sister organization of the SS Security Service, the Sicherheitsdienst, in 1935, and he became a Nazi party member in 1937, serving under Himmler, head of the SS and the Gestapo. Posted to Amsterdam, Barbie's duty was to locate and apprehend Jews and members of the Resistance in hiding for the Gestapo. In 1942, Barbie was sent to Dijon, in eastern France. Transferred to Lyon a year later, he personally interrogated and tortured his victims at his infamous Hotel Terminus headquarters. His sadism and perversion included electric shocks and sexual abuse. Barbie was known to have skinned a man alive before immersing his head in a bucket of ammonia. As head of the Fourth Section of the Gestapo, he sent 44 Jewish children from a nearby orphanage to Auschwitz and was responsible for the torture and death of Jean Moulin, the highest-ranking member of the French Resistance ever captured by the Nazis. Allegedly responsible for the deaths of more than 26,000 people, Barbie was a sadist who received the First Class Iron Cross with Swords from Hitler, in person. American intelligence agents reputedly protected Barbie after World War II, from 1945 to 1955, due to his "police skills," even though Barbie had been convicted of war crimes in abstentia and accorded the death penalty. When the French government demanded Barbie be sent to trial, it is possible the Americans did not cooperate because a trial could reveal he had worked for them. In 1965, Barbie worked in the West German Foreign Intelligence Service under the code name Adler. Evidence exists of him receiving a monthly salary of 500 Deutsch Marks and making at least 35 reports to BND headquarters. The U.S. helped Barbie to escape to Bolivia where he became Klaus Altmann. Barbie and his family gained citizenship in Bolivia in 1957. There he allegedly prospered as an interrogator and torturer for dictatorships in Bolivia and Peru, even after he was identified by Nazi hunters. With connections to the CIA, it is possible that Barbie was one of the key figures in the successful capture and execution of Ernesto Che Guevara, the Argentinian-born Cuban revolutionary who was murdered in Bolivia in 1967. When a politically moderate regime was finally elected in Bolivia in 1983, Barbie was left unprotected. Deported to France, he was tried in Lyon in 1987. Like the Eichmann trial in Israel, the trial was filmed for historical purposes.

Although 730 witnesses testified to his crimes, he adamantly refused to confess. He was sentenced to life imprisonment in Lyon and died there in 1991 from leukemia and spine and prostate cancer. According to the book's publishers in Vancouver, taped evidence provided by Wilson to the *New York Times* directly led to the Ryan Commission investigations that resulted in a formal American apology to France.

[Other B.C. books related to the Holocaust include *Stand in Hell* by Dennis Bolen, *Felice: A Travelogue* by Robert Harlow, *Finding Home: A War Child's Journey to Peace* by Frank Oberle and *Singing From the Darktime: A Childhood Memoir in Poetry and Prose* by S. Weilbach. *Killing Me Off: The Many Lives of Rubin Thau* (as told by his son Isaac Thau) was privately published in 2021. Forthcoming works include Ron Burnett's work of fiction, *The Lost Painter*, centred on the relationship between art, creativity and trauma, and Mariette Doduck's memoir, co-written with Lauren Faulkner Rossi, describing her survival in Belgium as the youngest of eleven children.]

PART FOUR

One Doctor, Two Rabbis

FEW PEOPLE IN THE 21st century know the Nazis and their allies established more than 33,000 camps, ghettos and other sites for the detention, persecution, forced labour and mass murder of Jews, according to the *U.S. Holocaust Memorial Museum Encyclopedia of Camps and Ghettos, 1933–1945*, edited by Geoffrey P. Megargee

That's because few people in the 20th century knew it either.

The Nazi concentration camp most people can name is Auschwitz, also spelled Auschwitcz. It is a rare person in the 21st century who can list—or recognize—the names of the 22 other designated killing grounds where millions lost their lives. Twenty of these murder factories had significant subcamps (most notoriously Birkenau as an extension of Auschwitz). Arbeitsdorf, Niederhagen and Warsaw were the 'stand alone' exceptions.

Jews were murdered in a variety of ways, among them gassing, shooting, burning, drowning or burial alive, exhaustion through forced labor, starvation, epidemic diseases, deprivation of medical care and minimal hygienic conditions, and more. Some Jews took their own lives in order to escape arrest and further persecution, or to end their relentless suffering.

An estimated 15,000 labour, death and concentration camps were established by Nazi Germany from 1939 to 1945 (based in the information compiled in *Le Livre des Camps* (1979) by Ludo Van Eck, *Perpetrators Victims Bystanders: The Jewish Catastrophe 1933-1945* (1992) by Raul Hilberg and *Atlas of the Holocaust* (1993) by Sir Martin Gilbert.

1. Arbeitsdorf
2. Bergen-Belsen
3. Buchenwald
4. Dachau
5. Flossenburg
6. Gross-Rosen
7. Hertogenbosch
8. Hinzert
9. Kaiserwald
10. Kauen
11. Krakow-Plaszow
12. Majdanek
13. Mauthausen
14. Mittelbau-Dora
15. Natzweiler-Struthof
16. Neuengamme
17. Niederhagen
18. Ravensbruck
19. Sachsenhausen
20. Stutthof
21. Vaivara
22. Warsaw
23. Klooga
24. Rumbula Rorest
25. Ponary
26. Westerbork
27. Treblinka
28. Chelmno
29. Sobibor
30. Starachowice
31. Drancy
32. Belzec
33. Auschwitcz-Birkenau
34. Janowska
35. Theresienstadt
36. Babi Yar

Somewhere in Germany

Dr. Tom Perry

DR. THOMAS L. PERRY was born in Asheville, North Carolina in 1916. Growing up in the "Jim Crow" American South, his own observations of daily life for African Americans led to a strong and permanent antipathy to racism and injustice. He was educated at Harvard University and Oxford (as a Rhodes Scholar), and graduated from Harvard Medical School in 1942. In 1941 he married Claire Lippman, whom some of his family initially rejected because of her Jewish heritage.

During World War II Dr. Perry served with the US Army Medical Corps within the 174th Medical Battalion under General George Patton. Nine days after the Americans liberated the Buchenwald Concentration Camp, Dr. Perry took a series of rarely-seen photos that his widow Claire Perry donated to the Vancouver Holocaust Education Centre in 1994 along with a five-page letter he wrote to her from "somewhere in Germany," describing his feelings and impressions of Buchenwald.

After the war, Dr. Perry trained in pediatrics in New York City, soon moving to Los Angeles to work at the Los Angeles Children's Hospital and University of Southern California Medical School. He witnessed the transformation of universally fatal diseases like tuberculous meningitis through the "miracle drug" streptomycin. Dr. Perry's activism on behalf of African American physicians who were not allowed to join the hospital staff, and his forceful opposition to atmospheric testing of nuclear weapons led to a summons to testify before the House Committee on UnAmerican Activities, notorious during the "McCarthyism" witchhunt of the 1950's. Dr. Perry's refusal to collaborate with the witch hunt cost him his hospital privileges and university appointment and research grants, but he maintained his private practice as an extremely popular pediatrician to children of both the Hollywood elite and of poor black people in Los Angeles. Later, the Nobel Chemistry and Peace Prize winner Professor Linus Pauling invited Dr. Perry to work in his laboratory at the California Institute of Technology, studying inborn errors of metabolism.

In 1962, Dr. Perry seized an opportunity to move to Vancouver for a professorship in the UBC Department of Pharmacology & Therapeutics. He won Medical Research Council grants right up to his death at age 74, becoming an international authority on inborn errors of metabolism in children and on the biochemical changes occuring in the brains of people with Huntington's chorea and other neurodegenerative diseases. After gaining Canadian citizenship in 1970, Dr. Perry became increasingly active in the movement against the Vietnam War and the proliferation of nuclear weapons. He edited *End the Arms Race: Fund Human Needs* (Gordon Soules 1987), based on the 1986 Vancouver Centennial Peace and Disarmament Symposium, and *Peacemaking in the 1990's: A Guide for Canadians* (Gordon Soules 1991). Dr. Perry was a co-founder of the B.C. Chapter of Canadian Physicians for the Prevention of Nuclear War and a member of Veterans Against Nuclear Arms. Along with thousands of other physicians, he shared the Nobel Peace Prize awarded to the International Physicians for Prevention of Nuclear War in 1985, and received the B.C.'s Citizen Peace Award shortly before his death at age seventy-four in 1991.

Dr. Perry's 1945 eyewitness reportage from Buchenwald in his letter home to his wife, Claire, and his unsanctioned, personal photographs of the concentration camp have not been published previously.

"Typhus and dysentery easily spread at Buchenwald. Six prisoners were required to sleep in each compartment in the barracks. Living quarters, April 1945." Photograph by Tom Perry Sr., Tom Perry collection, item 93.08.0095. Vancouver Holocaust Education Centre. https://collections.vhec.org/Detail/objects/4614. Reproduced with permission.

Somewhere in Germany,
20 April 1945

Darling Claire:

I want to write you tonight about one of the most moving experiences I have ever had, as well as of the most horrible thing I have ever seen. Something that has cemented my anti-Fascist convictions more solidly than xxxx andything I have ever seen or heard of or read of before.

I managed to get a ride on a trip for some distance from her to visit a recently liberated German concentration camp. It was the Buchenwald Concentration Camp near Weimar, in central Germany. I'll try to jot down while it's freash in my mind some to the things I saw there. With the idea not of pleasing you, for what I saw there was really too horrible to be seen by any decent human being. But with the thought that as my wife you would want to share with me my most horrible as well as my pleasant experiences. And because I think the rest of the family and our friends should know from personal observations what bestial things the Nazis have done, and what a dreadful menace they have been to people all over the world. I think the details of this place can be mentioned without violating censorship regulations. The press has seen the place, and I shouldn't be surprised if the place receives some publicity in the next few weeks. General Patton has said he wants as many of his troops as possible tonsee this place.

The Buchenwald Camp is located in a dense beech forest on a high hill a few miles from the large town of Weimar, birthplace of the Weimar Republic. It seemed to be about one half by one quarter mile in dimensions. Surrounded by a high barbed-wire fence which was charged with electricity so that anyone who tried to cross it would be immediately electrocuted. Outside the wire were grim wooden log forts with protruding machine guns pointed toward all sides of the camp. Inside the fence were scores of long low wooden, windowless barracks.

Before we got to the gate we passed many of the freed prisoners wandering around in a dazed sort of way trying to grasp the meaning of their new freedom. 9 days ago the Nazis were planning to exterminate the entire camp when our Third Army troops broke in and saved the more than 20,000 prisoners. An MP stopped us and showed us an ancient living skeleton lying in the grass along the edge of the road. He was a prisoner too weak and sick to walk up the hill to the Camp. We nade room for him and helped him into our vehicle. I talked to him in German as we drove up to the Camp. He was a Hungarian, only 49 years old, although he looked at least 75. He had been a professor of economics in Budapest. Now he's a broken wreck of skin and bones, living his last weeks. He pointed to a great gap in his mouth. The Nazis had pulled out his teeth for the gold in them. Then he broke down and weeped uncontrollably.

At the Camp entrance (iron grilled gates under a great rustic logged tower surmounted with machine guns) I turned this man over to a committee of freed prisoners running the place, under the command of an xxxx American officer. Then I asked for an English

"A small pile of corpses at Buchenwald seven days after it was liberated. They died in the few hours before we got there of disease and starvation, April 1945." Photograph by Tom Perry Sr., Tom Perry collection, item 93.08.0107. Vancouver Holocaust Education Centre. https://collections.vhec.org/Detail/objects/4626. Reproduced with permission.

- 2 -

speaking guide.

In a few minutes a young and very pleasant Dutchman came up to serve as our guide around Buchenwald. He had been an assistant professor of biology at the University of Amsterdam before the war; he was picked up by the Nazis because he belonged to an illegal Dutch patriotic society. He had spebt the last 4½ years of his life at Buchenwald and knew the place thoroughly. He had been relatively well treated and had been able to preserve his health. He had been engaged to a Dutch girl at the outbreak of the war. A year or two after he had been imprisoned he got a rare le ter fro her telling him that she was breaking their engagement. Just before the Americans liberated the Camp an order had been issued for his immediate execution, since he knew too much about the place. He only escaped by stealing the clothes off a dead French prisoner, shaving off all his hair, and pretending that he was a French prisoner.

We entered the Camp amid a throng of freed prisoners going in and out, American soldiers and officers, war correspondents, etc. We came into a great courtyard full of wasted human beings from every corner of Europe. Thousands upon thousands of gaunt faces dragging around rags of clothing on spindly legs. Faces yellow and sunken. People limping from the advanced peripheral neuritis of prolonged malnutrition. Most wore small red triangular cloth badges. (I'm sending you as a souvenir the badge of our guide). Red badges meant prisoners of war or political prisoners, and 90% of all the inmates wore them. Each bore a black letter. R for Russian, F for French, N for Dutch, T for Czech, J for Jew, P for Pole. A few wore violet triangles; they were said to be religious fanatics or conscientious objectors. And a few wore pink patches. They were ordinary German criminals, mostly homosexuals and murderers. Over the barracks there fluttered in the bright April sunlight flags erected by the freed men. The Stars and Stripes. Many buildings flew the Hammer and Sickle. And there were several Czechoslovakian and French flags.

Our guide first showed us two different types of apparatus of torture set up in the big courtyard. A rack to which the prisoners were tied face down and frequently beaten to death. And a cross from which recalcitrant prisoners were hung by their hands with their feet only a few inches above the ground. Then we went to a building which served as combination execution chamber and incinerator. There were big holes in the plaster of the walls from which the prisoners had recently torn hated hooks from which the men were hanged to death. There were 8 great ovens. Several still held partially burned skeletons, plainly recognizable as such. They had been prisoners who had been incinerated ten days ago while still alive!

We then learned that the normal capacity of the Camp was 50,000 prisoners. There are now a little more than 20,000 still living there, and in spite of adequate food now and medical care are dying at the rate of 50 a day from the effects of long s arvartion, disease and torture.

We went outside and there, right out on the ground with

people milling around, lay a heap of about 20 bodies. Those who had just died and no one had had time to identify them or bury them. The most ghastly corpses I have ever seen. Greyish-yellow baggy skin, bones protruding through, legs swollen with the edema of starvation. Near them but somewhat separated lay two naked blue bodies, young fat men with bestial feature, blue and cyanotic. They were two of the SS guards of the Camp who had been caught the day before in Weimar dressed in civilian clothes. They were xxxxx recognized by their former prisoners and arrested. During the night they had hung themselves. A twisted Russian walked up to them and spat on them. I felt like vomiting.

We walked on and learned of the life of the prisoners. What did they eat? Here is what I was told by our guide, and then later by a Belgian doctor. During all these years there the ration for one man had been: a sixth of a loaf of bread (200 grams) a day, plus a liter (quart) of turnip or potatoe soup a day, plus a half a liter of ersatz coffee a day. Once a week each man received 50 grams (an ounce and a half) of sausage, 10 grams of margarine, and a spoonful of marmalade. There was no other food except a few Red Cross packages which were allowed to come in. And the Belgian doctor later told me that those packages literally meant the difference between life and death for thousands of prisoners who have lived to be freed. What was a day at Buchenwald like? Roll call winter and summer at 4 a.m. Work from 6 until 12, and from 12:30 to 5 in winter and 6 in summer. Then rollcall from the endø of work often to as late as 10 p.m. The prisoners worked on farms around the Camp, in a quarry where hundreds xi died from sheer physical exhaustion, in a rifle manufacturing factory, and in a plant making parts for the V-1 flying bomb.

We walked on to visit several typical living quarters. On the way I took lots of pictures of the prisoners (and xxx of the gruesome things I have described above). And gave away all the cigarettes and soap and chocolate I had on me to the revenous prisoners. When they saw you give a man something they came running and struggling from all directions like wild animals, a look of the most ecstatic delight in their eyes as you handed them one ci arette. Some lay on the ground tooweak to rise and pleaded in high-pitched, whining, tearful voices: "Shokolade, Kamerad, Skokolade! Zucker, Kamerad!" I learned from our Dutch guide as we went along that there were many German "Bolsheviks" imprisoned here, as well as people of Nazi-overrun nations. There had been a few British, and some American fliers. At least half of these had been shot here for the "crime" of bombing German cities. I asked who was treated worst and our guide told us the Jews got far the worst treatment; then the Russian prisoners of war.

We passed through several of the barracks. Windowless and dark, and filled with the most overwhelming, nauseating odor of death and human ordure. Each wall had three tiers of shelves. These shelves extended some 8 feet back from the corridor to the wall, and were separated by partitions every six feet. In each of these six foot xxxxx sections lived six men. No bedding, no straw, no blankets. Feces everywhere, because almost all the prisoners had and still have dysente

- 4 -

Then our tour took us to the "experimental" hospital. Here crack Nazi doctors experimented on living human beings against their will. Mostly they gave the patients typhus in efforts to develop a vaccine of their own against the disease. Hundreds are said to have died of this artificially produced typhus. The operations performed are said to have been chiefly new types of surgical procedures on the stomack. The laboratories of this hospital were beautifully equipped. The finest instruments, refrigerators, flasks, culture media, all spotlessly clean. And contrasting incongrously with the squalor of the rest of the camp. There was a little pathological museum, full of pathological specimens from autopsied victims of the experiments. There were a number of death masks of former prisoners. I examined them. The inscription on one read:"Polish Jew, aged 38". Another said: "Aryan from Breslau, married a Jewess, aged 52". Another was of a Negro, whom a prisoner who had know him said was a former African Negro scholar who had traveled over the whole world. Then there were collections of human skin bearing artistic tattoos. Our guide said this hobby was stimulated by the arrogant wife of the brutal camp commander. She used to attend the inspections of the prisoners for lice. They were naked. Whenever she saw a nice tatoo, she took the prisoner's number. He was shortly killed, his skin tanned, and the tattooed sections presented to the Commander's wife. She made a great lampshade of them; and this has been removed to serve as an exhibit in the future war criminal trials. As further proof of this story, our guide pulled out of his pocket a 3 by 3 inch tanned section of a human breast bearing a brilliant and intricate tatoo. He had stolen it from the museum.

There's ten times this much to tell, but it's very late and I must finish. We went on to see the kennels where the SS guards kept 45 large and ferocious dogs specially trained to hunto down excaped prisoners and tear them to pieces. This they did on numerous occasions. Then to a huge indoor riding school built for the Commander. Here 7000 Russian prisoners of war were shot during a very few days when the camp was getting too crowded a few years back. Then to the rock quarry, to see huge miner's railway carts which the prisoners had to haul up a long steep incline by hand.

Finally we visited a hospital outside the camp which had been used for the SS guards. During the last few days the prisoners have taken it over and organized their own hospital there. In it are several hundred of the most seriously ill prisoners. There I met a very fine Belgian doctor, educated at the Univ. of Montreal. He was called to active duty in the Belgian Army in 1939, captured by the Germans in 1940, excaped and fled to France where he carried out sabotage work against the Nazis. Recaptured in 1943, imprisoned for a year in Paris and then moved to Buchenwald. Here he had been a field laborer for 6 months, and had then worked in the V-1 plant. He proudly said he had sabotaged many a V-bomb destined to fly against London. He told me that a great proportion of the prisoners had Tbc, many beriberi and other serious vitamin-deficiency diseases, peripheral neuritis, some typhus, many chronic skin infections. He took me on rounds, and I saw thinga I have never seen before. Bodies thinner and more wasted than the last stages of carcinomatosis, yet still alive. All incontinent of feces. One man had just died in bed. One 16 year old boy weighed 40 lbs, had advanced Tbc, and was deeply pigmented

"Dummy on a torture rack where prisoners were flogged. Model of apparatus on which prisoners were beaten, April 1945." Photograph by Tom Perry Sr., Tom Perry collection, item 93.08.0091. Vancouver Holocaust Education centre. https://collections.vhec.org/Detail/objects/4610. Reproduced with permission.

\- 5 -

from concomitant Addison's disease, or so I guessed. Most were completely deteriorated mentally as well as physically, and you could clearly see that they absolutely don't care two cents whether they live or die.

But I should add that there are lots of the prisoners, thin and sick as they are, who are still full of hope. They cheered us and waved at us everywhere we went. A crowd of Frenchmen gathered around a Major from Louisana who speaks fluent New Orleans French. I had a good chat with three young Russians from Gorki, who are itching to get back into the Red Army. We parted with shouts of "Dosvedanya!".

I asked our Dutch friend as I took his picture and shook hands in parting how he felt about the Germans after four and a half years in Buchenwald. Did he think they should all be exterminated? He said the SS and leading Nazis should certainly be killed. But what good to take revenge at this date on the whole German people. He did not want us to stoop to their level. I asked him whether he thought the German people as a whole knew and approved of what the Nazis had done. He said he certainly thought they did. He had worked on labor gangs in Weimar several months, and said that all the inhabitants of that city knew perfectly well what was happening in the dark forest up at Buchenwald, and approved of it, and mistreated the prisoners working down in their town. Were there any good Germans? Yes, there were a few left amomg the prisoners at Buchenwald.

That's what I saw today. The unadulterated, entirely unexaggerate truth. There was much more than that, but I can't begin to describe it in words. One has to see and <u>smell</u> it to realize its full horror. And Claire, I wouldn't want you to know more than this letter sets down.

As to my feelings: I'm filled tonight with a deep loathing for the German Nazis, for their people who allowed them to do this thing, and for persons anywhere who mimic these Nazis. I'm filled with amazement that people living in a country so physically beautiful as this part of Germany is, can do such vile, filthy things to their fellow men. And I'm filled with alarm that men can be so degraded in a dozen years by the pernicious creed of Fascism. I'm tremendously glad to be part of the force that's destroying Nazism, not by parliamentary methods and strong words, but by fire and flying metal. And determined to fight hard to keep such a curse from ever spreading over this earth again.

"Letter from Tom Perry to his wife Claire, April 20,1945." Tom Perry collection, item 94.08.0011. Vancouver Holocaust Education Centre. https://collections.vhec.org/Detail/objects/4627. Reproduced with permission.

"Dummy on a torture rack where prisoners were hung by their hands, April 1945." Photograph by Tom Perry Sr., Tom Perry collection, item 93.08.0101. Vancouver Holocaust Education Centre. https://collections.vhec.org/Detail/objects/4620. Reproduced with permission.

TIM GIDAL PHOTO

Seen here holding a flag in a refugee compound near Haifa in 1945, Israel Meir "Lulek" Lau was the youngest survivor of Buchenwald. He maintained his family's 1,000-year chain of rabbis and served as Ashkenazi Chief Rabbi of Israel from 1993 to 2003.

Lulek's Story

Rabbi Meir Lau

THE ICONIC PHOTOGRAPH of a boy clutching a Buchenwald banner was taken by one of the founders of photojournalism, Tim Gidal, on July 17, 1945. The Polish-born boy known as "Lulek" was two years old at the outset of World War II and almost eight years old when American soldiers liberated him from Buchenwald. The photo was taken just prior to the saddest day on the Jewish calendar, *Tisha B'Av*, an annual day of fasting to recall disastrous events in Judaism (including the destruction of the first Temple in Jerusalem by the Babylonians in 586 BCE, destruction of the Second Temple by the Romans in 69 CE, and the expulsion from Spain in 1492).

The cheerful and resolute child had disembarked from France with an English visa on a refugee ship that docked near Atlit, Palestine (south of Haifa, before the state of Israel was founded in 1948). At the time, the boy believed that the only person who knew him in Israel was his brother who had endured the camps with him.

Entitled "*Survivors of Buchenwald Concentration Camp, arrival at Atlit, Palestine, 1945*," this image was purchased by Yosef Wosk from Tim Gidal when they met in Jerusalem in 1994, two years before Gidal died. Known only as "Lulek" in the concentration camps, the boy in the photo would become Rabbi Meir Lau, Ashkenazi Chief Rabbi of Israel 48 years later, at which time he invited the crusty Jewish photographer Gidal to a private reception in order to share emotional reflections regarding the photo.

When Rabbi Lau visited Vancouver for an event at Congregation Beth Hamidrash in February of 2008, Yosef Wosk showed him the photo and Rabbi Lau confirmed he was the subject. In Hebrew, on the back of the picture, Rabbi Lau wrote "With the help of Heaven. Vancouver, 22nd of Adar I, 5768. To Rabbi Yosef Wosk, may God give him life and guard him. Dedicated with the best of blessings and heartfelt wishes. Israel Meir Lau."

In the camps, youngsters were usually considered useless as workers and were mostly disdained and murdered by the Nazis as "useless eaters." During the final days at Buchenwald, Lulek was kept hidden in a trash container to prevent him from being murdered. For several years, he had been steadfastly protected, first by his older brother Naphtali, nicknamed "Tulek," who was thirteen when the war was declared, then by an eighteen-year-old Russian who Lulek knew only as Fyodor. More than twice his brother's age, Tulek had been told by his father that he must save Lulek so that one of them could continue the family's rabbinical tradition that stretched for 37 generations. Another brother, Chiko, had left for Romania shortly before the war and also survived but their oldest brother, Samuel Yitzchak ("Milik"), was sent to Treblinka where he and their father perished.

When Tulek and Lulek became separated in Buchenwald, Tulek's parting words were to get to *Eretz Yisrael*. At age seven, Lulek did not know *Eretz Yisrael* was the Jewish term for the land of British-mandated Palestine, or where it might be. He learned more about this wonderland called *Eretz Yisrael* when, as part of a remarkable rehabilitation program for 426 displaced children, he was sent to an abandoned sanitorium at Ecouis in Normandy, France. Psychologists assumed such traumatized boys would not successfully re-integrate into society but the diminutive "Lulek," born on June 1, 1937 as Yisrael Meir Lau, became Chief Rabbi of Tel Aviv and Chairman of Yad Vashem Holocaust Memorial Museum Center, and his protective brother Naphtali, the heroic "Tulek," became a journalist, served as General Consul of Israel in New York, worked as an assistant to both Moshe Dayan and Shimon Peres in the Ministry of Defence, and wrote a memoir, *Balaam's Prophecy*.

"My earliest memory," Rabbi Lau told *Mishpacha* magazine in

2006, "is that of my father, standing with the rest of the Jews in the courtyard of the main shul, as the Germans 'selected' those who would be deported that day. That's the image that stays with me always, wherever I go."

Everyone in the Jewish community of Piotrkow Trybunalski had gathered near the Great Synagogue where his father, the chief rabbi of the town—and the last one—at age fifty, was confronted by the chief Gestapo officer Herdorf who was always accompanied by a large and threatening dog. (Of the 60,000 inhabitants of Piotrkow, there were 26,000 Jews. Nearly all of them perished. The synagogue still stands but for seventy years it has been used as a library.)

"I'm a five-year-old boy, stretching myself up as high as I can, to see my father. He's standing in the centre, with his impressive beard and his black rabbinical garb, and all the Jews are crowded around him. Suddenly a member of the Gestapo strides over to him and hits him hard on his back (with a rubber club). My father reels forward from the blow, but straightens himself immediately. He's mustering all his strength so as not to fall at the feet of the German and cause his fellow Jews to lose morale.

"Then comes another blow, and another. My father makes a mighty effort not to lose his balance, to help the members of his *kehillah*, his community, keep up their courage."

The excuse for the beating was that his father, Rabbi Moshe Chaim Lau, had not shaved his beard. All older Jews had been instructed to shave their beards in the ghetto, and he had been the only one who had refused. If he had shaved his beard, Rabbi Lau has avowed, the people would feel they would never be Jewish again. Lau's father had two Ph.Ds from the University of Vienna, and he was an author. "He was a nice man, a very-very charming person, tall and handsome," Rabbi Lau told interviewer Sophie Shevardnadze [granddaughter of Edouard Shevardnadze] in 2015. "They used to see him as the spiritual leader of the city."

Rabbi Yisrael Meir Lau can shut his eyes and still hear the sounds of barking dogs and boots pounding on pavement as children are torn from their parents' arms with the Gestapo wielding clubs and screaming, "*Schnell, schnell!*" (quick, quick!)

"The worst part of it was witnessing the humiliation," he has said. "A child can't bear to see his father, the hero he looks up to and identifies with, being demeaned. Today, as I look back on those six years of war, it's clear to me that it wasn't the hunger, nor the cold, nor the physical pain of being hit, but the humiliation.

"To see your father beaten with a club, kicked by hobnailed boots, threatened by a dog, almost falling to the ground, degraded before everyone—that's a picture that stays with a child.

"But I hold on to the other part of the memory, too. I see my father, with tremendous moral courage, keeping himself from falling, not begging for mercy, standing up straight in front of the Gestapo officer. This erases my feelings of helplessness."

Lulek's older brother, Naphtali, at age sixteen, was grabbed in the street by the Nazis and forced to help build the railway tracks from Auschwitz to Birkenau.

At age six, Lulek accompanied his mother and another brother from their house next to the Synagogue to Jerusalimska Street in the ghetto. She saved him on several occasions, and had always comforted him as best she could. Once, returning to their empty house at 21 Pilsudski Street, he had heard a scream in the street. "I stood on the bed to look. A young woman with a baby in her arms was lying in a pool of blood in the street while a Gestapo man was kicking her, looking for jewelry." His mother soothed him back to sleep.

"I feel amazed when I contemplate the chain of miracles that happened to me." — Rabbi Lau

Approximately 24,000 Jews from Piotrkow were herded into cattle cars between October 14 and 21, 1942.

Initially, Lulek's mother managed a community kitchen in the ghetto. Eventually, she went into hiding with Lulek for three days in the attic of a deserted house. His mother made honey cookies for when the Gestapo troops searched the house. That way children could be persuaded to stay absolutely quiet. Ten people in an attic, above a bathroom, were not found.

Lulek's father believed his family would never be able to escape from the city if he stayed with them. He was too well-known. "They would search every place until they found me," he told them. "If I try to hide, they will also find other Jews who have a chance to survive."

Lulek is haunted by the memory of being separated from his mother, Chaya Lau, in November of 1944. At age seven-and-a-half, Lulek found himself on a train platform where Germans were once more shouting, "*Schnell, schnell!*" He remembers his mother giving him an abrupt shove, sending him over to her husband and his older brother Tulek on the other side, away from the women and children. "Tulek!" she called out. "Take Lulek! Goodbye, Tulek! Goodbye, Lulek!"

His brother Tulek remembers the moment differently. "At the last possible moment," he has said, "I tore Lulek out of my mother's arms."

Lulek only knew that he had been separated from his mother. He took out his rage on his brother, Tulek, hammering on his chest with his little fists. Tulek could barely restrain him. Lulek had no way of knowing this was a calculated gamble, hoping his life could be saved if he could somehow survive with his brother as a labourer. It was terribly cold at the train station as his mother was pushed towards the train. The gates were closed. The women were likely sent to Ravensbruck.

"The last picture I remember," Rabbi Lau said in 2015, "was the fog of the locomotive and beyond this fog we saw Mother."

When the men made it to the Czestochowa labour camp for the Hassag Werke, a factory for the repair of tanks, Lulek was initially hidden under a bed while the men went to work. Inevitably, he and some other children were discovered and taken before the Gestapo leader, named Kiesling. There were about ten children. This time it was Lulek's turn to be brave. Possibly it was seeing his father's show of pride in the courtyard of the main *shul* that emboldened him.

"We boys were standing in a row in front of the German commander, each of us with his father behind him. In my case, since I was already an orphan, my brother Naphtali stood behind me. The commander was shouting, 'What do I need these accursed children for? They're non-productive and they're costing me money. We'll have to get rid of them!'

"While the other boys trembled with fear, I used my foot to push some snow and gravel into a little pile. It was about two inches high, but I imagined that if I stood on this little hillock, I'd look taller and my words would carry more weight, and maybe then the commander wouldn't kill us all.

"I took a step forward, stood on my 'platform,' and said, 'Sir! Why do you say we aren't productive? In the Piotrkow ghetto, I worked in the glass factory for eight hours a day non-stop, carrying huge bottles of drinking water for the workers in the factory, where the temperature was 140 degrees. For a whole year I did this, in snow, in storms, in heat, carrying heavy bottles into that blazing hot room. And then I was only five-and-a-half years old. Now that I'm so much bigger, I can do more than that. If I could work in the Hortenzia glass factory, why can't I work here?'

"If witnesses hadn't told me that this really happened, I wouldn't believe it myself; I would think my memory was playing tricks on me. But the fact is that the Nazi officer was convinced. The Almighty gave me confidence and put the right words into my mouth. This was my first speech. He was amazed—a child, a Jewish child, dares to speak to him! And this was the end of 1944, and still, a Jew has opened his mouth and said something.

"As a result of my little speech, the commander let it be known that he would redeem any child in the camp for a price of 1,000 marks. Our mother had foreseen circumstances like these and provided us with two diamonds and a gold watch."

A Jewish dentist had filled her tooth with a half-carat diamond, and she had sewn a two-carat stone into the lining of her coat. These valuables were transferred to her sons and proved to be lifesavers, first in the Czestochowa munitions factory, and later in Buchenwald where they facilitated the subterfuge that he was Polish rather than Jewish.

Meanwhile, the heroism of Lulek's brother was seemingly inexhaustible. In January of 1945, when they were being gathered onto another train station, a Gestapo officer noticed how young Lulek was. He was separated and flung into a group of about fifty women, with a few children, on a train car that was slated to be detached and sent elsewhere from the rest.

Naphtali was in a crowded car of all men. It was at the front end of the transport. During the night, whenever the train stopped, Naphtali somehow managed to extricate himself, crawl along the tracks and call out, "Lulek! Lulek!" After doing this seven times, he finally located his little brother, in the women's car, clinging to a feather pillow his mother had given him. Lulek had to crawl over dead bodies to be extricated. The brothers crawled back to the men's car. In the darkness. Before they climbed in, Naphtali had the foresight to fill a hat with snow for some clean water to drink.

The women's car was later detached. The brothers learned they were headed for a new concentration camp near the city of Weimar, in east-central Germany. The first thing they saw was a group of men in striped uniforms, shovelling snow. "We asked them where we were," Rabbi Lau later recalled. "In reply, they drew their forefingers across their throats."

Malnourished, Lulek didn't have even one tooth. He was much closer to being a baby than a man. Although he was a child of seven-and-a-half, he looked more like a five-year-old. Tulek understood this would be a place for men only. Knowing the Gestapo would likely kill Lulek on the spot, Tulek emptied his sack of belongings and said, "Lulek, get in." In this way, the future Ashkenazi Chief Rabbi of Israel was smuggled into Buchenwald, carried in a sack over his brother's shoulder.

When they got off the train, there was an oven into which they had to toss all their belongings. They imagined the worst. Tulek quickly concocted a story. Lulek was a Polish boy who had been unfairly captured while playing with some Jewish friends. They conversed only in Polish. The gold watch their Mama had given Tulek was used to bribe one of the German wardens to ignore the presence of Lulek, who would otherwise have been deemed dispensable.

"We were taken to a tunnel equipped with a row of showerheads. By 1945, everybody knew what to expect from showerheads in a Nazi camp, and we prepared to die a miserable death. One of the men in our group suddenly fell down dead. Ever since we left the Piotrkow ghetto, he'd been keeping a cyanide capsule hidden under a temporary filling in his tooth, and he'd decided this was the moment to use it. But when the showerheads were turned on, ice cold water sprayed out. I don't know how to describe the life-giving warmth we felt from that icy water."

After they had been doused in chlorine, a Czech vaccinator at the end of another long queue realized Lulek was too small for a full dose of vaccine. Clearly his older brother, Tulek, was lying when he said the boy was fifteen. The line-up had to proceed quickly. They had only seconds to decide Lulek's fate. "I am a Communist," said the man. "I don't want to kill him." Instinctively, Tulek told the truth and Lulek was given a half-dose. Only then could the boys be certain this medical officer was a fellow prisoner.

Tulek's prisoner number was 117029. Lulek became 117030. Only in Auschwitz-Brikenau were such numbers tattooed onto the prisoner's skin. In Buchenwald, unless a prisoner had previously been in Auschwitz, the numbers were sewn onto their shirtsleeves. "I was humiliated," Rabbi Lau later wrote, "when I found out that other deported persons had real tattoos. Nobody was going to believe that I had been in camp! So I wrote my number on my arm with ink but it disappeared after the first bath."

Sometimes it was twenty degrees below zero. The men wore wooden clogs, without socks. Often, they would be forced to stand outside for three hours with no blanket, no sweater. No medicines. Rotted teeth. The beatings. The diseases. "They talk about those who were murdered and those who survived," Rabbi Lau has said, as an old man, "but *how* did they survive? I am not even talking about mentally surviving—or psychologically. But physically, you cannot explain it. As much as we will tell you about the Shoah, you will never fully comprehend it. Never. Even those who were there cannot really understand. So, explaining it is impossible.

"Many ask, 'Why did you not escape?' I wouldn't know where to go. I did not know the alphabet in any language until I was eight. I never went to school, not even one day."

At first, they joined about 2,000 men in Block 52 where the stench was unbearable. It was customary to relieve oneself right in the barracks. Each prisoner's striped pajamas were adorned with a red patch on which there was printed a black letter. P was for Pollaks. R was for Russian. G was for Germany. J was for Juden. With a diamond as barter, a piece of cloth from a dead Polish prisoner was affixed to Lulek's sleeve.

Tulek was sent to Barracks 59, the Jewish barracks. He was hitched to a wagon with three other prisoners and forced to haul corpses to the crematorium. When they became separated, a German named Hamman took pity on Lulek. First, he was moved to Barracks 8, for relatively privileged senior inmates; then he was taken to Barracks 66, with mostly Russians. There he met a Russian boy, aged 18-and-a-half, from Rostov-on-Don, named Fyodor Mickhailichenko, who soon became his main guardian.

In order to qualify as a labourer, Lulek was accorded the job of cleaning the entire barracks daily, arranging beds and mattresses, cleaning the toilets. Fyodor gathered his Russian friends and made a speech: "Lulek has no father, probably has no mother. Now he's going to lose his childhood also. We can save his childhood, at least, if not his parents. We will do the cleaning job instead of him." Thereafter Fyodor and his friends woke up one hour earlier, at 5 o'clock, before the work, and did all his work for him each day.

Buchenwald was a strange amalgam. There were political prisoners that included Konrad Adenauer, the anti-Hitler mayor of Koln who would later become the first Chancellor of West Germany. Leon Blum was a former Prime Minister of France. There were two Nobel laureates in literature, one from Spain, one from France. Tiny Lulek was deemed special and favoured almost like a mascot. Promising to one day adopt Lulek if they ever escaped, Fyodor stole potatoes and cooked up soup for him and knitted him earmuffs with some stolen wool. "When the Germans yelled hats off at roll call in assembly," he later told Robert Krell, "my ears stayed nice and warm."

In 2008, Rabbi Lau made contact with two of Fyodor's daughters Elena and Juliya who had made a documentary about their father. Until that time, Rabbi Lau had never known his savior's name. The only time Fyodor had ever been beaten was not by German guards, but rather by some fellow Soviets. From this documentary, he learned that Fyodor had once stolen a bicycle for him so that Lulek could have the experience of riding a bicycle. Bizarrely, when Fyodor was teaching Lulek how to ride, they were on the bicycle together and fell. "He was sitting behind me and we were injured and I had blood on my face. I was bleeding. I learned his friends had beaten him because they were angry. They said, 'Why didn't you take care of the child? Look at his face, he's bleeding because of you!'"

By early April, 1945, rumours had reached the prisoners that Germany was losing the war. The last time they saw one another in Buchenwald, Tulek said, "They're taking me away. This is the end of the world." Lulek felt every word was engraved on his heart. "You're going to be left alone now. But you still have friends. Maybe a miracle will happen and you'll survive. I just wanted to tell you: There's a place called Eretz Yisrael. Repeat after me: *Eretz Yisrael*."

The words meant nothing at the time. "Eretz Yisrael is the home of the Jews," Naphtali explained. "It's the only place in the world where they don't kill us. If you survive, there will be people who will want to take you to live with them, because you're a cute little boy. You're not going any place. Only to Eretz Yisrael. We have an uncle there. Say that you're Rabbi Lau's son, and tell them to find your uncle. Goodbye, Lulek. Remember: Eretz Yisrael."

In their last weeks in Buchenwald, some older boys hid Lulek, the youngest, in a rubbish box. Naphtali was put on a train. During the night he managed to jump out the window with two others, but instead of hiding, he walked for two days and two nights towards Buchenwald. "I did not want to lose Lulek," he wrote. With supernatural strength, he crawled into the camp, and then he collapsed.

"He hadn't forgotten our father and the promise he had made to him," Rabbi Lau says, "or the sound of our mother's voice shouting, 'Take care of Lulek!' Not a day in my life goes by without my thinking of Naphtali. He was given a mission: to save my life. And he carried it out."

[Tulek would not marry until 1956 when he felt financially secure as a journalist. He believes he has led a normal and satisfying life in the Holy Land. He has written: "Other people make plans, strive for success, while I have the impression that I have achieved more than I could ever have hoped for and will do nothing extraordinary to improve my status. I must be the only person in Israel who has never asked for an increase or a bonus. I am happy with what I have."]

On April 11th, Tulek was put into quarantine with typhus. Lulek had the measles. They both heard the American planes flying low over Buchenwald. Liberation was another nightmare. The forces under General Patton were bombing the Buchenwald area.

Lulek's Russian protector Fyodor understood a bomb could easily destroy their barracks. From their barracks, they ran towards the main gate but it was still closed. Around them were many injured people and a heap of corpses. Fyodor threw Lulek to the ground and covered him with his own body during the bombings and a flurry of bullets.

In the confusion, they became separated. Tired of running, Lulek hid behind the corpses. Finally, an American command car broke through the gate. Naturally, when uniformed American soldiers appeared at Buchenwald in 1945, Lulek was frightened. More men in uniforms with guns. The liberators were themselves frightened. They looked at the ghastly corpses and the emaciated Jews with horror. Although Lulek wanted to flee, there was nowhere to go.

A Jewish chaplain wearing a helmet, Rabbi Herschel Schachter, got out of an army jeep and moved towards the pile of bodies. He had driven five miles to reach the site with his assistant, Private Hyman Schulman, after the German guards had fled earlier in the day.

Schachter later recalled, "I caught a glimpse of a tall chimney with billowing smoke still curling upward.... I scarcely could believe my eyes. There I stood, face to face with piles of dead bodies strewn around, waiting to be shovelled into the furnace that was still hot. It was just an incredible, harrowing sight. I stood there for a while in utter confusion and disbelief. I then began to really feel what this horror was all about."

Lulek did not take flight. Rabbi Schachter, a Jew from the Bronx, took out his pistol and slowly walked around the pile. There he says he saw two eyes with life in them. He discovered an almost-eight-year-old boy, staring back, wide-eyed and distrustful. Trembling, Rabbi Schacter put his gun away. The American rabbi picked him up, held him tightly, and cried. He was mystified. What was a child doing in hell?

"How old are you, *mein kind*?" he gently asked, in Yiddish.

"'What difference does it make?' Lulek answered. "I'm older than you, anyway."

The American rabbi was startled. Perhaps this child was insane. Was it meant to be some kind of riddle. He played along.

"Why do you think you're older than me?"

"Because you can smile and cry like a small child," Lulek replied. "I haven't laughed in a long time, and crying is not something I've done for years. So, which one of us is older?'"

Rabbi Lau himself used to question if this story really happened. For many years, like so many other survivors, he never mentioned the camps, not even to his uncle. The first time he began talking about his experiences was during the Eichmann trial. His brother Naphtali had been sent to attend the trial as a reporter for the *Haaretz* newspaper, but he found the strain too great and left Jerusalem. It was only then that Lulek and Tulek exchanged their memories of the camps for the first time.

Rabbi Lau had kept the details of liberation to himself until he heard Rabbi Hershel Schachter repeat the same story to President Ronald Reagan when the three of them were brought together on April 11, 1983 (exactly 38 years after liberation) in Annapolis, Maryland. The details that Rabbi Schachter repeated to President Reagan were the same as he recalled.

"I thought that it is my imagination, a fantasy," Rabbi Lau recalls. "But he told it the same way. He saw someone looking at him with vivid eyes, he was afraid that it was a German that wanted to kill him. He took out his pistol and very carefully went around this heap, and he saw a child, hiding himself, full of fear. He understood that child must be a Jewish child. He took me in his arms, he embraced me and started to cry..."

After Rabbi Schachter had repeated his version of their meeting, the U.S. Navy orchestra played the Song of the Partisans. This was the sign for Rabbi Lau to come from behind the curtains onto the stage. He hugged Rabbi Schachter. Then President Reagan came forward to shake Rabbi Lau's hand. The President of the United States spoke clearly, so that all the microphones would pick up his words: "Let me touch a living legend."

"YOU CANNOT EXPLAIN one moment of my survival without miracles," Rabbi Lau has written. "When I get up in the morning and say *Modeh Ani*, Thank You to God for restoring my soul, I also have an additional intention—that God *did* return my soul.

"For three years I was surrounded by corpses. Every morning in the block many people did not wake up. I carried the wagon of dead to the crematorium each day. Even after liberation, 60 percent of the survivors of Buchenwald died of typhus and other diseases before they could even begin to start their lives again. I was in the valley of dry bones.

"When I say Thank You, I really mean it. God performed countless miracles for me. This gives me an extra motivation not to waste my life and to do something to justify all the miracles that happened to me. I could have ended up on the street amongst the criminals but God trusted me. I am forbidden to disappoint Him."

Not a day goes by when the Holocaust does not re-enter Rabbi Lau's awareness. For this reason, he cherishes a second photo that was taken only slightly earlier than the first, in 1945. In this image, given to him as a gift by Robbie Waisman and Robert Krell, via Elie Wiesel, Lulek is holding a small suitcase, preparing for his journey from France to a new homeland.

"An American soldier donated an old suitcase to me from the army surplus storehouse," he has recalled. "It went with me to Eretz Yisrael, and it held everything I owned, as I wandered from one educational institution to another.

"By the time I got married, it was so shabby that my wife wanted to throw it out, but I refused to part with it. 'This was my house [referring to the little suitcase],' I told her. 'If our children ever complain, I'll show it to them and say, 'This is what your father had when he was a boy.'

"I put it up in the storage loft of our building, and when we moved to another apartment, I came back for it. I climbed seventy-five steps to retrieve it, but I found nothing there but the handle. The suitcase had disintegrated. But I have the photo. Elie Wiesel, who was with me in Buchenwald, presented it to me at a Bundist event; he'd first seen it in Vancouver."

The story of how Elie Wiesel came to present the framed photograph from Vancouver to Rabbi Lau at the Museum of Jewish Heritage in New York has been told by Robert Krell:

> We invited Elie Wiesel to Vancouver for an event. During that visit, Leon and Evelyn Kahn threw a cocktail party.

Robbie Waisman had undergone gall bladder surgery but he and Gloria wanted to come. Marilyn and I picked them up and we brought them. Robbie got out of his wheel chair and walked in under his own power. I had asked Robbie to bring his photo album of the Buchenwald boys, with pictures mainly taken by American soldiers. That night, Elie, Robbie and I found a corner to hide in and they identified everyone in the photos. One was of eight-year-old Lulek with the suitcase and another was the cover photo of the boys at Ecouis that we used for the book *The Boys of Buchenwald*, showing both Robbie [Romek] and Rabbi Lau [Lulek] on the cover.

Later, when I was invited to speak at the Museum of Jewish Heritage in New York, I told Elie I was coming. He asked Marilyn and me to attend an evening in honour of Rabbi Lau, who was then chief Rabbi of Israel. I reminded Elie of Robbie's suitcase photo and wondered if Rabbi Lau had it. Elie asked me to bring it. I borrowed it from Robbie and made an 8 x 11 enlargement. At the event, when Elie was preparing to go on stage, we were sitting quite far back when I spotted a slight commotion with him motioning to get to him quickly. I ran down, passed it off and Elie calmly walked to the lectern. He made some beautiful, touching remarks to Lulek and then handed him the photo.

I shall never forget it. Obviously, Rabbi Lau had prepared some remarks but he was speechless. He covered his face with both hands. For one of those minutes that seem like an eternity, he composed himself and then began a probably quite different address. He had not seen the photo before. He showed the photo to everyone and said, 'Here I am with my possessions,' he said. 'That little suitcase was my apartment.'

And from there he soared.

Returning to Vancouver, Robert Krell told Robbie Waisman about the occasion, whereupon Waisman wrote to his long-time friend in

Jerusalem. The Rabbi wrote back to say he had placed the picture on the wall near his front door so that he would see it every day.

"It came as a complete surprise to me," says Rabbi Lau. "As soon as my children saw it, they all said, 'There's the suitcase!' Now, when I leave my house every day, on one side of the door is the mezuzah; on the other side is this photograph. [A mezuzah fixed to a doorpost reminds a Jew they have a covenant with God.]

"Each time I see it, it says the same thing to me: 'Yisrael, look at Lulek. Now your task is to justify the fact that you were saved. You must carry out your parents' mission; you must keep the chain unbroken. This is from whence you came.' And across from the photo, the mezuzah tells me 'before Whom I'm destined to give an accounting.'"

THE HOLOCAUST CAN never be forgotten by those who lived it. Rabbi Lau has stressed it must also never be forgotten by those who didn't live through it, particularly Jews.

In 2017, he told interviewer Sophie Paatovna Shevardnadze:

> "The Germans did not want to only annihilate the Jewish people physically. They wanted to annihilate Judaism and not only the Jews. Also, the Jewish culture and tradition. A proof of that is that the first thing they did ten months before the war began was the Kristallnacht. 1,046 synagogues throughout Germany were destroyed in one night. This was planned in the night between the 8th and 9th of November 1938. This is what makes the Jewish people so special and what makes them a people: Their synagogues and the Torah scrolls, the siddur, the Tanach, the Chumach, and everything else. They destroyed the synagogues because they believed that this is how they can break the spirit of the Jewish people. They fought against the body and the Jewish spirit. Now you need to understand one thing: If I, G-d forbid, leave my tradition behind: no Tallit, no Tephillin, no synagogue, no

The future Rabbi Lau, 1945, carrying his suitcase and rifle.

> Siddur, no Shabbat, no Sedder and no Chanukah, no Kosher and no Mikveh, and no nothing, I am letting them win. I will be doing exactly what they wanted to achieve. My grandfather wanted me to remain Jewish, and also my father. The Nazis did not want me to remain Jewish. They did not want any Jew to remain. So whom should I listen to? To my father and my grandfather? To my grandmother and my mother? Or should I have listened to those murderers? One thing is clear to me: if I want to help the Nazis finish their work, I must divorce myself from my Judaism, from my religion, from my tradition and my faith. Is that what I should do? Or should I show them, by hook and by crook, 'I was Jewish, I am Jewish and I will remain Jewish?' We shouldn't play into the hands of our murderers. We must show them, and to the whole world, that we are a people with a rich history and with a great future. *Am Chai Vekayam*."

Rabbi Lau's memoir in Hebrew, *Al Tishlakh Yad'kha El Ha'Na'ar* (Yediot Safarim 2011) has been translated into many languages, including English, as *Out of the Depths: The Story of a Child in Buchenwald* (Sterling 2011), translated by Shira Leibowitz Schmidt and Jessica Setbon. Referring in 2017 to the Holocaust, Rabbi Lau told interviewer Sophie Shevardnadze, "It was a very, very long and dark, six-year tunnel."

Liberated from Buchenwald, Lulek was given a Hitler Youth uniform because there was simply no other viable clothing. According to his autobiography, it was an American soldier at Buchenwald who gave him a rifle (slung over his shoulder) after asking what he wanted to do with his life. "I want to take revenge," he said, at age eight. "Hearing this," Rabbi Lau writes, "he gave me his rifle, and I kept it with me on my trip through Germany to Paris, then on to Lyon, Marseille, Genoa."

Capture of Jerusalem — Prise de Jérusalem by Marc Chagall[1]

Out of Hiding: Questions and Answers from the Depths

Afterword by Yosef Wosk

THERE ARE MILLIONS of ways to discuss the Holocaust. Every victim had a story to tell, a life to live, a dream to fulfil. This, however, is a condensed essay. It is guided by the Talmudic dictum: "A hint is sufficient for the wise."[2]

Ideas presented are an attempt to make sense of the catastrophe. This is not an exercise in right or wrong but rather in harvesting reactions from across vast fields of speculation. It reminds me of the time I asked Jonathan Berkowitz, a prominent statistician at the University of British Columbia, "What are the odds of being born?" He responded that there were too many variables and that it was impossible to calculate. When I pressed him further, he paraphrased a famous retort: "That is my answer. If you don't like it, I have others."[3]

The stories you read about in this book tell of tender tears conceived in hiding, stories of how millions of adults and children—seeds of innocence born of nostalgic love, defiled by self-sanctified madmen—were violated by the horrific actions of state-sanctioned terror.

Before we enter a maze of ideas and search for meaning, please take a moment to sweep away other people's theories and imagine yourself in a ghetto, or in the forest with rebel partisans. Place yourself hiding under a false identity, fearful of being discovered, nervous of being

Yosef Wosk and Elie Wiesel in Vancouver, 1996. As Director of Interdisciplinary Programs in Continuing Studies at Simon Fraser University, Wosk organized Elie Wiesel's two-day visit to Vancouver. Photo by Dina Goldstein.

betrayed at any moment. Situate yourself in exile, a new immigrant, trusting no one, suspicious even of God and your own thoughts.

Impossibly, consider yourself in the living hell of a concentration camp. No place can ever be compared to the camps with their singular reputation as places where murder was manufactured on an industrial scale, reaping profits while extinguishing hope with gas, ovens, bullets, disease and starvation. While millions were exterminated and countless others suffered, one thing survived: hope. Appropriately, the national anthem of the resurrected State of Israel is called *Hatikvah,* "the hope," to signal the rebirth of the aspirations of a decimated people in the only country that has planted more trees, trees of life, than it had one hundred years ago.

Menachem Rosensaft, founding chairman of the International Network of Children of Holocaust Survivors, emphasized that "we are at a critical stage of history because this is a moment of the transfer of memory" from one generation to the next. When something is transferred it can be corrupted, dissipated and imperfectly transmitted or received. It is similar to perfume being poured from one bottle into another: most of the liquid may flow but some of the fragrance is lost.

Our mission is to be good listeners; to record and read history; to never forget.

Kinds of Hiding

Hiding in Paradise

Whether you accept the story of Adam and Eve in Paradise literally or as a metaphorical legend, everyone knows something about the narrative of the first people, the first transgression, the first hiding, and the first question.

After creating the world, God planted a garden in the east of Eden. Adam and Eve were placed there and given all plants to eat except the fruit of the Tree of the Knowledge of Good and Evil, and also the Tree of Life. These two trees were the most open, the most visible, the most not-in-hiding at the centre of the garden. The woman and man violated their trust, ate from the Tree of Knowledge and committed the first transgression. The consequences lead to not only the *knowledge* of good and evil but also the ability to *act* on it, to do good or commit evil. They became conscious of self as distinct from the other; they even became strangers to themselves.

The roots of the Holocaust were planted in Eden.

Adam, whose name derives from *adamah,* the earth, and Eve, *Hava*—translated as the mother of all life—became the progenitors of genocide as much as mavens of culture. The garden that was pleasant was now polluted. Upon exile from the garden they gave birth to Cain and his brother Abel. When Cain became angry at his brother and murdered him, it was the worst genocide in human history. One quarter of the population was killed.

These early biblical mythologies relate universal principles. There is nothing more complex than a simple story; nothing more true than fantasy; nothing more waiting to be revealed than that which is deep in hiding.

Two questions are asked in this Garden of Eden story. The first is asked by the serpent; the second by God. After ingesting the forbidden fruit whereupon their eyes were opened, Adam and Eve heard God in the garden and hid in fear. "But the Lord God called to the man, 'Where are you?' He answered, 'I heard you in the garden, and I was afraid because I was naked; so I hid'" (*Gen.* 3:8-9).

This is the first mention of fear and hiding. God's interrogation of Adam became the one eternal question that has echoed throughout human history. "*Ayeh'kah?* Where are you?" Not just where are you hiding physically but also where and how are you concealing yourself emotionally, intellectually and spiritually? It is the question that contains all others. Everything that we as humans—the best of species and the worst of species—do, is a response to that cosmic query.

Ayeh'kah is not just a question, it is also a lament[4] for the unintended consequences of an experiment in creation gone wrong. The Creator then decided that the only recourse was to drive the first people out of their favoured abode and leave them, for better or for worse, to their neurosis. *Behind the wound lies the genius.* We remain the most conflicted of creatures.

Hiding in Nature

HIDING IS A UNIVERSAL EXERCISE. It can take the form of back and forth flirting between lovers or commercial negotiations between business parties. Jewish tradition reminds us that even God hides.

There are many ways to hide. Hiding does not always carry a negative connotation. Often it is nurturing and generative. The egg hides in the primal womb prior to fertilization and then continues to evolve before being birthed into an expectant world. Most seeds germinate underground—buried before they are born—and then work their way to the surface where they break through the soil into sunlight.

Nature provides camouflage for the sake of survival. Animals develop hiding skills for protection from threatening weather and escape from predators. Hiding—the right to personal privacy—has existed as a fundamental practice throughout the ages. It is not always done out of fear or embarrassment. It is also found in the whisper of intimate love. We hide secret presents to be revealed at just the right moment for that particular person; we hide the end of jokes, the punch line, for the end to preserve laughter and dissipate darkness.

In a bivalent universe, for everything that is revealed, something is hidden. Hiding is a cosmic principle. Our thoughts are hidden from others and our essence manifests from the Hidden, the unformed basis of all existence. Through a series of incalculable coincidences we coalesce into an embodied consciousness that is simultaneously unique and yet also a mere footnote, inconsequential for the most part, in the midst of eternity. Nature has no favourites. Individual lives soon expire. Everything has a beginning and an end, even space caught in the web of time. Existence is precarious.

No wonder we're anxious. No wonder we hide.

Aspects of hiding described in this Afterword, with a few exceptions, have relevance to persecution, most notably traumatic concealment during and after the Holocaust. Some ideas utilize ancient biblical stories and related teachings from rabbinic literature. They can be interpreted in tens of ways from the literal to the allegorical and from the plain to the esoteric. Do not discard these treasures of world literature by considering them to be foolish scribblings of an earlier naïve age. Many mysteries have been packed into a few seemingly simple words.

Following every major national catastrophe, people have searched their traditions for something that would lend meaning. Reporting on a theological debate in the search for meaning, the Talmud in *Eruvin* 13b records one such doctrinal struggle. It took place in the generation following the destruction of Jerusalem by the Romans and exile of the majority of the population. These disastrous events felt like the abandonment of the people by the God of Israel and produced great existential reflection.

> For two and a half years, the Academies of Hillel and Shammai debated. The House of Shammai maintained that it would have been better if people had never been created while the House of Hillel was of the opinion it was better people were created rather than not. They finally concluded on a compromise: Never being created would have been better than being created but now that we are here we should examine our past and scrutinize our future deeds.

Is the Creator good? Are people progressive? Or is this a neutral, indifferent universe with no particular mind or meaning, no justice, hope, or care? Perhaps we exist for no reason, we come from nowhere and return to nothing. We tell ourselves stories as insulation against madness and as a crutch for survival.

Some of these stories are quite wonderful. In their service we have built ethereal temples and extended kindness to those who suffer. But we have also weaponized stories, worshipped beliefs and saluted prevailing loyalties. There are always those who have harassed, murdered and destroyed what the other half has built.

When the Romans destroyed Jerusalem two thousand years ago, they were far less efficient than the Nazis in terms of eliminating Jews from their empire. In the continent of Europe—not just one city—the Nazis achieved a kill rate of approximately 70% throughout their conquered realm; 92% when it came to children. The Nazis never forgot a sheaf in the field and if they ever did, they did not leave it for the benefit of the disenfranchised. They murdered most of those as extra mouths to feed and as defective examples of the master race. They sent armies into the fields, stealing every grain for the military and destroying the rest so their enemies might starve. They hid their evil intentions from their victims while demanding abject obedience unto slavery and death. They burned the Hebrew Bible as well as its adherents as contrary to the German spirit.

The Nazis did not only eliminate Jews and Roma (Gypsies) as racially inferior. They also slaughtered Jehovah's Witnesses, homosexuals, blacks, the physically and mentally disabled, political opponents, dissenting clergy, resistance fighters, prisoners of war and individuals from the artistic communities. The deaf, the blind, the physically disabled, homosexuals, the mentally ill and alcoholics were either to be sterilized or killed simply because they were viewed as genetically defective. Slavic people, though labeled racially inferior by the Germans, were allowed to exist as slaves in order to supply the Nazis with free labor.

Hiding from the Light

THE HEBREW BIBLE mentions the idea of hiding over two hundred times in various contexts. Sometimes it is even God who is in hiding and occasionally the prophets. Prophecy, by its very nature, is something that is hidden from the vast majority of people and only revealed to a few chosen individuals who are tasked as messengers for making God's will known to the nation. Even the greatest prophets had to hide.

At the Burning Bush, Moses was suddenly confronted by a miraculous occurrence—the presence of an angel in the ethereal fire that burned within the bush but did not consume it, and then the voice of God. "At this, Moses *hid his face*, for he was afraid to look at God" (Ex. 3:6). During a subsequent encounter Moses asked God to reveal more of Itself to him—"Show me, please, your Glory"—but God agreed to reveal only a part by proclaiming the essence of Its name. He then warned Moses that he could not be shown more: "You cannot see My face, for no one can see Me and live." Moses is then hidden in a crevice of a rock on the heights of Sinai where God further protects him by covering him with His hand until the Presence passes by. "Then I will take My hand away and you will see My back, but My face will not be seen" (*Ex. 33:18-23). These four levels of protective hiding were necessary to transmit a certain amount of information—more than any person had ever experienced—and yet preserve his life.*

To shelter Abraham from a frightening revelation concerning the future of the nation that would issue from him, and also about the land upon which they would settle, God causes him to fall into a deep sleep: "As the sun was setting, Abram fell into a deep sleep, and suddenly great terror and darkness overwhelmed him (*Gen.* 15)." History has corroborated that the history of the Jewish people and the land of Israel would not be easy. Abraham had to be hidden from the "terror and darkness." something that would have been too much to bear if awake.

A third example takes place in the midst of a prophetic dream vision where Elijah is transported to the desert Mountain of God, Horeb, also known as Mount Sinai. He took refuge in a cave from where he heard a wind powerful enough to shatter rocks, but God was not in the wind; then an earthquake struck, but God was not in the earthshaking; "After the earthquake there was a fire, but the Lord was not in the fire. And after the fire came *kol demama daka,* a still, small voice. When Elijah heard it, he *wrapped his face in his cloak* and went out and stood at the entrance of the cave. Suddenly a voice came to him and asked, "What are you doing here, Elijah?" (*1 Kings* 19).

Hiding from the Mission

JONAH, HIDDEN INSIDE the belly of a whale, is perhaps the most famous of the reluctant prophets. He is instructed to travel to Nineveh, a large, non-Jewish city, to preach warning of imminent destruction unless the inhabitants changed their corrupt and heartless ways. Certain of failure and ridicule "Jonah got up to flee to Tarshish, [as far] away from the presence of the Lord [as he could get]. He went down to Jaffa and found a ship bound for Tarshish. So, he paid the fare and went aboard to sail for Tarshish, away from the presence of the Lord (*Jonah* 1)." God, however, caused a great storm to assail the ship at which time Jonah's identity and purpose are discovered and he is thrown overboard. Swallowed by a whale to both protect him and give him three days to reconsider his calling, he is hurled up on shore from where he makes his way to Nineveh. His prophecy ends with success, one of the few times in biblical history.

When God appeared to Moses and told him his mission—"Go! I am sending you to Pharaoh to bring my people the Israelites out of Egypt"—Moses demurred, "Who am I that I should go to Pharaoh and bring the Israelites out of Egypt?" God assured him, "I will be with you." But even that was not enough for Moses. According to a rabbinic *midrash* teaching story, he continued to argue with God for seven days and seven nights in an attempt to recuse himself from the appointment. He doubted the enslaved Israelites would believe him and asked God, who hasn't been around for a long time, "By the way, what is your name?" God is patient and gives him tactics to use as well as signs and wonders to perform yet Moses continues to excuse himself claiming that he is not eloquent, is slow of speech and one who stutters, to which God counters: "Who gave man his mouth? Or who makes the mute or the deaf, the sighted or the blind? Is it not I, the Lord? Now go! I will help you as you speak, and I will teach you what to say." To which Moses, in desperation, cries out: "Please, Lord, send someone else." At this, God got angry at Moses and would harbour no further excuses, telling him that his older brother, Aaron, who was eloquent and a leader among the people—but someone Moses had never met—would assist him (*Ex.* 3). That is how Moses, the humble outcast hiding from the Egyptians, his own people and now God, became the reluctant prophet, liberator of his nation, negotiator with Pharaoh, mediator with God, and vehicle of divine revelation, the Torah.

The final example of hiding from one's mission with reluctance is Jeremiah. God said to him, "I have appointed you as a prophet to the nations." Jeremiah's response to this sudden numinous invasion of mind, body and soul was both humble and deflective: "Ah, Sovereign Lord, I do not know how to speak, for I am only a youth." God reassured him, "Do not be afraid, for I am with you." "Then the Lord reached out his hand, touched my mouth, and said to me: 'Behold, I have put my words in your mouth'" (*Jer.* 1). Jeremiah ended up preaching his message for forty years but few listened. He lived to witness the destruction of Jerusalem and exile of its inhabitants. He also joined them in exile, for the prophet's final act is not to gloat and further demean a dejected people—"I warned you! I told you this would happen!"—but rather to console and give them hope for renewal.

Hiding from Persecution

POSSIBLY THE MOST famous example of Biblical hiding—in terms of being known to non-Jews—remains the story of Moses as an infant. When the Hebrew population began to increase and the Egyptians felt threatened, Pharaoh decreed that all the newborn boys were to be sentenced to death. Moses' mother, Yokheved, hid him for three months and then put him in a basket and floated it in the Nile. The basket was discovered and he was saved by none other than Pharaoh's daughter who drew him from the river, redeemed him from hiding, and then raised him as her own in the palace. In recognition of her defying her father's decree to kill all the male babies, rabbinic tradition rewarded her with a Hebrew name, Batyah, the "daughter of God." In appreciation for her revolutionary act and becoming a Righteous

Elijah's Vision by Marc Chagall. Elijah entered a cave and spent the night. A great and mighty wind tore into the mountains and shattered the rocks, but the Lord was not in the wind. After the wind there was an earthquake, but the Lord was not in the earthquake. After the earthquake there was a fire, but the Lord was not in the fire. And after the fire came a still, small voice. When Elijah heard it, he wrapped his face in his cloak and went out and stood at the entrance of the cave. Suddenly a voice came to him and asked, "What are you doing here, Elijah?" (*1 Kings* 19).

Among the Nations, she was elevated: "No longer are you just the daughter of a pharoaoh, you are now considered a daughter of God."

Hide & Seek

IN A HASIDIC STORY, the grandson of Rebbe Barukh of Medziboz (1753–1811), Yehiel Mihal, was playing hide-and-seek with another boy. He hid himself well and waited for his friend to find him. After waiting for a long time, he came out of his hiding place but the other boy was nowhere to be seen. He suddenly realized that his friend had not sought him out at all. The distraught child broke into tears and ran to his grandfather's study. As the boy told his story, tears fell from the rebbe's eyes and he said, "That's exactly what the Almighty Himself says: 'I hide myself but nobody wants to search for Me.'"

During the Holocaust, however, the game was transformed into a matter of life and death. Some were able to conceal their Jewish identity and continued to live in the open under the guise of counterfeit identification papers. Others were assisted by non-Jewish friends who secreted them—at great risk to themselves—in places such as attics, cellars, barns or forests. Some survived the war but countless others were discovered and killed.

Rabbi Joseph Polak, born a Dutch Jew in The Hague, really did play hide-and-seek in the concentration camps. He was not yet three when the war ended. He survived imprisonment in Westerbork and Bergen-Belsen with his parents. His father died in Bergen-Belsen but he survived with his mother and, after moving to Montreal and then Boston, sought for decades to reclaim memories that were not yet preserved because of his youth. He studied the history and gathered stories, struggled with childhood health problems and hidden emotional trauma, but could not consciously remember the starvation, disease and death all around him.[5] He writes:

> Mother died when I turned 40. Freddie, a tad older than I, came to sit with me at her shivah. "Do you remember, Joseph," he said, "do you remember how we used to play

> hide-and-seek around the corpses in Bergen-Belsen?"
>
> I did not remember, but it was this question, coming from him, that allowed me to accept myself as a survivor. And it has taken nearly three decades following that shivah for me to have learned that what my mind does not remember, my body does, and so does my soul.[6]

Hermit in Hiding

HIDING AS A RECLUSE is as old as caves. Some people are more comfortable living in obscurity, off the grid, withdrawn from society, a hermit in hiding. John Donne, 17th century English poet, asserted that "No man is an island" but some people hide so well and protect themelves with so many defensive layers of separation, that some of us *are* islands. During the Holocaust and other persecutions, while most people refused to leave their families, even when they had an opportunity to escape and were doomed, some individuals were saved because they travelled lightly and alone.

Hiding in Dreams

WE SPEND ABOUT A third of our lives in sleep. Sleep and hosting dreams can be a retreat from day's demanding activity. During the Holocaust every day was filled with terror. It was a time when dreams, even nightmares, were a relief and dawn itself the horror. Sleep was a temporary escape from a daily routine controlled by others. Decades after liberation, however, many survivors wake up screaming in the night, haunted by memories from which there is no escape.

Human existence is a precarious braid composed of an intertwined series of revelations and hidings. We emerge from an almost impossible union, are conceived in passion's flowered cave, are born to improbable odds, and emerge crying into a strange world. According to the Torah we are born into a world of light, "And God said, 'Let there be light,' and there was light. And God saw that the light was good, and He separated the light from the darkness" (*Gen.* 1:3-4). Many, however, have been condemned to the Kingdom of Night, the Valley of *Tsalmavet,* the Shadow of Death (*Ps.* 23:4). The metaphoric themes of light and dark have also been debated in the curatorial world of museums. For example, James Belgin, content leader of Holocaust Galleries at the Imperial War Museums in London, commented: "There are good reasons for [most Holocaust museums] to be [presented] in the dark. It feels appropriate to the nature of the subject. But the problem is that it also tacitly suggests the Holocaust is something that happened in the shadows. We wanted to be really clear with visitors about the fact that these things happened in our world. We need to accept that fact, that this didn't happen *despite* Western culture; it happened *within* it and *because* of it." Excerpt from "The dress that gave hope after the horror of the Holocaust" by Etan Smallman, *The Daily Telegraph,* January 27, 2021.

Life is a temporary reprieve between two hidings—pre-existence and post-existence. For those few years we are condemned to be free. It is an often awkward dance. Hiding can nonetheless be as comfortable as forest moss in the gentle shelter of gnarled trees, subtle beauty that is only shared in low light, rust that reveals as much as it conceals, and erotic fantasies that are best stimulated beneath evening's seductive veil.

Once protected from the "fear of night" (*Ps.* 91:5), one can merge with the evening and sing with the stars. The dream of Zion, the aura of Israel, kept millions alive during the darkest of times.

Pathologies of Hiding

THE NAZIS WERE NOT the first enemy to burn Jews alive. Paranoia can be triggered by having been in threatening or stressful situations. The Jewish people have experienced so many of those as to live in a constant state of legitimate low-level suspicion.

There are also pathologies of hiding, such as irrational feelings of being persecuted, accused and followed. Paranoia has also often been reported by Marranos—crypto-Jews who had been forced to convert to Catholicism by the Spanish or the Portuguese Inquisitions in the late 15th century. There are still descendents of Marranos today, five hundred years after the persecution, and as they pass down hints of secret Jewish traditon they are still held back by a centuries-old residual fear of being discovered. The consequences, they fear, would be arrest, punishment, excommunication or even death.

Hiding in Humility

HUMILITY CAN BE another type of hiding. Holocaust survivors know a unique humility. They live in a place that is inaccessible to the rest of us and they are understandably reluctant messengers as to its reality.

Out of a sense of politeness, modesty, manners, and social etiquette, we have been taught under most circumstances not to ask others certain probing questions, and not to listen to particularly embarrassing answers or to engage in gratuitous gossip. Complete revelation of ones thoughts and actions would be unbearable. We protect one another's privacy by the mutual suppression of information and label its desecration as we would a war: an *invasion* of privacy.

Humility, knowing one's place and not boasting, is one of the highest virtues in Jewish moral tradition. Maimonides (1138–1204) advised that we should follow a middle path when expressing any character trait but that excessive humility was a virtue.[7] Humility, however, does not necessarily imply weakness or having a low self-regard for oneself. Moses, for example, conversed with Pharaoh, leader of the most powerful country in the world; he led a nation of slaves to emancipation, including forty years of wandering interspersed with multiple issues and uprisings; and, as an appointed prophet of the ancestral God, he often found himself in heated negotiations with the Almighty. And yet, in conjunction with his strong personality, according to the Torah, "Moses was a very humble man, more so than anyone on the face of the earth" (*Num.* 12:3).

Another lesson in humility is drawn from the giving of the Torah, the Ten Commandments, at Mount Sinai. The first tablets were written with the "finger of God" in the midst of the fire and presented with great pomp as part of a forty-day ritual punctuated with deafening thunder and blinding lightening that was so disorienting that the people ran from the mountain in fear for their lives while experiencing synesthesia during which they "saw the sound and heard the visions." The dramatic experiences, however, were not sustainable. Moses descended the mountain to find that the people had reverted to familiar Egyptian slavery practices of building and worshipping a Golden Calf. He threw down the divine tablets, shattering them against the mountain. The second set of tablets were given and received in subdued humility. These were the ones that lasted.

Strength and humility are often intertwined in the biblical text. Rabbi Yohanan observed in the Talmud that "Wherever the power of the Holy One is mentioned, you also find his humility" (*Megillah* 31a). Biblical literature is replete with examples of the humble and humiliated ones elected to fulfil the working of divine history: the unassuming shepherd, the deformed prophet, the crippled patriarch and limping God, the younger brother, the smallest nation, the weak and poor, the stranger, exile, widow, outcast and disenfranchised. That which is concealed in humility is exalted in other realms.

And so "greatness tempered by humility" is a common theme. Consider the Burning Bush (why was a lowly bush chosen for the revelation instead of a tall, strong tree?), Mount Sinai (why was a modest desert mountain chosen instead of a more prominent peak or one situated by the great sea?) and Moses (why did God choose an inexperienced person with a speech impediment as his ambassador instead of a clever orator, a leader known and respected by the nation?).

Abandonment and Invisibility as Acts of Hiding

THE EXACT PERCENTAGE of Jews who chose to conceal their identities throughout the centuries remains necessarily hidden. There were those who became invisible, crypto-Jews, and continued to engage in some form of secret remnant of Judaism, those who abandoned their religion and converted to other religions, and those who simply gave up transmitting the tradition to the next generation so that the terrible burden might die with them. Even then, however, much has been passed on unconsciously in the epigenetic, subconscious cellular memory of an ancient people who entered into an eternal covenant with transcendent forces of history.

Hiding in Silence

THERE ARE MANY KINDS of silence just as there are multiple ways to hide.

"The world" hid in silence and denial in reaction to Hitler's provocations in the pre-war years including the annexation of Austria and Czechoslovakia, his blatant anti-Semitic persecution, abuse of human rights and massive rearmament in violation of the Treaty of Versailles. The principle response from the West was diplomatic appeasement. The reluctance to use stronger language and forceful containment led to even greater forays by the Germans. The results of this fearful silence were World War II, the destruction of Europe, the Holocaust, the deaths of approximately 45 million civilians and soldiers, with another tens of millions wounded.

Just as the worst war in history was preceded by silence, it was also followed by silence. Initially, Holocaust survivors were too shocked to be able to speak or write about what they had experienced. Trauma from persecution and concentration camp horrors resulted in some survivors feeling as if their tongues had been severed and hung on the gallows of Auschwitz. Horrified, many naturally chose exile from their native lands and Europe altogether.

Jewish life began in exile when Abraham was instructed to "Leave your country, your place of birth, and your father's house, and go to the land that I will show you" (*Gen.* 12:1). Exile follows as one of the recurrent themes in the Bible until there is a return to the Promised Land of Israel. Consequently, the bible reminds us at least 36 times—

more often than we are directed to believe in God—not to oppress the stranger.

You, too, must love the stranger, for you were strangers in the land of Egypt (*Deut.* 10:19).

> When a stranger dwells with you, a stranger in your land, do not cheat him. You should consider him as one of your [natural] citizens, that stranger who lives with you. You shall love him like yourself. I am the Lord your God.[8]

Being a stranger in exile makes one a *visible* minority and it is therefore the opposite of hiding. The new immigrant, however, is one who is constantly living on edge, trying not to be conspicuous as an identifiable "other." Two familiar mottos for Jews in exile throughout the centuries were "To endure, be obscure"[9] and "Be a man in the streets and a Jew at home."[10]

The Nazis depicted the Jewish people as the consummate outsiders and therefore they were scapegoats for every perceived offence to the "pure Aryan German race." The more the Jews tried to assimilate, the more they were suspected of being a fifth column, infiltrators and desecrators of German society. It only took the Nazis a few years to arrive at the logical conclusion to their accusations: "The Final Solution", the deadliest genocide in history. Now we know why the Torah considered the directive to "love the stranger"—or at least to assist the immigrant—to be as important as belief in God and why we were reminded so many times over.

Hiding from Truth

A NUMBER OF RECENT case studies have uncovered varying results in attempts to determine how many lies a person tells every day.[11] Some studies estimated that we are lied to as much as 200 times a day. The Bible contains several admonitions against lying including the ninth commandment "You shall not bear false witness against your neighbor." However, during the Shoah, we had to become masters of masquerade. Jews used concealment as an act of survival, and lied for the sake of truth. We dressed as the other in order to preserve the self and deceived evil to redeem whatever scraps of goodness still managed to defy the chokehold of authority.

Such deception and concealment to preserve who we are is reminiscent of the Jewish holiday of Purim, originally celebrated 2,500 years ago, when Esther the queen managed to hide her Jewish origins until revealing them helped to save her people. It was a time of *ve'naha'foh hu* (*Esther* 9:1), when everything had been turned upside down and inside out. "On this day the enemies of the Jews had hoped to overpower them, *but their plan was overturned* and the Jews overpowered those who hated them." To this day we celebrate the holiday by dressing in costumes to commemorate the creative deception that lead to salvation. Even the presence of God is not mentioned once in the entire book of Esther. Ironically, when all things official reek of skull & crossbones, of corruption and chaos, masking the truth sometimes results in the greatest veracity.

There are times when pretending to be someone else is the only way to preserve yourself. While biblical literature champions honesty—its foundational injunction being "Keep far away from anything false"[12]—it is also replete with examples of deception and disguise for the purpose of survival, to usurp blessings, to obtain information, for the sake of love, for generational continuity and as political strategy.

A few examples of deception: Sarah who told Avimelekh, king of Gerar, that she was Abraham's sister, not his wife; obedient Jacob who disguised himself as his brother, Esau, at the behest of his mother, Rivka, in order to receive his blind father's blessing; Esther who hid her Jewish nationality from the king until revealing it in a bold move to save her nation; David who feigned insanity among his enemies to save his life; Tamar who veiled her face and dressed as a prostitute to become pregnant and carry on the family lineage by stealth; Leah who was instructed by her father, Lavan, to pretend under the cover of night and modesty, that she was her younger sister, Rahel, and trick Jacob into marriage; Moses who, in his early life, passed as an Egyptian; the twelve spies, one representing each tribe, who were sent to scout out the land; Joseph, who, when prime minister in Egypt, concealed his identity from his brothers who had attempted to kill him and then sold him into slavery. King Saul also disguised himself as a commoner to consult the forbidden augury of the witch of Eindor. The Christian bible describes an extra-dimensional level of deception when it submits that "Even Satan disguises himself as an angel of light" (2 *Cor.* 11:15).

During the Holocaust, in a nightmarish world where you were condemned just for being yourself and were guilty by birth, you often had to lose your previous identity and become someone else in an effort to survive. Possessions were reduced to a minumum; all that was important was saving your life. You had to become invisible even in plain sight. You were given a new name, foreign and false. Your past was erased, your future was only as secure as the next knock on the door.

Those in hiding were only safe as imposters. Some boys posed as girls to avoid being searched for marks of circumcision. Many hid under the guise of different religions—as Catholics, Protestants or Muslims—and learned their prayers and rituals. Those in hiding had to keep their identity secret from even their closest new friends. They could not even afford to have cluttered thoughts, for those, too, might be detected by an eager enemy. Their silence must be perfect. Concealed. A secret disguised with deception beneath a well-rehearsed mask reciting someone else's lines in a theatre of the absurd. A wayward comment, an honest sharing of information, or the murmurings of inquisitive neighbours could lead to betrayal and death.

During this most terrible of all wars, the biblical passage—"Life and death are in the power of the tongue" (*Prov.* 18:21)—was never more true. The Nazi search for the hidden was incessant. There were harsh punishments for gentiles who hid Jews and rewards to informers who turned them in. There were raids, threats, blackmail, checking identification papers again and again. The pressure was intense both for those in hiding and those who hid them.

Some rescuers may have been kind at first and some protected their charges for the duration of the war but others only took them in for money, then turned around and handed the children or others in hiding over to the Nazi authorities for an additional reward. More often it was fear that finally drove the benefactors to have the desperate Jewish refugees, often children, removed from their homes.

At first, some Jews who were not as assimilated into German culture and still maintained their Jewish sounding first and last names, tried becoming less conspicuous in society by altering them to more common Germanic appellations.[13] They changed them to more common Germanic names. This offered some protection until the Nazis instituted a law forbidding such changes. On August 17, 1938, the Nazis issued a further Executive Order concerning the Law on the Alteration of Family and Personal Names. It required German Jews bearing first names of "non-Jewish" origin to adopt an additional identifying name: "Israel" for men and "Sara" for women. Later, all Jews were forced to sew six-sided yellow Stars of David onto their clothing to make their presence more obvious. Hiding became even less possible when even your clothes shouted your identity.

Hiding when you are "Disappeared"

DURING THE SHOAH, millions of Jews were ostracized and declared pariahs; they were deported, enslaved, forced to flee and murdered. The Nazis then engineered a cover up of mass graves, crematoria and other concealments. Never were so many "disappeared."

En route to that disappearance, millions were removed from society by arrests and incarceration, expelled from school, fired from their jobs, bullied or made to feel invisible. Nazis and their collaborators considered Jews as "parasitic vermin," a deadly virus, and marked for eradication. Incessant propaganda legally declared Jews to be criminals in and of themselves or portrayed them as Bolshevik agents out to subvert European society.

"The vast majority of Jews in German-occupied Europe never went into hiding, for many reasons. Hiding meant leaving behind relatives, risking immediate and severe punishment, and finding an individual or family willing to risk providing refuge. Any one caught rescuing them was under a threat of severe and immediate penalties. Many Jews, no doubt, held out the hope that the threat of death would pass or that they could survive until the Allied victory."[14]

Approximately 1,500,000 Jews were able to escape the Nazi killing machine by fleeing to neighbouring European countries or to a few other states worldwide. More than 90,000 German and Austrian Jews fled to neighbouring countries between 1933 and 1939; nearly 300,000 Polish Jews fled German-occupied areas of Poland and crossed into the Soviet zone between 1939 and 1941; while after the German attack on the Soviet Union in June 1941, more than a million Soviet Jews fled eastward into the Asian parts of the vast country.

Yellow Judenstern "Jew's Star" that German Nazis forced Jews to sew onto their clothing.

Children in Hiding

1.5 MILLION JEWISH children were murdered during the Holocaust. "All Jews were targeted for death, but the mortality rate for children was especially high. Only 6 to 11% of Europe's pre-war Jewish population of children survived as compared with 33% of the adults. Of the almost one million Jewish children in 1939 Poland, only about 5,000 survived."[15]

The effect of all this trauma—living through years of terror confronted by history's most efficent and cruelest killing machine—forced some children to mature beyond their years. One child survivor described them as "old people with children's faces, without a trace of joy, happiness, or childish innocence."[16]

Although the following encounter is mentioned in the preceding segment called "Lulek's Story," I believe it bears repeating here in the context of hiding. In 1995, fifty years after liberation, Rabbi Israel Meir Lau—a child survivor of Buchenwald called Lulek who eventually became a Chief Rabbi of Israel—described how an American rabbi, a chaplain with U.S. forces [Rabbi Herschel Schacter], had taken him in his arms after the camp was freed on April 11, 1945.

> "He came in and met a child of less than eight years old—that was me—taking him in his arms, weeping and trying to smile and laugh. Holding me in his arms he asked [in Yiddish]: 'How old are you, my child?' And I said, 'What does it matter? I'm older than you.' 'Why do you think you are older?' he asked me. I said, 'Because you cry and you laugh like a child. I don't cry and I haven't laughed for a long time. Tell me who is older: me or you?'" Rabbi Lau added: "After fifty years we are permitted to cry."[17]

After the war, many children who had been in hiding experienced the trauma of reunification with their birth parents. Due to their young age and the passage of so many years, some children forgot who their parents were and didn't want to go with them. Others did not want to be Jewish: it represented danger; they felt safer with their Christian foster protectors who had also grown fond of the children and wanted to keep them. For many hidden children, the years of separation became permanent when their murdered parents or siblings could not return to rescue them. The reverberations of being hidden never fully subsided once World War II officially ended.

The Enemy also Hides

EUROPE IS LITTERED with buried bones, scattered ashes and destroyed archives—all attempts made by perpetrators to cover up their crimes.

The Nazis engaged in fraud, deception and secrecy on a massive scale. With only a few exceptions, "the fact of deliberate physical destruction of human beings, and particularly of the European Jews, was never mentioned in published Nazi documents." The "solution to the Jewish question" was generally spoken about in code words and euphemisms such as "emigration" and "evacuation" or "the final objective" or "total solution" or that "they be appropriately dealt with." The secrecy of the operation was guarded so as not to arouse international reaction, panic by the Jewish population, and to elicit gradual cooperation by the Wehrmacht, the combined armed forces of Nazi Germany.[18]

As an example of the attempted cover up: At Auschwitz, where over one million people were murdered, "bones that did not burn completely were ground to powder with pestles and then dumped, along with the ashes, in the rivers Soła and Vistula and in nearby ponds, or strewn in the fields as fertilizer, or used as landfill on uneven ground and in marshes."[19]

"The secrecy was complete and, to a large extent, effective. The very monstrosity of the crime made it unbelieveable. In fact, the Nazis speculated that the unimaginability of their *Aktionen* would work in their favor. Commenting on a report of such an *Aktion*, Heinrich Lohse, Nazi commissioner for Ostland, observed: "Just imagine what would happen if such occurrences became known to the enemy and were exploited; but probably such propaganda would have no effect since those who hear or read it would not be willing to believe it!"... Despite all the efforts, Himmler's expectation that 'the extermination of the Jewish people... this glorious chapter in our history... should never be told,' was frustrated by the Allied victory. [What remained of] Nazi archives were opened, contemporary Jewish documents were discovered, and facts were ferreted out by courts and scholars. Moreover, by 1942 the Free World had gradually learned the truth, albeit not always complete and precise."[20]

Some Last Words

EVEN THOUGH THE all-consuming fire of the Holocaust Sacrifice has been extinguished, embers still glow in the service of memory.

Hannah Szenes [see entry Hay, Peter] penned this poem when she was 22 years old, days before her capture on June 9, 1944, leading to her execution by a firing squad on November 7, 1944:

Hannah Szenes in Budapest, circa 1937–1938

Blessed is the match consumed in kindling flame.
Blessed is the flame that burns in the secret fastness of the heart.
Blessed is the heart with strength to stop its beating for honour's sake.
Blessed is the match consumed in kindling flame.

May these words enlighten your path and illuminate your heroic journey of discovery.

There is much to remember and even more to know as the Holocaust comes out of hiding.

Notes

1 This etching with hand colouring by Russian-French Jewish artist Marc Chagall (1887-1985), was produced as one of 105 images from *Bible,* a project initiated by Vollard in France in 1931 and published by Tériade in 1956. It, too, has a history interrupted by the Holocaust: see the online article "Marc Chagall's Bible Series: How the Artist Brought the Bible to Life", Park West Gallery, Southfield, Michigan. It is part of the Yosef Wosk Collection, purchased with the assistance of Susanna Strem, owner of the Vancouver-based Chali-Rosso Gallery. Strem's family was from Hungary. Many were murdered in Auschwitz; a few survived the Holocaust but were then forced to live under Communist rule after the war. Strem—who left in 1986, emigrated to Israel in 1992 and then to Vancouver in 1996—relates how "my father and his parents were saved from the ghetto by a Nazi party member. The building they lived in before and during the war had a caretaker. She was from the countryside, with very little education. Before the war broke out, she became a member of the local chapter of the Nazi party for nationalistic reasons and to rectify the wrongs Hungarians felt had been imposed upon them by losing territory after WW I. Late in 1944 all the remaining Jews of Budapest were forced to leave their homes and move into a ghetto. Soon rumours spread that the entire ghetto was booby-trapped and was going to be blown up killing everyone. This simple-thinking janitor, when learning that my family was locked in this place, managed to find her old Nazi membership card (which she has not used before), and went to the ghetto to pick up my family. She marched in with great dedication and soon all of them marched out from the ghetto, she with a big Nazi salute. She even went back to bring out other families whom she knew. She would have been shot on the spot if the police knew what she was doing...What always shocks me is the timeline of history. The frenzied speed of the deportation of hundreds of thousands of Jews from Budapest took place when Paris was being liberated. France was free! While the French were celebrating the war being over, not far away the death marches and transports to Auschwitz were being accelerated in Hungary." In May 1944 the deportation of Hungary's Jews to Auschwitz began. In just eight weeks, some 424,000 Jews were deported. By the end of the Holocaust less than a year later, some 565,000 Hungarian Jews had been murdered ("Murder of Hungarian Jewry", *Yad Vashem*).

2 *Dah'ee la'hakima bi'remizah* (*Midrash Proverbs* 22:15).

3 "Those are my principles, and if you don't like them...well, I have others," attributed to Groucho Marx. Cf. quoteinvestigator.com/2010/05/09/groucho-principles/.

4 The same word of four Hebrew letters—*aleph, yud, khaf, heh*—in a slightly different grammatical form is used as the first word in the Book of Lamentations. It is a cry of despair asking *Eikha,* "Ai, how does the lonely city once full of people exist?" It is an agonizing lament written, according to tradition, by the prophet Jeremiah after the destruction of Jerusalem and exile of her population by the Babylonians in 586 BCE. It is the same question expressing divine disappointment with humankind—whether in the

Garden or in Jerusalem—spoken thousands of years apart. We did not learn our lesson then nor have we now.

5 "On April 15, 1945, British forces liberated Bergen-Belsen. The British found around sixty thousand prisoners in the camp, most of them seriously ill. *Thousands of corpses lay unburied on the campgrounds.* Between May 1943 and April 15, 1945, between 36,400 and 37,600 prisoners died in Bergen-Belsen. More than 13,000 former prisoners, too ill to recover, died after liberation. After evacuating Bergen-Belsen, British forces burned down the whole camp to prevent the spread of typhus. During its existence, approximately 50,000 persons died in the Bergen-Belsen concentration camp complex including Anne Frank and her sister Margot. Both died in the camp in February or March 1945. Most of the victims were Jews." (Holocaust Encyclopedia, United States Holocaust Memorial Museum).

6 *After the Holocaust the Bells Still Ring* by Joseph Polak, foreword by Elie Wiesel (Jerusalem, New York: Urim Publications, 2015).

7 See Maimonides (Rambam) *Hilkhot Deot,* II:3 and his commentary on *Avot* IV:4. Cf. his *Shmonah Prakim,* Eight Chapters on Ethics, Chapter IV, for a more attenuated position in which he counsels the middle position—"the mean between two equally bad extremes, the too much and the too little"—for the exercise of all characteristics.

8 *Lev.* 19:33-34 and also see *Bava Metzia* 59b.

9 Related to me by Lilian Broca; this is what her parents used to say in Bucharest, Romania before the war.

10 A statement first coined by Yehuda Leib Gordon (1830-1892), a Lithuanian-Russian scholar and Hebrew poet of the *Haskalah,* Jewish Enlightenment.

11 "People Lie for a Reason: Three Experiments Documenting the Principle of Veracity" by Timothy R. Levine, Rachel K. Kim and Lauren M. Hamel, *Communication Research Reports,* Vol. 27, 2010, Issue 4, pp. 271-285; *Liespotting,* book and online presentations, by Pamela Meyer (New York: St. Martin's Press, 2010); "9 things you should know about liars" on *Science of People* website; and "UMass researcher finds most people lie in everyday conversation", University of Massachusetts at Amhert; among others.

12 *Ex.* 23:7; also see *Gen.* 18:23; *Ex.* 20:16 and 23:1; *Lev.* 19:11 and 19:16; *Deut.* 25:1 and 27:25; *Ps.* 119:29, etc.

13 "How Nazis used personal names to spawn the Holocaust", *Ideas Program,* CBC Radio and online: November 27, 2020. The episode featured University of Cologne professor Iman Nick and her work on forensic onomastics—the scientific study of personal names. For further reading on anti-Semitic trolling of Jewish sounding (((names))) see en.wikipedia.org/wiki/Triple_parentheses. Also see "The Etymology of Hate", article in the *Baltimore Jewish Times,* August 13, 2020. For an even more comprehensive list of this constantly evolving hate base, visit "The Racial Slur Database" www.rsdb.org/race/jews.

14 United States Holocaust Memorial Museum.

15 United States Holocaust Memorial Museum.

16 *Ibid. www.ushmm.org/exhibition/hidden-children/insideX/.*

17 "When a person has reason to cry, and he wants to cry, but is not able to cry—that's the greatest cry of all." — *Rabbi Menachem Mendel of Kotzk (1787-1859).*

18 An active debate among historians questions how much Germans and others, in Europe and around the world, knew about the Holocaust while it was being carried out. Opinions range from it being an open secret, to active collaboration in the events with intimate knowledge of the mass murders, to claims by others of only hearing some rumours but knowing nothing about actual killings. (See the Wikipedia article "Knowledge of the Holocaust in Nazi Germany and German-occupied Europe".)

There were also a series of reports from credible sources during the war but they were often treated as exaggerated and seldom inflamed the Allies to take specific action, outside of the ongoing war effort, in an attempt to prevent the murder of millions of civilians and prisoners of war. See "What did the World Know?" on *Facing History & Ourselves* website, and *Holocaust in the Name of the Fuehrer* by R. Gordon Grant, pp. 55-56 (Trafford Publishing, 2003). Also see the *United States Holocaust Memorial Museum* exhibit "State of Deception: The Power of Nazi Propaganda", and their entry on "Frequently Asked Questions about the Holocaust". As for the complicity of the German Army: Although there were a small minority who spoke out against participating in such atrocities, after Nazi Germany invaded the Soviet Union in June 1941, an estimated 1,500,000 Jews alone were shot to death by the *Einsatzgruppen* (mobile killing squads) in what has become known as the Holocaust by Bullets.

19 "The extermination procedure in the gas chambers," Auschwitz-Birkenau Memorial and Museum webpage.

20 *Encyclopaedia Judaica*. Volume 8, pp. 854 – 856 (Jerusalem: Keter Publishing House, 1972).

Author's Statement

The death camps of Europe were closed one lifetime ago, six million lives too late. Here then is a roadmap back to places and experiences that must never be forgotten, offering a wide range of perspectives from the Holocaust-related books of British Columbian authors.

I have written *Out of Hiding* (with Yosef Wosk) because I believe that if the most-heinous, most-planned and most extensive genocide can be deep-sixed by mankind, all genocides thereafter can be shrugged off as natural—as inevitable as forest fires, plagues, droughts, locusts or tidal waves. If the Holocaust is untaught and therefore unlearned—and therefore denied—it will be easy to believe that each genocide thereafter is actually some form of a natural disaster, like earthquakes or tsunamis, usually faraway and therefore someone else's problem.

As made shockingly clear by Leon Kahn in his memoir, *No Time to Mourn*, mass murder and vicious cruelty towards Jews during the Holocaust were not the sole preserve of Germans. The human species needs to own the Holocaust, front and centre, because the Holocaust serves as an essential reminder as to what the human race can do. Canada's well-entrenched anti-Semitism was vile and the Allies never bothered to bomb the railroad tracks.

Soon all witnesses will be gone. The Holocaust must not be relegated to being merely the psychic preserve of Jews and Germans.

A.T.

About the Author

ALAN TWIGG IS HIS PROVINCE'S leading man of letters having founded the *BC BookWorld* newspaper, the *ABCBookWorld* reference site (for 12,500 B.C. authors), the *BC BookLook* news service, the *Literary Map of BC*, the *Indigenous Literary Map of BC*, the *Ormsby Review*, the George Woodcock Walk of Fame at the Vancouver Public Library and many of the province's major literary prizes. He has made seven literary documentaries and published 20 books in 40 years. A fifth-generation builder of British Columbia and a Shadbolt Scholar at SFU, he was made a Member of the Order of Canada in 2015.